Project Management Checklists

Checklists

FOR
DUMMIES®
A Wiley Brand

by Nick Graham

FOR
DUMMIES
A Wiley Brand

Project Management Checklists For Dummies®

Published by: **John Wiley & Sons, Ltd.,** The Atrium, Southern Gate, Chichester, www.wiley.com

This edition first published 2014

© 2014 John Wiley & Sons, Ltd, Chichester, West Sussex.

Registered office

John Wiley & Sons Ltd, The Atrium, Southern Gate, Chichester, West Sussex, PO19 8SQ, United Kingdom

For details of our global editorial offices, for customer services and for information about how to apply for permission to reuse the copyright material in this book please see our website at www.wiley.com.

The right of the author to be identified as the author of this work has been asserted in accordance with the Copyright, Designs and Patents Act 1988

Wiley publishes in a variety of print and electronic formats and by print-on-demand. Some material included with standard print versions of this book may not be included in e-books or in print-on-demand. If this book refers to media such as a CD or DVD that is not included in the version you purchased, you may download this material at http://booksupport.wiley.com. For more information about Wiley products, visit www.wiley.com.

Designations used by companies to distinguish their products are often claimed as trademarks. All brand names and product names used in this book are trade names, service marks, trademarks or registered trademarks of their respective owners. The publisher is not associated with any product or vendor mentioned in this book.

For general information on our other products and services, please contact our Customer Care Department within the U.S. at 877-762-2974, outside the U.S. at (001) 317-572-3993, or fax 317-572-4002. For technical support, please visit www.wiley.com/techsupport.

For technical support, please visit www.wiley.com/techsupport.

ISBN 978-1-118-93143-1 (pbk) ISBN 978-1-118-93142-4 (ebk)

ISBN 978-1-118-93141-7 (ebk)

Printed in Great Britain by TJ International, Padstow, Cornwall.

10 9 8 7 6 5 4 3 2

Contents at a Glance

Table of Contents

Introduction

*P*roject management is a challenge and it can also be great fun . . . when you're in control. However it can be a miserable existence being a Project Manager if you're not in control. Part of the secret of success is being organised, thinking things through thoroughly and not leaving important things out only to get tripped up later in the project. That's where the checklists and templates in this book come in. They help you develop an orderly approach where you can be confident that you've covered all the bases because you have everything you need checked off on the list.

As explain in the first chapter though, this isn't a list ticker's paradise. It's not about mindlessly ticking off the points just to fill the boxes. Rather it's about taking a professional approach to get things right and getting them right first time.

So, which would you prefer? A smoothly running project where you've thought things through up front, or fire-fighting one crisis after another because you forgot stuff? Of course that's not to say that you'll have a perfect project once you've read this book – projects are always unpredictable to some extent. But you'll have the pleasure of seeing your project in control and knowing that you're not encountering problems that were both predictable and avoidable if only you'd had a list to make sure that you'd covered everything.

About this Book

For Dummies books are designed so that you can dip in to them at different points according to what you need at the time. That's true of this one too, but you'll find it will help if you read Chapter 1 first anyway because that explains more about using the checklists and templates. And this book really is all about the checklists and templates.

Inside *Project Management Checklists For Dummies* you'll find essential checklists covering everything you need to do to run your project smoothly (and plenty of advice on what you don't need to do), as well as vital questions to ask yourself to check that you've overlooked nothing. You'll also find lots of hints and tips to help you every step of the way.

Parts II-V of the book are made up of Checklists and Templates. The Checklists serve as to-do lists for certain activities, as reminders of documents to complete, and as failsafe lists to make sure you've thought of everything you need to. The templates, are typical documents that you need to complete during the course of a project. The Templates are included in the book and also on Dummies.com – so you can download and customise them to suit your project.

Foolish Assumptions

When writing this book, I assumed that those reading it will mostly be Project Managers. However, it's also suitable for:

- Senior managers involved with setting up good project control and management (project governance) in their organisations.

- Project Steering Group members (such as the project's Sponsor) who want to perform their role well and be effective in the project.

- Team Leaders who want to control their work well and perhaps go on to become Project Managers

- Project administration staff who want to be professional and highly effective in supporting Project Managers and Team Leaders.

I have assumed that you want to run, or help run, projects well. I have assumed that you want real project success not merely a pile of documentation and that you will use the checklists in this book intelligently.

If you're a project auditor then you'll find a chapter especially for you, and here I assume that you too are focused on project delivery and success, not on superficial compliance with documentation standards. In the chapter covering the audit role I've said that project auditors can make a valuable contribution if they approach the task correctly, and I assume that's exactly what you want as you start a project audit.

Icons Used in This book

The small icons in the left margins of the book are to alert you to special information in the text. Here's what they mean.

This icon gives a real or hypothetical situation to illustrate a particular point in the text. Projects are a rich source of examples, so most of them are real life.

This icon points out important information you should keep in mind as you use the checklists and work on your project.

This icon lets you in on handy advice and shortcuts that can save you time and effort.

This icon highlights potential pitfalls and dangers.

Beyond the Book

In addition to the material in the print or e-book you're reading right now, this product also comes with some access-anywhere goodies on the Web. Check out the free Cheat Sheet at www. dummies.com/cheatsheet/pmchecklists for some helpful key checklists.

You can also find many of the most important templates from this book reproduced as editable Word files at www.dummies. com/extras/pmchecklists.

Where to Go from Here

You can dip into this book to find help on the bit of your project that you're currently working on. However, as pointed out earlier, you'll find it helpful to read Chapter 1 first.

When you look at a particular checklist, bear in mind that you may need to alter it to fit the exact needs of your project. So where you go may be to grab a pencil or a computer and set up an adjusted checklist that will be of maximum help to you.

For documents, you don't have to key in all the headings into your own document template. In the true spirit of helpfulness of the *For Dummies* books we've put Word and Excel versions of the templates in this book up on the website such as for a Risk Log and a Project Charter.

Although there's a lot of help in this book, if you're new to project management or some approaches such as 'product based planning' you may feel in need of a bit more help. If so, don't despair. Where you can go from here is to get a copy of the UK edition of *Project Management For Dummies* which is designed to give much more help and advice.

Part I

Understanding Projects and Checklists

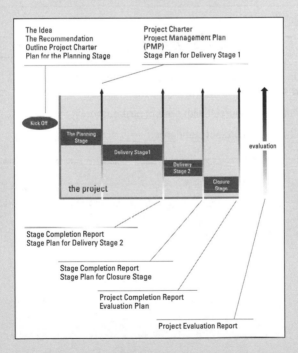

The Idea
The Recommendation
Outline Project Charter
Plan for the Planning Stage

Project Charter
Project Management Plan
(PMP)
Stage Plan for Delivery Stage 1

Kick Off

The Planning Stage

Delivery Stage1

Delivery Stage 2

Closure Stage

the project

evaluation

Stage Completion Report
Stage Plan for Delivery Stage 2

Stage Completion Report
Stage Plan for Closure Stage

Project Completion Report
Evaluation Plan

Project Evaluation Report

It can be a bit tough seeing where key documents fit into the project. If you find that, this diagram may help a bit. Don't think though that the focus is the documents. It isn't, but the documents – done well and kept concise – should prove to be a very helpful and powerful support.

In this part . . .

✔ Understand how to use the checklist and templates to full effect.

✔ Familiarise yourself with project structure.

✔ Find help on project standards.

Chapter 1

Using Checklists and Templates in Projects

. . . .

In This Chapter

▶ The power of project checklists

▶ The types of checklist in this book

▶ Avoiding checklist pitfalls

▶ The templates and how to use them

▶ Understanding the Project Structure

. . . .

*T*his chapter, and indeed the whole of this first part of *Project Checklists for Dummies*, may seem a bit strange in a book of checklists. You may think that you just want to get going with your project and start ticking some boxes. However, to get the best out of the checklists and templates and use them really effectively you need to appreciate how to use them . . . and also how not to.

The checklists are designed to help you make sure that you have got everything right at different points in the project and haven't missed out anything important. It's so easy to make mistakes that are actually avoidable. As well as helping you to think things through for each project, the checklists also draw on lots of experience and help you make sure that you get it right for 'this' project, whether 'this' project is your first one or just your latest.

> *History repeats itself because nobody listens the first time.*
> *Anonymous*

If you're new to projects, it will also pay you to go through the last part of this chapter to understand the project structure that the checklists are designed to fit in with. If you're already familiar with project structure you can skip that section if you prefer.

Using the Checklists

When running any project you'll find that checklists are a very powerful tool. They help you to ensure that you produce sound, well thought-out plans and control documents the first time around. That will not only save time and trouble later, but will also help you develop a deserved reputation as a thorough and effective Project Manager.

This section gives you a few pointers on using the checklists, including tackling problems where you want other staff to use them too, but where they are not quite as keen as you. Some don't like things like project methods and checklists, and say that they have no need of them because of their experience and knowledge.

I like the example of an airline pilot here. Imagine that you're standing in an airport waiting to check in for your flight over the Atlantic Ocean. The captain and co-pilot for your flight happen to walk past you and you overhear what the Captain is saying. 'I'm not bothering with the pre-flight checklist on this trip. I've been flying aircraft for years, I'm very experienced and I'm sure I'll remember everything important.' You might feel slightly unhappy about that and start scanning the departure board to see if you can find an alternative flight. You certainly wouldn't take the captain's words as a sign of expertise and professionalism.

Using checklists is not unprofessional; rather the reverse. As far as you possibly can, you want to be sure that you get things right and that you don't miss anything important. Quite apart from the consequences for the project if you get things wrong, avoiding problems will also save you a lot of time and hassle later.

I'm sure that you will use the project checklists in this book intelligently and appropriately, but to make absolutely sure you do, here are a few pitfalls to avoid.

✔ **Use the checklists thoughtfully:** Adjust them to the needs of your project, then use them. Otherwise you may be in danger of, for example, applying large project controls to a small project that simply doesn't need them. Continuing with the aircraft analogy from the start of this section, different aircraft have different pre-flight checklists.

✔ **Be extra careful in audit:** Following on from the last point, if you're using checklists to check up on someone else's project (Project Audit) don't apply some generic checklist to every project and ignore the individual project characteristics and specific control needs.

✔ **Don't get 'tick happy':** The objective is not to fill up all the boxes with ticks, but to do the project work so that you can tick the boxes – if you see the difference. When you tick a box it should mean that the item is properly dealt with.

✔ **Add to the checklists:** If you need extra things on the checklists because of the nature of those projects, then add them.

✔ **Take away from the checklists:** As a reverse of the last point, if you never need to do something that's on a checklist then take it off. Always keep the checklists relevant to what you are doing.

In short, keep your brain in gear and don't drive up project overheads by doing unnecessary work because you haven't thought through whether everything on a checklist is relevant to your project.

Using Lists As An Expert – Or Not

You'll find the checklists useful if you're a project expert – back to the analogy of an experienced aircraft pilot. You'll also find them useful if you are less experienced in project management and need a bit of help. The format used for the lists in the book looks like this:

❑ **Item:** Explanation and help.

If you're very experienced, you can just run down the bold
headed items to be sure that you've covered everything you
need to. If you're less experienced, or just unsure of a particular point, you'll see that each checklist item is followed
by a short explanation to help you see why that item may be
important in your project.

Understanding Checklist Types

There are four different types of checklist in the book.
Although you'd probably have spotted that anyway, it helps to
explain up front what the types are so you can watch out for
them.

- ✔ **Activity checklists:** The activity checklists are to make
  sure that you are doing, or have done, everything you
  need to at a particular point in the project. For example,
  if you're approaching the end of a Delivery Stage, have
  you done all the necessary checking and preparation for
  the 'Stage Gate' review?

- ✔ **Thinking checklists:** This type of checklist helps you
  think across different areas to make sure that you've
  looked into all the areas that you need to. For example,
  when considering who the stakeholders in your project
  are, have you remembered customers and suppliers?

- ✔ **Completion checklists:** The completion type of checklist is to make sure that you've got everything. So, when
  you're doing the organisation chart of who is needed for
  the project, have you got all of the management roles
  covered or have you missed one?

- ✔ **Information checklists:** These tell you about the range
  of things in a particular area. For example, when you're
  writing a Business Case for your project, you have to
  be really clear about the three sorts of benefit, because
  they're very different. There's a checklist to say what the
  three types of benefit are and to briefly explain each one.

Using Templates

Templates are helpful, they really are, but of course you should use them intelligently as you do the checklists. In fact the same do's and don'ts apply that are in the bullet point list in the 'Using the Checklists' section earlier in this chapter. Templates can work powerfully for you in four ways:

- ✔ To save you significant time and effort 're-inventing the wheel', such as in designing a document from scratch when it would be much quicker to use a template.

- ✔ Even if you can't quite use the templates in this book 'as is', you can use them as a starting point and adapt them. That's usually a whole lot faster and much less effort than starting from scratch. You're bound to want quite a few of the sections even if you take a few out and add one or two others in.

- ✔ To help instruct others on how documents should be completed, improving the relevance and accuracy of the information that they enter.

- ✔ To help make sure that you haven't missed anything.

Following on from the second point in the list, many people assume that their organisation and its projects are going to be very different from everyone else's. In fact the core of project management is very similar, so you may well find that you only need minor changes to the templates, or even none at all, in which case you can relax and go home early today.

In each main part of this book you'll find one or two chapters of templates for things like documents, reports and logs. You, or your project team members, then replace the 'advice' text in each section with the actual content. Easy, huh? And it's that ease of use which again demonstrates the value of project templates.

On the *For Dummies* web site (www.dummies.com) we're also making the templates available in Microsoft Word format. That way you can load a template straight into your computer and you don't have to copy all of the information out of the book. Helpful of us and sensible too, don't you think? But then that's why you bought a *For Dummies* title in the first place.

Understanding Project Structure

To understand how the checklists are used at different points in the project, the first step is to be clear on what those points are.

Figure 1-1 shows the main parts of any project. Some of it may be familiar to you, such as the use of *project stages* – or you may know them as *phases*. Having said that, this book starts with the work that's needed before the project gets underway; and that part is both extremely important and frequently underestimated. Before you dive in and check whether you are setting up the project correctly, you first need to establish whether it really is a project.

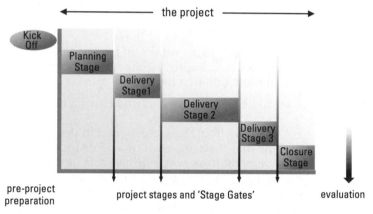

Figure 1-1: The Project and What Comes Before and After.

The next few sub-sections cover the elements of Figure 1-1 in turn.

Kicking off the project

Some people say that just about everything is a project: Even, they claim, making a cup of tea. That's a common myth and it's absolutely untrue, so don't be fooled for a moment. Projects have overheads, such as the work needed for planning, risk management, quality management and progress control. Not all work justifies such overheads. Sometimes you can do things as 'normal' work, perhaps even using a few project techniques, and it doesn't justify putting in full project controls and structure. If that's the case it's not a problem, it just isn't a project.

Before starting a project, you need to do three important things:

1. **Get an understanding of what will be involved and make sure that the work is worth doing – one way or another.**

2. **If the job is worth doing, decide whether it's a project or should be tackled as 'business as usual' type work.**

3. **If it does look like a project, get some idea of what resource will be needed, find out whether that resource is available and then when the project could start.**

And guess what? A lot of the pre-project work in Kick Off is about those three exact things in the list above. Too many projects start. Many get a long way into planning or, even worse, begin the delivery work and then find out that actually the project isn't worth doing. Getting into that position is bad news for two reasons. First, all of the people involved feel – very understandably – disappointed that all their hard work was a complete waste of effort. Second, your organisation has wasted valuable staff time and money. There may even be a strategic dimension to the impact. Another project may have been ruled out in favour of investing time and money in this one, and that project would have been genuinely worth doing. The strategic part of the impact can be very significant and it's easy to underestimate it.

You'll know from your own experience that most ideas sound great at first. It's only when you start working on an idea that you begin to realise that it's not quite as shiny and wonderful as you first thought and, to be brutally honest, there are an awful lot of drawbacks and problems. The idea of the Kick Off is to do a limited amount of work early on to investigate the idea and stop the project before it's even started if you discover that it isn't worthwhile after all.

Dealing with Kick Off in three steps

A good approach in Kick Off is to take it in three sequential steps. Don't think that all this pre-project work is going to take a long time, though, because almost always it won't. The approach actually reflects normal business handling of ideas.

1. **Rough out 'the idea' on a single sheet of paper.**

   Set down what it is and the advantages of doing the work. If that looks good when discussed with an organisational manager then . . .

2. **Work up the idea into a bit more detail and create a recommendation.**

   Your task here may include looking into a few different options for the way that the work is done and getting a bit of expert input if it's needed to make sure that the recommendation is realistic and technically sound. When the recommendation is reviewed by organisational managers, if it still looks good then you can . . .

3. **Develop an Outline Charter (sometimes known as a Project Brief.)**

   This is a more detailed view and should be done by people including some with project experience not just business expertise. If, when the Outline is reviewed, it still looks good then the project can be started, a project team appointed and work begun in earnest on the full planning. If you're not sure what documents like the Outline Charter are all about, then don't worry a bit because they're covered in Chapter 2.

The three steps can normally be completed in the space of two or three days, even for quite substantial projects. Notice too how the work increases through the steps. You only put more effort in if the idea is still looking good. If it turns out to be not such a good idea after all then the earlier you drop it the better, when less resource has been used investigating it.

Putting key roles in place

When the project starts it's important to have project roles filled and defined clearly, so that people know what they are supposed to be doing and what everyone else is supposed to be doing too. There's a checklist of roles for projects in

Chapter 6. To make sense of later sections in this chapter though, I need to explain some now.

> ✔ **Project Steering Group:** The small group of senior managers with overall responsibility for the project, including its *project governance* (that it's run properly). In a very small project, the Steering Group might be a single manager covering all of the roles.

> ✔ **Sponsor:** The chairperson of the Project Steering Group and the business manager ultimately responsible for the project.

> ✔ **Project Manager:** A manager with responsibility for the day-to-day running of the project. The Project Manager is accountable to the Project Steering Group and will attend all of its meetings. However the Project Manager isn't a part of that group.

Finding the Kick Off checklists and templates

You can find checklists to help you with Kick Off in Part II. That includes one for the roles and responsibilities in the project because as part of your Kick Off work you need to start thinking about who is needed for the project. You'll also find templates for the Idea, Recommendation and Outline in Chapter 7 within Part II.

Doing the Planning

If the Outline Charter (or just 'Outline' for short) shows that it's worth starting the project off, then the first stage of the project should be a planning stage. It's a bad mistake to rush into the work without proper plans. You'll only waste time and get confused when things start to go wrong, such as when you discover additional work that you hadn't realised would be needed. Also, you won't be able to control the project. If you don't know where you are supposed to be (because you haven't got a plan) how can you tell whether you're on track or not?

Planning the work of the project

You'll normally need to develop a number of plans in the Planning Stage. For the project work itself you're going to need two plans. The first is a Project Plan covering the whole project but at a high level of detail. The second is a more detailed Stage Plan for the first Delivery Stage – the one that comes immediately after the Planning Stage. That way, if the Steering Group gives permission to go ahead with the first Delivery Stage, the plan is in place and you can get going without having a long gap.

It's easy to get plans wrong and, as touched on earlier in this section, that can so easily be because you've missed things. If you fail to spot part of the work needed in the project, then clearly it can cause you big problems later on. The project will get delayed while that extra, but essential, work is done. Perhaps you'll need additional people to do the extra work too– even specialists. But what if those people aren't available at short notice? No, it's a lot better to have a good plan at the start and one that's both complete and clear. What's that you say? A checklist or two might help? Now there's an idea.

Planning the other aspects

Unless your project is particularly small and straightforward, you'll usually need other plans as well. For example, how will you manage risk in the project? To explain that and to put the necessary controls in place you can write a Risk Plan. These tactical plans all form part of what is often called the Project Management Plan (PMP). The more strategic documents such as the scope and the Business Case go into the Project Charter. You'll remember from the 'Kicking off the project' section earlier in this chapter that there was an Outline Charter. Well, this is now the fully developed Charter. You'll find checklists in the book to help you prepare both the Charter and the PMP, and templates too.

Avoiding Paper Mountains

Before you start to think that the planning sounds like a huge amount of electronic 'paperwork' remember that some of the plans may be quite short and simple, though still necessary. However, you always need to be careful to only produce what you really need to control the project. Clearly a small, simple, low-risk project will need much less in terms of planning and control than a large, high-risk and business critical one. The documentation should reflect those different control needs.

Locating the Planning Checklists and Templates

Part III covers planning and you'll find checklists there covering three aspects: The plans themselves, the controls you need to set up and then the staff management aspects. There's also a chapter of useful templates, Chapter 11.

Delivering Project Products

The next stage of the project, the Delivery Stage, is where all the main project work gets done. You will give one or more teams work assignments to build the project deliverables.

In terms of the project structure, the Delivery Stage repeats. In a very small project you may have a single Delivery Stage, but in most projects you'll have several. Figure 1-1 shows three Delivery Stages, but you may well need more than that for your project, and you could need less.

The Delivery Stages are important. They give you clear units of work that you can then plan in detail as you approach them (the Stage Plans). They also provide a powerful Project Steering Group (PSG) control, because at the end of each stage the PSG will meet to check up on the project and ensure that it makes sense to carry on with the next stage. If it doesn't, then the project must be stopped.

The PSG check at the end of each stage is usually called a *Stage Gate*. That's a great term because it gives the clear picture of a barrier where you stop, but one that can be opened to allow you through to the next section. The Project Manager will attend to explain how things went on the stage just finishing, set down the current state of the project and then provide the plan for the next stage.

The term Stage Gate is used all over the world including in the USA, and by users of software such as Microsoft Project, where people usually refer to these sections of the project as phases rather than stages. But how on earth can you have a 'Stage' Gate at the end of a phase? Surely it should be a Phase Gate. It just goes to show that Project Managers influenced by the UK approach, and similar ones, which use stages and Stage Gates are more consistent, more logical, more intelligent . . . and of course more modest too.

Naming conventions aside, don't underestimate the Stage Gate. It's a very powerful control and is emphasised in most project approaches as well as the international ISO Standard. You'll find a substantial checklist later in the book dealing with the Stage Gate, and it reflects the strong ISO emphasis.

The main heading for this section refers to products. This book assumes that you'll want to use the powerful *product-based* or *product-led* approach to planning. Before you start to think about the activities and resource you need in the project, you first investigate what it is that you are going to produce. So, you have to build a wall. What exactly do you mean by 'wall' then? Is it something like the Great Wall of China, or a small wall around a flower bed in your back garden? Until you're clear on what you have to produce (the products), you can't be accurate with planning the activities and resource. If you're interested in reading more about this approach to planning (which is powerful for progress, financial and quality control as well as for planning) have a look at the UK edition of *Project Management for Dummies* (Wiley).

Finding the checklists and templates

Running a Delivery Stage is all about control, so you'll find that Part IV is called Checklists for Project Control. In it you'll find chapters with checklists for things like stage checks and Stage Gates. Then there are two chapters of templates. The first, Chapter 16, covers templates for control documents while Chapter 17 provides useful reporting templates. Part IV also includes the checklists and templates for the next two areas, closure and evaluation.

Closing the Project

In many projects you'll find it sensible to have a Closure Stage. Some take the view that once the final delivery has been made at the end of the last Delivery Stage then that's it, you turn the lights out and everyone can go home. More often than not though, there's still work to be done and you'll still need people on the project to do it. Typical closure work is the 'handholding' help you need to give the people using what the project delivered, to explain things and help while they get used to it all. Then there are often adjustments needed to project deliverables to fine-tune them. You'll still need your project team members around to carry out those adjustments.

On the project management side of things, you'll also need to record how the project went and report things like the final cost.

Only when that 'tidy-up' work is all complete can you shut the project down and finally disband the teams.

Evaluating the Project

Even though the project is now closed, there's another job to be done and that's the evaluation. Sadly the evaluation work is often neglected but that doesn't mean it's unimportant. You can often do the final evaluation after a few weeks and you'll normally be checking out two aspects:

- ✔ **Measuring benefits:** A check to see whether the benefits originally claimed for the project when it was started have actually materialised. You can think of this as the 'Return on Investment'. What was the return in terms of business benefits?

- ✔ **Looking at operational effectiveness:** Do the project deliverables work well and have they proved appropriate for those using them after a period of time? For example, staff can be very happy with a new building at first. However, after a few weeks they've discovered that the layout is wrong and the building is very hard to work in. Equally, sometimes an initial negative reaction to deliverables can be reversed after a few weeks when staff find that actually the products are really excellent, but that they just took a bit of getting used to.

Chapter 2

The Key Documents

· ·

In This Chapter

▶ About documents and why you'll need at least some

▶ When a document needn't be a document

▶ Documents for Kick Off and the Planning Stage

▶ Documents for control, including progress reports

▶ Balancing the amount of documentation against the control needs

· ·

*C*hapter 1 contains a warning about not creating a 'paper mountain' in your project. However, unless you have a particularly good memory and nobody else will ever need to see any project information, you're going to have to write some stuff down.

This chapter explains the range of documents you may want to think about for your project. You may not need all of them, but you can use the checklists to think through what you will need, and then how much detail you should go into, which in turn will depend on the control needs of the project. Later chapters in the book contain checklists that will then help you make sure that you've thought through everything correctly. Those chapters also include templates to save you having to design documents from scratch.

A document needn't always be a document. To keep things simple, this book refers to documents, but a document needn't always be a document. For example, a progress report may be entirely verbal or given in the form of a short business presentation with visuals. In the early part of Kick Off, the Idea and Recommendation may each be an agenda item in a management meeting where someone explains the proposed project. The content is the same; it's just the medium that's different. In each case, think through the best way of communicating; the answer isn't always a document.

Kick Off

The three documents in Kick Off work up the idea for a project from a one-side overview to an Outline Charter. You add more detail at each point when you have established that it's worth progressing. The information from the earlier documents is not duplicated because in the later ones you expand on the information in the earlier ones.

- ❑ **The Idea:** A one-page overview of the basics of the idea for the project.

- ❑ **The Recommendation:** Typically five to ten sides of paper, exploring options, recommending one, recommending not to go ahead after all or perhaps recommending that while the work should be done, it doesn't need a project to do it.

- ❑ **The Outline Charter:** Okay, it's looking like a viable project now. The Outline Charter sets down the scope and an overview Business Case and is developed using project expertise, not just business expertise.

Project Planning

If the managers in overall charge of the project and its preparation, the Project Steering Group (PSG), accepts the Outline, it's time to start the project itself and that begins with the Planning Stage. You'll need some major documents here for project approval and then control, but you'll need to prepare other control documents too, such as a Risk Log and a Project Log.

The major planning documents

There are three major documents here, but the second one – the Project Management Plan – contains quite a few other plans.

As always, fit the documentation to the control needs of the document. There are no prizes for producing unnecessarily large documents – they merely drive up project overheads and waste everyone's time in preparing and then reading them.

❑ **Project Charter:** The strategic view of the project. This will be maintained throughout. Amongst other things it contains the scope statement to say what the project is, the objectives and, importantly, the full Business Case.

❑ **Project Management Plan (PMP):** The tactical view of how you'll manage the project. You'll need some or all of the following:

❑ **Project Plan:** With the product, activity and resource plans and also the budget.

❑ **Risk Plan:** How you will control risk on the project, including reporting procedures.

❑ **Quality Plan:** The level of quality to be achieved, and how you will achieve it.

❑ **Communications Plan:** What information will be needed and how it will be communicated.

❑ **Stakeholder Plan:** If you have a significant amount of Stakeholder management to do, how you will do it.

❑ **Procurement Plan:** If your project will involve a significant amount of procurement. This shows what will be bought and when, including lead times.

If you need to let a contract the lead time can be substantial, with Invitations to Tender and agreeing the contract. You may need to start the process several months before the actual purchase is due in the project.

❑ **Other Controls:** Details of any other controls to be used, not covered in the other plans in the PMP.

❑ **Stage Plan:** The plan for the first Delivery Stage so you can move ahead promptly when the Charter and PMP are approved.

The logs

Logs are working documents to keep track of things such as risks. You may not need all of the ones in the checklist, but you'll need most. You set up the logs in the Planning Stage, or sometimes before, ready for use throughout the project.

Don't dismiss logs as unnecessary and just over-formalised project bureaucracy. They are often logically necessary. For example, you may decide not to bother with a Risk Log. Instead you'll just keep a simple spreadsheet with each risk on a row. Okay, you'll need some columns with headings then. Perhaps things such as how severe each risk is, what actions you have planned to control it, who is responsible for taking any action, when you last checked the risk. You get the point; you've just re-invented the Risk Log.

- ❏ **Project Log:** This functions as the Project Manager's journal. It contains reminders, notes, records of important phone calls, lessons being learned from the project, and so on. It's both simple and really useful.

- ❏ **Risk Log:** Another simple yet powerful log, the Risk Log has information on each risk and how it is being managed. It should be made available 'read-only' to everyone on the project so that everyone is aware of the risks and is watching out for them.

- ❏ **Change Log:** Not mentioned by many of the project approaches except the PRIME method, this log is powerful. If you keep a list of changes in this log you can quickly track which changes have been accepted, which have been rejected, who suggested them and, importantly, what they cost.

- ❏ **Stakeholder Log:** If you have a significant number of stakeholders in your project, you can keep a list in the log, perhaps grouped according to their interest. For example, operations staff, suppliers, other organisations that you work with and who will be affected.

Two checklists

You'll use the two control checklists stage-by-stage, but you should decide the format during the Planning Stage.

❑ **Quality Checklist:** A list of tests and other quality activities being done in a stage. Each item is then ticked off when it is done. The checklist is a simple but powerful tool for making sure that a planned test hasn't simply been overlooked.

❑ **Work Checklist:** A list of products to be developed in a stage, and then the date when each is delivered having been completed and successfully passing any tests. This is an extremely powerful progress checking tool.

Project Control

During the Delivery Stages, Closure Stage and evaluation of the project you'll need some further documents. This checklist is to help you think through what you'll need, and perhaps what you won't need.

❑ **Stage Progress Report:** For the Project Manager to report progress to the Steering Group, possibly copied to others such as organisational managers and Project Managers of any interfacing projects.

❑ **Team Progress Report:** Where you have a project with multiple teams working, the Team Leaders will need to inform the Project Manager of progress on their current work assignments.

❑ **Stage Completion Report:** Produced at the end of each stage, this report is used by the Project Manager to inform the Project Steering Group of how the stage went. So, what was the final time and cost? Were there any problems that will affect future stages? This report may be given as a presentation at the Stage Gate.

❑ **Project Completion Report:** Produced by the Project Manager at the end of the project, it reports how the whole project went. It should also record any lessons learned during the project, good and bad, that may be of value to future projects.

❑ **Project Evaluation Report:** Produced after the end of the project, this sets down information on benefits realisation (what the actual benefits were compared to what was expected when the project started) and the suitability of project deliverables after an initial period of use.

❑ **Project Issue (or Project Memo):** A communication from anyone in the project to the Project Manager, but you may choose to use them for written communications between the Project Manager and the Steering Group too.

❑ **Work Package:** A work assignment given to a Team Leader by a Project Manager. It sets down what work is to be done and how. A project team will work through one or more Work Packages in a Delivery Stage.

Thinking About What You Need

Your decision on the level of documentation in the project is a control decision and it's a balancing act. On the one hand you don't want excessive or unnecessary documents. On the other hand you need to keep the project in control and other people need to check up on it too – they can't check what isn't there. Overall with documentation, follow the KISS principle of Keep It Simple, Stupid.

The control requirements may be dictated in part by your organisational standards. However, even here think hard. If something is set down as mandatory for every project, be prepared to challenge it if there's no value to your one. You may need to get the Project Steering Group (PSG) on board to do that, but it's not in the PSGs interest to incur unnecessary overheads and divert effort from getting the project delivered successfully.

In some cases, it's not so much the organisational standards that are dictating the degree of documentation but a Project Management Office that is getting a bit carried away. As with standards, though, question the value to your particular project of what they're doing. You really have quite enough to do without spending time and effort on unnecessary bureaucracy.

Chapter 3

Using Project Standards

*O*n the one hand there are a number of standards, approaches and methods around, which you may find helpful; on the other there are some you may actually be required to work with. This last, and short, chapter in Part I is to explain them briefly and then to say how the checklists in the rest of this book fit in.

If you don't need to be too bothered with international standards and professional bodies, you may like to skip most of this chapter and move on to the section 'Using a Project Method' because that's something you may want to consider.

Standardising Internationally

The International Standards Organisation (ISO) have issued an international standard for project management . The current one at the time of writing is ISO 21500:2012, published in September 2012.

The ISO standard is short but very practical . . . as far as it goes. It has some really solid content based on a lot of project management experience. For example, as mentioned briefly in Chapter 1, it emphasises the importance of Stage Gates for effective control and *governance* (good management). The checklists in this book are influenced by ISO, but necessarily go beyond it because the standard doesn't have the space to go into much specific detail.

Although it looks simple enough at first sight, complying with the ISO is harder work than you might think. It has a straightforward process model including, for example, planning and then execution and control. The problems start when you realise that you have to apply that model at project level, then again with overlaps at stage level. Clearly you are still working on the execution of one stage when you start to plan the next one. Then, taking into account other ISOs such as the one for project quality, running an ISO-compliant project becomes a much bigger job.

Following a PMBoK

The rather strange acronym stands for *Project Management Body of Knowledge*. Predictably there are a number of professional project management organisations. The biggest single organisation worldwide is undoubtedly the Project Management Institute (PMI). The PMI is a USA-based organisation but has chapters (branches) worldwide. The PMI has produced a book which is its *Project Management Body of Knowledge*. It's available from booksellers, so you don't have to join the PMI to get hold of a copy.

In the UK, the Association for Project Management (APM) – of which I happen to be a member – also has a PMBoK. Other countries have their own national bodies and many, including the APM, are affiliated to an international federation, the Swiss-based International Project Management Association (IPMA). If you are thinking of making project management your career, you might like to consider joining one of these professional bodies.

The PMBoKs say what you should include at particular points of a project, and if you are following one then you will need to factor that in when you come to use and adapt the checklists in this book. Because the book doesn't follow any one single standard, it can't be a 'one-size-fits-all'. Rather it is focused on what most readers should find really practical and helpful. While the PMBoKs give you the 'what' they don't try to say much on the 'how', or sometimes the 'when' either, and that's where project methods come in.

Using a Project Method

Most Project Managers that I've come across say that they find some structure useful when planning and running a project. If that describes you too, then you may like to use a project method.

A method provides a structure, suggests what you should do at each point, and sometimes offers some techniques to help do it. Don't worry that you will get locked into a series of steps from which you can't escape, though. To use a method properly you need to adjust it to the exact needs of each project. That can be quite a bit of work, or just a little, depending on the method involved.

Probably the biggest and most well-known project method is PRINCE2®. This is particularly high-profile in the UK, but it's also used worldwide. The method goes through the project to say what activities you should do at each point. However, its format is quite complicated since, like the project management ISO, it has overlapping project processes. Most people need a training course to understand PRINCE2, and they go on to take exams in it.

PRINCE2® is a registered trademark of AXELOS Limited.

Strangely, PRINCE2 leaves out a number of important elements of project management, even within its scope of project planning and control. For example it doesn't include the vital area of project budgeting, and has very limited content on financial control. The manual also covers the full complexity of the method in one go, so if you have a simple project to run your first job is to think through how you will cut it down, which all makes for extra work.

Another method is PRIME® – the PRoject Implementation MEthod. As joint author of PRIME I have to declare an interest and more than a little bias. PRIME has set out to be comprehensive but also simple to use. In contrast to many other approaches it offers a straighforward, linear path through the project with no complex overlapping processes. The main part of the manual is also simple, aimed at 'normal' projects so you don't have a big job to strip out the bits you don't need. However, it then extends its reach considerably with PowerPacks that you add in when you need to, but only when you need to. For example, if you have a very high risk project, or a very long one, or both.

PRIME covers all of the main areas of project management, including financial control. Unlike PRINCE2 it is also compliant with ISO 21500:2012, and with the ISO standards on risk and project quality management. By using PRIME you will comply with the international standards but without the complexity.

There are still more methods around. For example many of the large management consultancies have their own project method. Perhaps that's because they want to be seen as experts and not needing someone else's! A lot of large organisations have also developed their own standards and methods. If yours has, be careful to comply with any mandatory ones and adapt the checklists in this book if you need to.

Using Checklists with Standards

If you are following a PMBoK or a project method or standard, you'll have contents lists in that particular approach. In that case simply use them as your checklists for things like the key documents. Other checklists in this book will still be extremely useful though, for example to help ensure that you have thought through the full range of benefits that could come from your project or the things to think through if you have a problem with team performance being below that which you expected and planned for.

Chapter 1 included a 'heads up' on avoiding paper mountains on projects. Where your organisation has a standard for projects, you'll need to be particularly careful. Standards can be really sensible but always check to make sure that the standard fits your project, and work hard to get exemption where it doesn't. If you don't check, you're likely to end up with a lot of documents which are neither helpful nor necessary. That may be because you just don't need certain documents at all this time around, or because they are too complex for your project. Don't get led down the path of having 'well documented failures' where the focus shifts from delivering the project successfully to filling in unnecessary forms and keeping over-zealous compliance staff happy.

PRIME® is a registered trademark.

Part II
Checklists for Kick Off

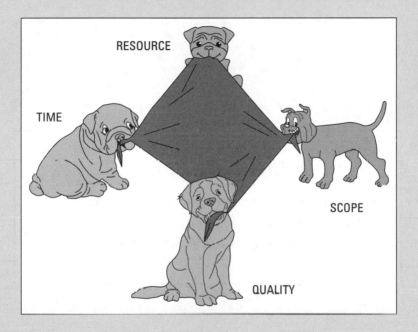

A lot of projects fail and the failure is predictable; the project wasn't in the right balance across four key areas. It's like four dogs pulling on a piece of project canvas – the canvas has to be in the right tension. In both Kick Off and full planning, ask if the project can deliver the required scope, to the necessary level of quality, with the given resource by the stated deadline? Is that 'do-able'?

The model is good for change control during the project as well. If a dog pulls, representing, for example, the project being required to deliver earlier, then you must adjust the other things to get the project 'canvas' back into the right tension in order to keep it achievable.

In this part . . .

- ✔ Come to grips with what your project will actually involve.
- ✔ Decide whether your project is really worth doing.
- ✔ Chart your way through the Kick Off period before your project gets fully under way.

Chapter 4

Kicking Off the Project

•••

•••

*B*efore you get deep into the full planning of your project, it pays to be sure the overall idea is viable and that it looks like it is worth pursuing. Even if the project is mandatory and so must be done, it will pay you to get a high-level view of what it's all about before you plunge into the detail, and that includes getting an idea about costs, staff resource, risk and timescales.

In his book *The Seven Habits of Highly Effective People*, published by Simon and Schuster, Steven Covey has as his second habit:

> *Begin with the end in mind.*

Covey's advice is sensible when it comes to projects as well as general effectiveness, and too many projects get started without being clear or agreed on the objectives or what the project is going to deliver; both of those are considered in Kick Off. However his example of the second habit is especially relevant and that is, before you climb a ladder you make sure that you've it propped against the right wall. Don't climb to the top and then think 'Whoops, wrong wall.' You just have to get down again, move the ladder and climb up all over again.

So, before you go to all the effort of producing the project plans, it's worth making sure that you have the basics right and that the ladder is against the right wall . . . and that everyone agrees it is against the right wall too.

If you're in a hurry you may be tempted to skip Kick Off and get straight on with the full planning. However Kick Off really will earn its keep and save you time. You get a clear view of what you're dealing with and, importantly, others do too. You can feel sure that you're clear on the project, and perhaps you are. But you run the risk of others disagreeing with you when they finally see the plans. It's a lot more work to change the detailed plans than ever it is to do Kick Off, make any adjustments there, and then get the planning spot-on the first time around.

I suggest in Chapter 1 that you sketch out an 'Idea' very briefly first, then, if that looks good, investigate any options for taking it forward and producing a more detailed 'Recommendation'. If everything's still looking good at that point, move on to develop an Outline Charter, or just Outline for short. As you go through the three you will put in increasing amounts of work.

Producing an Idea, then a Recommendation and then an Outline isn't duplicating the work. Rather, you are taking each one as a base to work into more detail for the next bit, and involving more people, such as project specialists, to do that. This approach allows your organisation to add resource gradually as you show that the project is worth doing, or to back out without too much waste of effort if it isn't.

As you produce the Idea, Recommendation and then Outline in turn (or your organisation's equivalent) use the checklists in this chapter to help make sure that you've got them right.

The Idea Checklist

The Idea should normally be on a single side of paper, or the equivalent – perhaps as a meeting item. In the Idea you should explain briefly what your project 'idea' is and get approval to do a bit more investigation and produce a Recommendation. You must spell things out very clearly in the Idea. Don't forget that while your head may have been buzzing with all this stuff for a while, the manager receiving the Idea may be considering it all for the first time.

❑ **Background:** Check the wording of the Idea to be sure that you've explained clearly and concisely why the project is needed or would be advantageous.

❑ **Description:** Check that you've spelled out what the idea actually is, and in terms that your manager will understand.

❑ **The business perspective:** Make sure that the proposed project would genuinely help your organisation and that it isn't merely something you'd like to do, perhaps because it looks interesting.

❑ **Advantages:** Have you been clear and realistic about the advantages and benefits of running the project, neither overstating nor understating them? If you are not sure of the amount of benefit, err on the side of slightly understating it rather than overstating it.

❑ **Resources and timing:** Double-check that the resource levels and timescale you have specified are realistic, and that you haven't been over-optimistic. You'll be aware from your own experience that many things take longer than you first thought they would.

The Recommendation Checklist

A recommendation normally takes up about five to ten sides of paper, or the equivalent in a business presentation. It provides information for a decision on whether or not to go on with the more extensive work to create an Outline Charter. It covers the same ground as the Idea, just in more detail, so you'll need to apply some of the same checks.

❑ **The options:** Have you thought of all of the viable options or are you still thinking 'inside the box'? Prepare to be dramatic to get maximum advantage. Are there further options that you haven't considered?

❑ **Workability:** Check that each option is genuinely workable and take out any that are just plain unrealistic. Contrary to the claims of one well known project method, there isn't always a 'do nothing' option; you may have to do something. So don't include 'do nothing' unless it is a serious and sensible option. It's usually advantageous to check things out with others to make sure that the options are sensible and workable, and you'll find a Consultation Checklist following this one with some ideas on who to talk to.

❑ **The recommended project:** Check that you've explained simply and clearly what the recommended project is. You'll often need to state the obvious, because it won't be obvious to people who are less familiar than you with this area of the organisation.

❑ **Reasoning:** Have you explained clearly why you are recommending the option that you are and why the others are less suitable? Don't go into huge detail here but rather keep things simple. However keep the additional detail readily to hand in case you're asked for it to back up your recommendation.

❑ **Terms and wording:** Check the terms you've used because the Recommendation may be seen by a wider group of managers, not just by your line manager. Those people may not understand the TLAs that you use day-to-day.

❑ **Justification:** Have you spelled out the justification clearly and accurately? That includes saying if the project is mandatory and must be done anyway even if there are no benefits. Check out the Justification Checklist in Chapter 5 to be sure you've got this right.

❑ **Benefits:** Again check out Chapter 5 to be sure that you have categorised the benefits correctly. Then check that you have been realistic about your claims of benefits. You might want to get someone else to have a look at your figures to confirm that the benefit levels are achievable; perhaps someone with some project or finance expertise.

Don't promise the moon and the stars when you can only deliver the moon. As mentioned in the checklist, the Recommendation is likely to go to more senior managers than just your line manager. Your 'promises' of benefits are likely to be remembered, even though you say that they're just an early estimate. Being over-optimistic now could result in your project being seen as a failure later. Your project turned out to be an astounding success; it cost just $10,000 and saved $1 million. However senior managers are disappointed because in the Recommendation you led them to believe it would save $2 million. Don't try to 'talk up' the project to get it approved and in doing so take it into the realms of the unachievable. This is a really important point, so don't be surprised when you see it crop up again in the book.

❑ **Resources:** Are the resource levels you have specified realistic, or have you been over-optimistic? You might want to check out your estimates with a few other people.

❑ **Resource availability:** Do you believe that the staff resource and finance will be available for this proposed project, or is there a problem that you should point out? Perhaps the project will need input from particular technical specialists and you know they're already heavily committed on other work.

By the way, the letters TLA mentioned in the list above stand for Three Letter Acronym. If you were unfamiliar with 'TLA', you'll now see what a problem it is if you hit an abbreviation or acronym that you don't understand. And your project is a whole lot more important than a single item on a checklist in this book.

Consultation Checklist

You might have a really good project in mind, but your Recommendation for it can be badly undermined if it contains factual errors. To be sure that the Recommendation is credible and that you've got things right, consider checking out the detail with people with specific expertise such as:

❑ **Legal and compliance:** To ensure that the proposed project will comply with any legal requirements, existing contracts and codes of practice.

❑ **Technical:** Engineers, for example, to be sure that the project outcome will be practical.

❑ **Business user management:** To be sure that the project will deliver things of genuine use.

❑ **Financial:** To check that benefits levels are realistic and that you've set them down accurately. The finance staff may also be able to advise on whether funding is likely to be available for the project or whether your managers will need a special case to secure it.

❑ **Senior management:** To ensure that the recommended project is in line with corporate objectives and strategy.

❑ **Project:** People with project expertise to help check that your cost, staff resource and time estimates are realistic, based on their experience of any similar projects.

The Outline Checklist

The Outline Charter, is really the foundation for the project, pinning down precisely what it is before starting the project and going on to full planning. You may think that you've already done that with the Recommendation, but the Outline now adds a project perspective to the business perspective on which the Idea and Recommendation were based. Consequently, the Outline should be produced by staff with project experience, and often including the person who will be the Project Manager if the project goes ahead. If the Outline is approved, the project will normally start soon after, so you'll also need people ready to take on the various project roles.

- ❑ **Scope:** Ensure that the scope of the project is clear and unambiguous. Is it crystal clear what the project will cover and what it will deliver?

- ❑ **Negative scope:** Make clear what the project won't cover, if any of those things could be misunderstood and people could otherwise assume they're included.

- ❑ **Justification and Business Case:** Are you sure that the project is genuinely justified? As you do more work on the justification to produce a Business Case for the project, stand back and be as objective as possible. Try hard not to be swayed by really wanting to do the project.

- ❑ **Benefits:** The benefits set down in the Business Case are still an approximation at the moment, but they should still be in the right ball park, so check them. Make sure that you've specified the benefit types correctly. See Chapter 5 for more on the three types of benefit.

- ❑ **Roles:** Ensure that you've identified people to take on all of the roles in the project. Use the checklist in Chapter 6 to help make quite sure.

- ❑ **Availability:** Confirm that people that you want to fill the roles in the project are both willing and available to take on the work. If anyone isn't sure that they will have the time to do the job properly, it's much better to find someone else now. You don't want to hit problems later on because someone doesn't have sufficient availability and then causes a whole series of delays.

❑ **Timing:** Is your estimate of how long the project will take realistic? How do you know? Should you check this out with others who have experience? Have a look back at the Consultation checklist that was before this one.

❑ **Costs:** As with the timing, are you confident that your figure is roughly right, even though it's still an estimate? If you're feeling uncertain, or it just looks wrong somehow, do the costing again. You may want to consult others again if you remain unsure. Other people with experience, particularly project experience, may be able to spot things that you've missed or confirm that actually you're right even though you were a bit unsure.

The Ready-to-roll Checklist

Unless the Project Steering Group (PSG) has decided that there will be a delay between the Outline and starting the full planning, the project can start with the Planning Stage immediately after the Outline has been approved. To be sure that you're absolutely ready to start that first stage, check the items on this list. They cover the things that you must have ready to pass on to the PSG, such as the Outline and the practical things that you'll need to have in place to be ready to roll.

❑ **Outline:** Check through the Outline to make sure that it's complete but also that it's clear and understandable.

❑ **Stage Plan for the Planning Stage:** Make sure that your Stage Plan for the Planning Stage is complete and realistic. This Stage Plan will go to the PSG for approval along with the Outline. There's another checklist after this one to help you think about the plan to be sure you've included enough time for the different parts of the planning work.

❑ **Staff for planning:** Check that the staff who will take part in the planning are aware of their involvement and also when they'll be needed.

❑ **Accommodation:** Check that the accommodation will be ready and available, such as a team room. Also make sure that you'll have the necessary equipment such as a large whiteboard, markers and flip charts.

❑ **PSG:** Be sure that Project Steering Group (PSG) members are aware of their involvement in the Planning Stage on things such as resource planning and the risk management. If you're intending to have a Planning Workshop (strongly recommended) then make sure that you've told the PSG members the date and checked that they'll be available.

❑ **Planning Workshop:** Check that the room is booked for the time that you'll need it, and that participants in the workshop know that they'll be needed and when. You may start the workshop with just the PSG and the Project Manager and then open it out to others later to tackle things such as the Project Plan. And don't forget to book the refreshments, unless you work in the UK government, where they're usually so terrible that you're better off without them.

❑ **Charter and PMP content:** Be sure that the PSG members and Project Manager are clear on the nature and content of the Charter and PMP for this project. PMP members can't work on the documents and make an effective contribution if they're unclear on what they are, why they're needed or how they'll be used.

❑ **Interdependencies:** A recurring theme on the checklists in this book, but interdependencies are important. Check to see whether your project is dependent on other areas of work such as other projects, and whether other areas are dependent on your project. If the project does interact with other ones you won't be able to create a workable plan if you don't understand the degree and nature of the interaction.

Planning Stage Checklist

The previous checklist included advice that you should make sure that the Stage Plan for the first project stage, the Planning Stage, is complete and realistic. Part of your check will be to make sure that you have put in enough planning time for the various elements. In turn, that will depend on the nature of the project. For example, if the project is high risk, have you allowed sufficient time for extensive risk analysis and planning? Here's a short checklist to help you make sure that your Stage Plan will be workable.

❑ **Scope:** If the scope is still a bit unclear, or if there may be hidden parts of the project making the scope bigger than everyone expected, be sure that you've allocated enough time to think about the scope and to discuss and amend the Scope Statement for the full Project Charter (developed from the Outline Charter that you prepared in Kick Off).

❑ **Risk:** Picking up on the point in the paragraph before this checklist, make sure that your plan includes enough time for risk analysis and deciding risk action, and also that you've thought about the people that you'll need to help with it. For example, you may want to run a Risk Workshop.

❑ **Quality:** If you have to hit a high level of quality you'll need a lot more time to think through your approach than for a lower quality level. Quality planning can be far reaching and time consuming so think about this aspect carefully.

❑ **Interdependencies:** Yes, this item pops up on yet another checklist. However, allow time for working on any interdependencies. Not just to identify them this time but rather to investigate the nature of the dependencies and co-ordinate the Project Plans.

I ran a workshop with a client recently to plan a series of projects. The interdependencies were significant. One project was producing a particular product and until that product was ready and passed to a second project, the second project couldn't get far at all. The second project then had to go on to produce a series of products, and one of the later ones was needed as an input back in the first project. The first project team suddenly found that there was going to be a big gap in their project. They needed the product from the second project and assumed that it would be ready quickly, but in fact it was going to take several weeks to produce so they had to recast their plan. If you think that's tough, the second project also had interdependencies with a third project with further timing implications, and in turn those affected the first project again. But wait there's more, so much more. Shall I continue? No, perhaps not as I guess you've now got the point about allowing sufficient time in the Planning Stage.

❑ **Resource levelling:** Resource levelling (making sure that the required resource for the project is within the limits of available resource) is time consuming at the best of times. The bad news is that if you are sharing a resource pool with other work or projects, then you'll need to resource level across projects not just within your own one. Six projects can't all have the electrical team in Week 17. The amount of work needed for resource levelling will jump up significantly if you have to consider other work areas. You'll have to talk to other managers and look at their plans, go back and adjust your plans, resolve new conflicts, go back to the other projects a second time to see if there are new implications (or they might have now found new things that affect yours), and even that might not be the end of it. There can be a lot to do but one thing's for sure; your project won't work without resource levelling.

❏ **Draft documents:** if the PSG wants to see a draft Charter and PMP before agreeing to the final ones, don't forget to allow time in the plan to produce and circulate the draft documents, time for PSG members to review them, ask any questions and comment, then time to process those comments and produce the final versions.

Chapter 5

Checking the Justification and Benefits

● ●

In This Chapter

▶ It's not just about benefits – looking at different justifications

▶ Being clear on benefit types, including non-quantifiable benefits

▶ Help to think through the possible benefits for your project

● ●

*T*he Business Case focuses on the justification for the project, including listing any business benefits that will result from the project. This chapter helps you check the justification for your project and write a sound Business Case.

Project Justification Checklist

It's easy to be too focused on benefits, or even a given level of financial benefits, when you're thinking about whether a project is justified or not. However, while achieving business benefits is the most common project justification, it isn't the only one. Have a look at this list to check your project out.

❏ **Benefits:** Okay, the most common justification first. The project will pay back with business benefits which outweigh the cost and effort involved in running the project.

❏ **Compliance:** You have to run the project whether there are benefits or not. That might be compliance with legal requirements or something like an HQ instruction that 'All regional offices will run a project . . .'

❏ **Enabling:** The project itself won't deliver benefits, but it will put something in place that will allow other projects or operations to deliver benefits. Infrastructure projects often fall into this category, such as a project to install a new computer network.

❏ **Maintenance:** The project just has to be done, even though there is not any benefit in the normal sense of the word and it's not mandatory (where it's needed for legal compliance). Replacing worn out equipment or redecorating the HQ building are often just 'maintenance' projects.

A senior UK police officer once asked me for advice on the Business Case for his project. He said he'd been working for a couple of days to identify benefits but he couldn't find any and so couldn't see how he could write the Business Case. I asked him why the police force was considering running the project and he replied 'Well, the Home Office has told us to.' (the Home Office is the UK government department that oversees police forces). I advised the officer that the main part of his Business Case – the justification – was 'The Home Office has told us to.' The project justification was 'compliance' based and very simple.

You may find that your project has a combined justification. Perhaps you must run the project anyway (compliance) but actually it will deliver a few benefits along the way which, although not completely offsetting the cost, will nevertheless contribute.

Benefit Types Checklist

Even where your project is benefits justified, you must be clear on what type of benefits those are. There are three different types and you need to be very aware of them because for sure your Finance Director will be.

The first distinction between benefits is whether they are measurable – quantifiable – or not. If a benefit can be measured, the next divide is whether it will be a financial gain or something else that is quantifiable. This breakdown is illustrated in Figure 5-1.

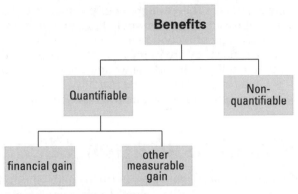

Figure 5-1: Benefits categories

❑ **Quantifiable – financial gain:** Cash savings are involved. If you replace a high-maintenance machine with a low-maintenance machine then you'll be able to see the unspent money in the maintenance budget. The 'financial gain' benefit is real money and is of particular interest to your Finance Director and to business managers.

❑ **Quantifiable – other measurable gain:** You can measure the benefit, perhaps even in financial terms, but isn't real money that you could draw out of an account and hold in your hand. Perhaps your project will improve the delivery schedule so customers get their orders in two days rather than the present four-day turnaround; that's a measurable benefit.

❑ **Non-quantifiable:** A benefit that you cannot measure meaningfully. In some cases it's pointless to try to measure something where the resulting figure will be vague or even misleading. In other cases you can see that you have no hope of accurately measuring the benefit at all. It may still be an extremely important benefit though – see the warning below.

Don't ignore non-quantifiable benefits, and be especially careful if you are using a method (such as the leading UK project method) that plays them down as if they don't matter. Non-quantifiable benefits can be incredibly important to the point of justifying the project without need for anything else. For example, running a project to improve the design of a commercial product may be essential so that you keep pace with competitors and hold market share. But it's hard to prove how many customers then bought your product solely because of the improvement; some would have bought it anyway and your sales were still good before the project. On the other hand, because they aren't measurable, it's easy to fool yourself that you'll get all sorts of wonderful non-quantifiable benefits when really you won't. Be brutally realistic then and try not to understate or overstate the non-quantifiables.

Benefits Consultation Checklist

You may have identified a lot of the benefits of running the project, but it can help to check things out with other people too. Sometimes they will see extra benefits that you didn't, and that could end up with your project being better justified than you'd realised.

Talking to other people can often make for a better project too. Someone may identify substantial benefits in a related area that you don't currently intend to include in the project scope. Yet you could easily take in the additional area and make the project very much more effective in the process.

Tom Peters, the American management guru, has said that all projects should be 'wow' projects. If any project isn't 'wow', he argues, you should rethink and reframe it until it is. I don't agree that every project can be a wow project. Being American, I'm sure Mr Peters doesn't know about projects to change the VAT rate across an organisation, for example, but I do think that he makes a valuable point. You can sometimes improve the value of the project considerably by adjusting the project boundary even if that adjustment doesn't result in the project being an organisation-changing watershed. The time to make such scope adjustments is now, during Kick Off, when the project documentation is still in sketch form and making changes is relatively easy. If you're interested in Tom Peters' take on this, have a look at his book 'The Project 50', part of the 'reinventing work' series published by Alfred A. Knopf.

My favourite example of taking a project to the next level is with a stationery supply company that put in a new computer system for customer orders. They realised that with small scope increase they could make use of the order data and make personalised special offers to customers, thereby increasing sales. So, suppose I buy a new fountain pen. On my next mailing from the company I see a tailored front page with a personal special offer on ink cartridges and blotting paper. I was impressed because that was a clever move; a lot of extra benefit from a relatively small amount of extra work using data that they were going to have to hold anyway.

As you're thinking about who you might ask about the benefits and potential benefits of your project idea, check out this list.

❑ **Business users:** Those who will use what the project will deliver. Ask them if there is anything that would make the deliverables even better. For example, including additional storage facilities in the new building extension may save staff time because currently people have to go to a more distant area to fetch things. Listen carefully to staff, including junior staff. Often junior people have been making sensible suggestions for ages only nobody's heard them.

❑ **Operational and maintenance staff:** Check out what ops and maintenance staff think about the project idea. They may be able to identify further benefits, or small changes that would lead to significant operational and maintenance savings, partly based on their experience of what's costing a lot at the moment.

❑ **Customers and sales staff:** It can be helpful to ask customers what they would find useful, or at least sales staff who understand customer needs. Some relatively small extra things can have disproportionately high benefits to customers, and make a good impression at the same time.

❑ **Managers:** Organisational managers may find benefits in small additions, such as being able to get additional reports in a new computer system so they can do a better analysis of usage patterns for hospital consumables. This wouldmake buying more cost efficient.

❑ **Senior managers:** To see whether additional functions would help achieve organisational targets. It could be that it isn't worth running a project just to hit one of those objectives, but adding that scope to yours would be a way of achieving it economically.

❑ **Similar organisations:** Particularly if you're in the charity or public sectors, talk to other organisations to see if they've done something similar. Ask what the scope of their projects was and what benefits they found. While you're at it, ask them if they would change the scope if they could go back in time and do the project all over again.

❑ **Suppliers:** Talk to suppliers, including internal suppliers within your own organisation, such as the IT Department. Draw on their experience of what would work well and make for an even better project, perhaps using new technology to give improved functionality or cheaper operations.

Measurement Points Checklist

Note against every quantifiable benefit that you list in the Business Case how and when it should be measured. It's a common misconception that all benefits are measured after the end of the project.

Think about what measurement points are appropriate for your project in the context of the benefits that you need to measure and when they will come on stream. Here's a summary of the main benefits review points.

❑ **During the project:** Some benefits may come on stream during the project. For example, if you replace a high-maintenance machine with a new low-maintenance machine early on in the project, you will start to see savings in the maintenance budget during the life of the project.

❑ **At the end of the project:** Particularly where you have a Closure Stage after the final Delivery Stage, the benefits from that delivery may be measurable before the project shuts down. In that case the benefits realisation can be included in the Project Completion Report.

❑ **After the end of the project:** Some benefits might not be clear for some time after the end of the project and so cannot be measured until then. For example, staff working on a newly introduced business procedure may not be working at normal speed for a few weeks while they get used to the new approach. It's only when things have settled down that you can take a meaningful measure of the savings in staff time.

❏ **Interim and final:** You might decide to use the last two points in combination. You could take an interim measure at the end of the project to give organisational managers and the Project Steering Group an early indication of the level of a benefit, then do a later and final one to give a precise measure.

❏ **At the end of linked projects:** Where your project is linked to others (perhaps in a programme), it may be that some of the benefits of your project can't be fully measured until after other projects have also delivered and the combined effect comes into play.

Benefits Checklist

Sometimes you may find it hard to spot all the areas of benefit, and if you miss benefits out then you'll understate the justification for your project. Use this list to help think through whether you've covered all of the possible benefits. The list is in the two areas of savings and gains. As always, adjust the list to fit your sort of project, and if you spot a new benefit area that applies to you then be sure to add it on. That way the list will be all the more useful at the beginning of each project.

Savings

A lot of business projects involve making savings in one form or another. Have a look through this part of the checklist to help make sure that you've spotted all the possible savings.

❏ **Staff time:** Staff time is expensive and often seriously so. Will your project mean that it will take fewer staff hours than the existing approach to operate a business or operational function?

❏ **Ease of use:** If something now needs fewer expert staff, your staff costs could be reduced.

❏ **Maintenance:** Check to see whether new equipment will be easier to maintain. You could find savings in three areas.

   ❏ **Engineer costs:** The number of staff hours needed for maintenance work.

❑ **Maintenance materials:** Service materials related to maintenance such as replacement oils and servicing kits.

❑ **Down-time:** The amount of down-time being reduced because maintenance is faster and/or because it is less frequent.

❑ **Durability:** If equipment will last longer it will not need replacing so often, and that may be a significant saving.

❑ **Disposal:** If the final disposal costs of any new equipment would be reduced, perhaps because it is constructed of less hazardous material and, related to the previous point, because of less frequent replacement.

❑ **Legal and compliance:** Reduction in compliance inspections or, for example, no longer needing an annual licence for something.

❑ **Materials:** If you are bringing in a new design for a product, or something like new product packaging, you may get a saving on materials and thus on production costs.

❑ **Consumables:** Check whether your project will save on consumables, such as with electronic long term records reducing consumption of paper, ink and toner.

❑ **Waste:** See whether your project will reduce waste. That could bring two benefits. First, a better 'green' image for your organisation; second, a reduction in waste disposal costs. Both benefits are especially significant if the waste is hazardous.

❑ **Energy consumption:** Check whether your project will make a saving on energy costs, or could be altered to do so. With escalating energy prices, this benefit is not only financially significant but very high profile.

❑ **Improved cash flow:** Things that will get money in more rapidly, such as faster issue of invoices because your project is introducing electronic invoicing.

❑ **Travel and overnights:** Reducing the need for staff travel and accommodation, for example with a comms improvement project that provides video-conferencing. Or this benefit may be linked to improved product quality where better reliability means fewer service visits.

❑ **Building accommodation:** See whether your project will reduce the demand for space, such as by reducing the need for storage. However, be very careful to think this one through, and do take on board the warning below. Remember that the accommodation saving may be very much greater if, for example, your project is an office move to a new headquarters in a less expensive, out-of-town, area.

Think very carefully when you come to consider savings on accommodation. If your project frees up a large storage room it won't save any money – an empty room in your headquarters building isn't cheaper to run than one filled with files. However, if you can convert that space into office accommodation which will mean your organisation won't now have to build that new office extension then perhaps you're on to something. Also watch out for cramming staff together to save space. If staff performance levels drop as a result, it may end up as a cost rather than a saving.

If your project is to solve a problem, solving the problem isn't the benefit. The benefit is the elimination, or reduction, of the negative impact(s) that the problem was causing. However, for the Business Case to make sense to organisational managers you'll usually need to describe the benefits in the context of the original problem.

Gains

The savings in the previous section are, in effect, a negative view as you are seeking to lower costs. In contrast, this next part of the checklist is the positive side. Can you increase revenue or service with the project?

☐ **Organisational objectives:** Achieving something that the organisation has committed to, in the five-year strategy plan for example.

☐ **Performance:** Check whether the project will increase staff performance, perhaps by giving people better computer tools to do the job or reducing the time it takes them to find essential information.

☐ **Service level:** Such as cutting waiting times in a hospital, or achieving faster delivery to customers.

☐ **Usability:** Such as making it much easier for your customers to place orders, thereby reducing the number of customers who give up part way through the process (a surprisingly common problem on web sites).

❑ **Production:** Gains through faster machines, for example, that mean you can produce more units in a given time.

❑ **Sales:** Some projects, such as those involved with re-branding or product improvement, may be justified because they will boost sales.

❑ **Quality:** Improving the quality of something your organisation is doing or producing. That may be a non-quantifiable benefit but an important one to maintain or boost the image of your organisation. That boost may happen through better design or by increased reliability, for example.

❑ **Staff facilities:** An improvement in the staff working environment. This benefit will normally be non-quantifiable, but important. You probably won't be able to measure a reduction in staff turnover that is due solely to the improvement in the working environment delivered by this project, but you know for sure that you'll continue to lose people if the environment isn't significantly improved by this and other projects.

❑ **Image and reputation:** Such as compliance where your project brings your organisation into line with ISO standards and codes of practice, and has a significant positive impact on your organisation's public image. This benefit may be very significant if the project eliminates a problem that was in the public eye. An announcement that the problem is now resolved may do a lot to help restore a damaged reputation.

Disadvantages Checklist

Sometimes running a project brings disadvantages, though of course these should be outweighed by the advantages unless the project is mandatory. Don't let people get taken by surprise with negatives but rather keep the Business Case realistic so that managers know what they are letting themselves in for, just as they do with project risk. Here are a few things that you might want to think about when warning of disadvantages as part of your Business Case.

❑ **Disruption:** Temporary disruption while the project is in progress, such as blocking an entrance to a building while extension work is done.

❑ **Delay:** Perhaps processing customer orders will be slowed down while the warehouse is being re-configured as part of the project.

❑ **Loss of production:** More 'down time' of computer systems or production line machinery while changes are made.

❑ **Loss of functionality:** Although things may be improved in one part of the operation, perhaps they are slightly degraded in another. For example, a new computer package that does most things a lot better but a few things that used to be automated will now have to be done clerically.

One project method refers to the disadvantages of running a project as *disbenefits*. However, that word isn't in common use. When was the last time you said to your partner 'If we go shopping at the weekend a disbenefit will be that it will take longer because the shops will be crowded.'? You'll want to minimise communication problems in your project so the last thing you want to do is use terms that people don't readily understand. For that reason you may agree with me that it's better to stick with the word *disadvantages* as suggested in this checklist.

Don't confuse disadvantages with what will happen if you don't run the project. Disadvantages, as set down in the Business Case, are the negative things that will happen if you do run the project. Note too that these things *will* happen; there *will* be disruption if you rip out the main reception area of your HQ building and fit a new one. If something just *might* happen then it's a risk.

Chapter 6

Tackling the Roles and Responsibilities

● ●

In This Chapter

▶ Roles and the fit with communications

▶ It's about roles, not jobs

▶ The roles you'll need in the project

▶ Role descriptions

● ●

*R*epeated surveys of the causes of project failure come up
with communication problems as one of the top reasons.
In turn, those communication problems frequently have their
roots in roles and responsibilities. People aren't clear on what
they should be doing, and they certainly aren't clear on what
other people should be doing, so things 'fall down the gaps'.

> *There were four people in the Body family. Their names*
> *were Everybody, Somebody, Anybody and Nobody. There*
> *was an important job to be done and Everybody was sure*
> *that Somebody would do it. Anybody could have done it,*
> *but Nobody did it. Somebody got angry about that, because*
> *it was Everybody's job. Everybody thought Anybody could*
> *do it, but Nobody realised that Everybody wouldn't do it. It*
> *ended up that Everybody blamed Somebody when Nobody*
> *did what Anybody could have done.*
>
> *Source unknown*

A lot of people talk casually about *roles and responsibilities*
without ever thinking about what that phrase means. In projects the use of the word *role* is crucial in two dimensions:

✔ **Roles are about function and not status.** A person who is very senior in the organisation may be a team member while someone who is their junior may be the Project Manager. The project organisation can take normal organisational reporting lines and turn them upside down.

✔ **Roles allow you to fit the project organisation around the specific needs of the project.** One person may have more than one role, and some roles can be shared between more than one person.

Figure 6-1 shows how the roles in the project fit together. This organisational structure is ISO compliant and builds in the important divide between the governance of the project (making sure that it's being run properly) and the operational aspects of the day-to-day management.

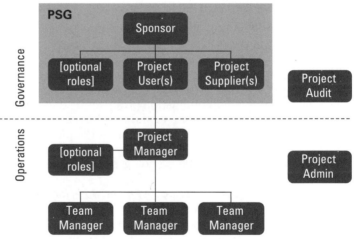

Figure 6-1: An ISO compliant organisational structure.

Project Roles Checklist

Use this checklist along with Figure 6-1 to make sure that you have all the bases covered when it comes to filling the project roles. The first three roles on the list make up the Project Steering Group (PSG), which is the small group of managers with overall responsibility for the project. The PSG is the Project Manager's boss.

❑ **Sponsor:** The 'business' interest in the project and in overall charge.

❑ **Project User(s):** The manager(s) representing those who will use what the project is delivering.

❑ **Project Supplier(s):** The manager(s) supplying most of the staff resource needed to run the project.

❑ **Optional PSG roles:** You may need someone extra to liaise with a programme level or to make sure that the whole of the business change runs smoothly.

❑ **Project Audit:** The person or persons responsible for checking the project to make sure that everything is okay.

❑ **Project Manager:** The manager responsible for the day-to-day running of the project.

❑ **Optional management roles:** Exceptionally, you may want to consider appointing someone to a specialised role to help the Project Manager, such as to keep an eye on business change or risk.

❑ **Team Leader:** Where the project has more than one team, you will normally need a Team Leader for each one.

❑ **Project Administration:** The person or people giving administrative support to the project. Administrative support could come from a Project Management Office if you have one.

Project Steering Group Checklist

The Project Steering Group (PSG) is made up of the three roles of Sponsor, Project User(s) and Project Supplier(s). Each role has specific responsibilities and you'll find those on individual checklists following this one. This checklist is about the joint responsibilities of the PSG.

In some organisations the PSG is known as a Project Steering Committee while in others it's called the Project Board. If you are unfamiliar with some of the terms used in this book, have a look at Chapter 21 in the Part of Tens which gives alternative names for documents and roles. You may well find that your organisation has exactly the same thing but uses a different label.

❏ **Ownership:** The project is not the Project Manager's project, it's the PSG's project. The PSG must take that fact on board and 'take ownership'.

❏ **Project governance:** Just as the senior managers in a department must make sure that the department runs well, so the PSG is responsible for making sure that the project is managed well. That involves checking that the project is set up properly at the start and then controlled properly throughout.

❏ **Review:** Following on from the previous point on governance, the PSG must have regular reviews to check that the project is running well. That doesn't mean putting undue pressure on the Project Manager, but it does mean getting the right information and actually checking it.

❏ **Audit follow up:** Considering the findings of Project Audit and ensuring that action is taken where that is justified.

❏ **Change:** Considering change requests that are beyond the authority the PSG has delegated to the Project Manager

❏ **Risk:** Deciding if the overall risk exposure is acceptable and then ensuring that the agreed risk management actions and procedures (such as how staff notify new risks) are actually working.

❏ **Quality:** Ensuring that the required quality is actually being achieved, not just talked about.

❏ **Support:** Just like any group of senior managers, the PSG members must support the Project Manager. The same principle holds true in projects as it does in general management – if your staff succeed, you succeed.

Don't accept a PSG role unless you can handle the responsibility and are available to take it on. If the project goes wrong because of poor management and poor control, you will be held to account by corporate management. That's not to say that the Project Manager isn't culpable too, but rather to emphasise that it's the PSGs project and the PSG members were appointed to their roles to make quite sure that the project was run properly. If that sounds a little harsh, just think about normal organisational management. If poor management somewhere within a department leads to failure, then it's the fault of the senior managers of that department and especially the head of department. An important element of a senior manager's function is to make sure that things don't go wrong and to put the appropriate checks and controls in place to monitor the work being done.

Sponsor Checklist

So, you're the Sponsor for the project? Congratulations. Here's a list to help you understand what your role involves, alongside your shared responsibilities as set down in the last checklist on the PSG. As Sponsor you are ultimately responsible for the project and of the three views of business, user and supplier, you represent the business view.

❏ **Leadership:** you are in overall charge of the project, even though day-to-day management of the project is delegated to the Project Manager. You must show that leadership to the point of encouraging and even inspiring the project staff.

Napoleon Bonaparte was an inspiring leader. The Duke of Wellington said of him that when he was on the field of battle he was worth 40,000 soldiers. Don't underestimate the value of being out and about and encouraging project staff. However, do your encouraging carefully without undermining the management position of the Project Manager and the Team Leaders, and without getting in the way. And don't go round asking silly questions; be an intelligent and informed leader, not a tourist.

❏ **Communication:** You must communicate as necessary with the corporate managers who appointed you to run the project. When it comes to senior organisational managers, you speak for the project; it's not the Project Manager's place to do that.

❏ **Business Case:** It's mostly down to you to ensure that the Business Case is sound and accurately compiled. That means checking that the benefits estimates are realistic and correctly calculated. You must also ensure that the Business Case is kept up-to-date throughout the project and that the project continues to be viable.

❏ **Value for money:** You must ensure that the project is value for money. Even if the project is mandatory, is it being done in the most cost-effective way?

❑ **Business impact:** You should check the impact the project will have on the rest of the organisation and ensure that other areas are aware of it. If you're running the PRIME project management method you must personally sign the Business Impact Statement, and that action indicates your personal responsibility for it.

❑ **Chair the PSG:** As Sponsor and the business interest in the project, you will chair PSG meetings. Those meetings are notably the Stage Reviews (progress meetings) and Stage Gates (the meeting at the end of each Delivery Stage to check the project and approve the next stage).

❑ **Decision making:** You will listen very carefully to the views of the other PSG members and also to those of the Project Manager. Normally the PSG will reach decisions on the project by consensus, but if there is disagreement you must make the final decision even if that goes against the views of all the other PSG members. It's like being a head of department.

❑ **Guidance and direction:** You must be available personally for the Project Manager when she needs direction or input from time to time. For example, she may want to talk to you about the impact of a newly discovered risk and get your views on it.

❑ **Emergency action:** If something goes wrong in a stage, or across the whole project, that's beyond the authority of the Project Manager to deal with, she will refer the matter to you. You must now step in and take charge of the situation. You'll listen carefully to the Project Manager's recommendations and to other PSG members, but you must now resolve the matter. That resolution may be to shut the project down.

Project User Checklist

So, you've been appointed to the Project User role on the Project Steering Group. It's an important role so have a look at this checklist to help you understand what it involves. This checklist accompanies the earlier checklist on the shared responsibilities of the PSG. Of the three views of business, user and supplier, you represent the user view. You may hold this role on your own, or alongside one or two other Project Users from different areas that will be affected by the project.

❑ **Fit for purpose:** As Project User your primary responsibility is to ensure that the project is delivering what the users can use.

❑ **Staff resource:** Most projects need user staff involved to help specify what's needed and then to test that the deliverables are okay, but the degree of involvement may be even more. Part of your role is to supply that user resource.

❑ **Project champion:** As well as bringing user information into the project, you're responsible for the reverse information flow too. You should be 'championing' the project in the business areas.

❑ **Guidance and direction:** You must be available personally for the Project Manager when she needs direction or input from time-to-time. For example, she may want to talk to you about the relative priorities of changes that have been requested by user staff.

Be totally realistic when you work with the Project Manager to discuss what user resource is needed and what is available. When you sign the plan, you commit that user resource, so make very sure that you can provide it. If you are not in personal control of all the user staff needed on the project, you may need to get agreements from other managers before agreeing to the resource provision on their behalf as well as on your own.

Project Supplier Checklist

Of the three views of business, user and supplier, you represent the supplier view. Congratulations on your appointment to the Project Steering Group. The supplier side covers those actually doing the work of the project – the project teams.

You may be alone in the Project Supplier role, or there may be someone else sharing the role. It's common, for example, to have one Project Supplier authorising staff resource from within the customer organisation and another Project Supplier from an external supplier company authorising their staff's involvement in the project.

Here's a checklist to help you understand the Project Supplier responsibilities. The responsibilities go in parallel with your joint PSG responsibilities as listed in the PSG checklist earlier in the chapter.

❑ **Advise on supply matters:** Advise the PSG on the supplier aspects of the project, including that the approach being taken is technically sound and achievable.

❑ **Translate:** Where the project involves technical things, other PSG members may struggle to understand what is involved and that will make it harder to make sensible management decisions. Part of your role is to explain any necessary technicalities to other PSG members in terms that they can understand.

❑ **Standards:** Ensure that any applicable technical standards will be met and that they are listed correctly in the Quality Plan.

❑ **Plans:** Work with the Project Manager on project resourcing and say what staff resource you will be able to supply and when.

❑ **Guidance and direction:** You must be available personally for the Project Manager when she needs direction or input from time-to-time. For example, she may want to talk to you about the implications for team resourcing if the project starts to run ahead of schedule.

❑ **Supply team resource:** You will authorise the team resource for most of the project work. The only staff resource you won't supply is user staff (they will be provided by the Project User on the PSG).

 Check the Project and Stage Plans carefully and make sure that you can provide the supplier staff resource that they show. When you sign a plan be very aware that you are committing the supplier resource shown on it.

 You may not be in direct personal control of all of the supplier resource – for example if different departments are providing staff. In that case you will need to get agreements from others, perhaps signed, before you sign a plan to commit all of the supplier resource needed for the project.

Optional PSG Roles

You really want a 'lean and mean' PSG with up to three people, but no more than six. However, sometimes it may be helpful to have an additional person in one of two specialised roles.

❑ **Change Manager:** If the project will require substantial change elsewhere in the organisation, you may want to have someone on the PSG keeping a special eye on this and making sure that all other areas will be ready at the point that the project delivers. An alternative is to have a Change Manager helping the Project Manager.

❑ **Programme Liaison:** Where the project is part of a programme, it can help considerably to have a member of the programme management team on the Steering Group to maintain a strong link between the project and programme levels.

Project Manager Checklist

As Project Manager, you have day-to-day responsibility for running the project and you're accountable to the PSG for that. If you already have some project management experience you might think that it would be simpler to have a checklist of what you're *not* responsible for in the project, but here goes anyway. Sharpen your pencil because predictably, it's a long checklist with a lot of boxes to tick.

❑ **Plans:** You'll normally be planning at two levels; project level and stage level.

❑ **Business Case:** Although the Sponsor has primary responsibility for the Business Case, you'll be doing a lot of the 'spadework' to research and write it.

❑ **Project Charter:** You'll be the driving force in writing the Project Charter, the strategic view of the project. Have a look at the template in Chapter 11 if you're not clear on the contents.

❑ **PMP:** The Project Management Plan or PMP is primarily your responsibility, though you will get input from others such as PSG members. It's a set of plans including the

Project Plan and Risk Plan. Again, have a look at the templates in Chapter 11 if you're unclear on the contents.

❏ **Flow of work:** You are responsible for controlling the flow of work to teams (or individuals if it's a smaller project) with Work Packages (work assignments).

❏ **Control:** Once the project is underway and the teams start on the first Work Packages, your job is to be at the helm to keep the project in general, and the stage in particular, on track.

❏ **Risk:** You'll be keeping an eye on identified risks and their related control actions and examining any new risks.

❏ **Quality:** There's no point in delivering unusable garbage on time and within budget. An important part of your function is to ensure that the project is delivering to the specified level of quality.

❏ **Plan updates:** A plan is no help for control unless it's up-to-date, so updating the plan must be a regular and routine part of your management.

❏ **Reports:** You're responsible for reporting to others, as set down in the Communications Plan in the PMP. Notably that's keeping the PSG informed of progress but there's other reporting too such as at the end of each stage (Stage Completion Report) and at the end of the project (Project Completion Report).

❏ **Change:** You're responsible for dealing with change requests and looking at the value and impact. For each change you can decide on it if you have the authority, or refer it to the PSG if not.

❏ **Problem solving:** It's absolutely normal for any project to hit problems. Part of the challenge of your role is solving them, but with input from others when you need it.

❏ **Co-ordination:** Where your project interfaces with other work (perhaps in a programme and perhaps not) you need to keep in touch with other project managers and organisational managers to make sure that everything works together.

❏ **Motivation and encouragement:** Although you may have Team Leaders running the teams, you have an important function to help motivate and encourage those doing the work.

❏ **Stage Gates:** At the end of each Delivery Stage you are responsible for preparing for the Stage Gate with all the information that the PSG will need to assess the project.

❏ **Lessons:** Note lessons that you've learned in this project, both good and bad things, which might be of help to future projects.

❏ **Capturing 'actuals' and maintaining records:** Hopefully you'll have a Project Administration function to cover this aspect. However if you don't then this job is down to you.

Optional Management Roles

The Project Manager is in day-to-day charge of the project, usually with Team Leaders reporting to her. In some circumstances, though, it's a good idea to have specialised managers working for the Project Manager but not involved in leading one of the teams.

❏ **Project Risk Manager:** In a very high risk project you may appoint a Risk Manager to assist the Project Manager and concentrate solely on risk.

❏ **Project Change Manager:** Where the project involves substantial organisational change outside the direct control of the project, you may find it helpful to have a dedicated Change Manager. If someone more senior is needed then this role could be at PSG level as described earlier in the chapter.

Team Leader Checklist

As Team Leader you're responsible for managing a team to work through one or more Work Packages (work assignments) in a stage. Here's a checklist to help you make sure that you're covering all of the important areas of responsibility.

❏ **Assist with stage planning:** Your input will be invaluable to the Project Manager when planning the stage. It will also help you to think through what will be involved in your own management.

❑ **Plan the Work Package:** If a Work Package is complex and the Stage Plan doesn't give sufficient detail to control it, then produce a Work Plan with the level of detail that you *do* need.

❑ **Control the work:** Keep track of the work as your team builds the products in the Work Package. Check that everything is on-track, and make adjustments if it isn't.

❑ **Check quality:** Make sure that products are being built to the right quality level as set down in the Product Definitions, and that tests and checks are being carried out properly.

❑ **Report progress:** Keep the Project Manager up-to-date with progress on the current work. That will be as instructed when you were given the Work Package and could be by report or by giving the same information in a Team Leaders' meeting for example.

❑ **Report problems:** Inform the Project Manager of anything that could affect the final delivery date of the Work Package or affect the stage in other ways.

❑ **Monitor risks:** Monitor the risks associated with the Work Package and inform the Project Manager of any new risks you see in the project or any change of status in existing risks. It follows that you need to be familiar with the risks in the project Risk Log.

❑ **Advise:** Advise the Project Manager as required, such as on the impact of a change that has been requested.

Project Audit Checklist

In Chapter 19 you'll find a whole range of checklists for auditing specific areas of the project. This simple one in the 'Roles and Responsibilities' chapter is about the role itself.

This checklist is rather different from others in the chapter because as well as saying what you are responsible for, it also makes clear what you're not responsible for. It's important that you're clear on your function because there are a lot of misunderstandings about, not helped by fuzzy thinking in some project methods and approaches.

What you're responsible for

These are the main areas of responsibility for Project Audit. The exact auditing requirements will be established at the start of the project and may be largely influenced by an organisational approach to project governance and audit.

❑ **Helping the project to succeed:** This may sound a bit odd as a first point, but it's important. Be balanced, helpful and constructive; don't nit-pick on trivia and make the life of the Project Manager more difficult than it need be.

❑ **Business Case:** Checking that it's sensible, not overstated, accurate and clear.

❑ **Appointments:** Ensuring that they're suitable both in terms of the competence of the people appointed and that those people have sufficient availability to do the job.

❑ **Completeness:** Making sure that documents such as the Project Charter and Project Management Plan are complete, as consistent with the needs of the project.

❑ **Plans:** Checking that plans are realistic, achievable and accurate. For example, that there's sufficient contingency and that work hasn't been scheduled by mistake over public holiday periods.

❑ **Standards:** Ensuring that any required standards are being met and in an appropriate way. That means looking out for where projects are exceeding requirements and incurring unnecessary overheads as well as where they may be failing to meet necessary parts of the standards.

❑ **Procedures:** Making sure that procedures within the project are functioning properly. So, when someone in the project notices a new risk and sends in a Project Memo, is it being correctly picked up and processed?

❑ **Actions:** Ensuring that intended actions are actually being taken. So if a regular monthly action has been planned to avoid a risk, is that actually being done?

❑ **Quality:** This point is related to the last one but worth spelling out separately. If a quality action such as a test is supposed to have been done, has it been done, and has it been done by the right people?

If you're doing your job correctly in Project Audit, the Project Manager should find you a real help and welcome you warmly when you visit. You should be like a helpful colleague and a 'second pair of eyes', in that you find errors and omissions. That doesn't detract for one moment from your independence and if the Project Manager is 'blindsiding' the PSG for example, you will report it.

What you're not responsible for

This isn't everything outside your role in Project Audit but just things that are confused sometimes or are just plain wrong.

❑ **Appointments:** you shouldn't be suggesting people for project roles. You can't audit to evaluate if an appointment is appropriate if you suggested that person in the first place. If you're familiar with a leading project management method and think that I'm criticising it in making this point, you're absolutely right: I am.

❑ **Project work:** You mustn't be involved in any way in the project work, even if you consider that to be a different role ('I'm a team member for four days a week and the Project Auditor on the same project for one day a week.') You can't be independent if you've been involved in doing the work.

❑ **Corrections:** You shouldn't be directly involved in correcting things that you found to be wrong. If you do, you lose your independence in any later check to ensure that corrections have been properly handled.

❑ **Finding something wrong:** Don't think that you have a responsibility to find something wrong in the project to justify your existence. If there's nothing wrong then say so in your audit report; you've still done your job. Also, keep a sense of proportion. Be very careful not to exaggerate minor things and report them as major things so that it makes the audit seem more worthwhile.

❑ **Running the project:** The PSG is responsible for the project. You are not there to instruct the PSG members on how to do their jobs any more than the financial auditors instruct a Finance Director on how to do hers. Neither should you give instructions to the Project Manager; remember that her boss is the PSG, not you. You can report problems or errors that you discover in your audit checks, but it is for the management of the project to take any necessary action.

Project Administration Checklist

In a Project Administration role you can make an enormous contribution to the success of the project. The important thing is to recognise that you are in a support function. Your role is not to run the project but to help the Project Manager (and possibly Team Leaders) run the project. If you're tempted to think that isn't very important, just think how essential a good PA (personal assistant) is to a top manager in a large organisation. That PA needs to be practical, intelligent, highly professional, thoroughly competent and thoroughly reliable . . . and so do you.

Here's a checklist to help you get to grips with the range of things where you can provide very real help and assistance.

❑ **Planning:** Assist the Project Manager and others with drawing up comprehensive and pragmatic project plans. You need to be fully familiar with product planning, activity planning, resource planning and budgeting.

❑ **Project setup:** Assist and perhaps advise the Project Manager on suitable records and record formats for the project. Your objective here is to help put in the right degree of control without unnecessary overheads. You may advise on simplifying forms and procedures for this particular project.

❑ **Meeting administration:** Making arrangements for meetings including sending out any invitations, booking rooms and ordering refreshments. Then in taking and distributing notes of meetings.

❑ **Logging 'actuals':** Entering 'actuals' such as timesheet and spending information into spreadsheets and project management software tools.

❑ **Drafting reports:** Doing the initial work to prepare reports such as progress and financial reports.

❑ **Giving advice:** Advising the Project Manager and Team Leaders on areas of project planning, control and administration, such as on the detail of using project management software tools.

❑ **Checks:** Making sure that documents are complete and accurate. For example, you might unobtrusively check the draft Project Charter to ensure that all sections have been completed, and warn the Project Manager if she's forgotten something. You might also check the mathematics of the benefits calculations in the Business Case to be sure that they're correct.

❑ **Version control:** Depending on the nature of the project, you may control the versioning system for the project to keep track of versions of technical products, such as design drawings, and management products such as the Business Case.

Chapter 7

Templates for Kick Off

- -

In This Chapter

▶ A template for the Idea

▶ A template for the Recommendation

▶ A template for the Outline Charter

- -

*T*emplates have the big advantage that they help you ensure that you have everything you need in a document. Note that word *need* though. If the templates in this chapter and elsewhere in the book have sections that you *don't* need, then simply edit them out. You should always guard against the problem where templates become the excuse for over-documentation that just wastes time.

The three templates in this chapter are to give you a steer on completing the documents in Kick Off. Following on from the thought in the last paragraph, you should find them particularly fast to complete. Unlike the templates in other chapters which are more generic, these are taken from the PRIME project method, with permission. PRIME is designed to go particularly quickly in its early stages. In fact you could be starting the project and moving on to full planning in two weeks, even for a large project, and in many cases much less than that.

Speed is important in most projects for two reasons. First, the longer the project takes, the higher the costs will usually be. Second, with benefits-driven projects, the longer the project takes the longer it is before the business benefits come on stream. Benefits delays can, and often do, dwarf the cost of the project itself. Now be careful with going fast. The emphasis here is on working intelligently, efficiently and moving things on promptly, not on being reckless and leaving out important plans and controls.

As you read through this chapter and look at the templates, you may think at first that the contents are rather repetitive and therefore wasteful. However, what you are seeing is levels of detail. Your efforts in the early documents are not wasted because you expand on those things and go into more detail in the later ones. If you find that you don't need to put in any more detail for an item as you move forward, that's fine; just cut and paste the information into the next document.

The Idea

The Idea is simply that, an idea for a project. This template is intended to be available to everyone in the organisation to use if they have a suggestion to put forward for a project. A member of staff will normally submit an Idea to their line manager but it could be linked in with a staff suggestions scheme.

The Idea should be short, ideally about a half to one page of text, or the equivalent as a discussion item in a meeting. The contents shown in the template will guide the author to provide the information that a more senior manager will need. That manager will then make a decision on whether or not to devote more effort to the proposal and go on to produce a Recommendation – the subject of the next template.

The Idea should be short. Most Ideas won't become projects and it simply isn't worth putting in more effort until a manager has decided that it's worth it.

❏ **Background:** How the Idea came into being. There may be, for example, a problem such as a delay in the supply chain. Or it could be a need to improve a service to keep up with competitors, or new technology opening the way to a new commercial product.

❏ **Idea description:** An explanation of the proposed project. This should be in straightforward terms to be readily understandable.

❏ **Impact of the Idea:** In two dimensions. First the extent to which the Idea will work, for example to solve a problem or at least part of it. Second, the organisational impacts. For example, will it require a change in the organisation's computer systems?

❏ **Business Advantages:** How the project will help the organisation.

❏ **Estimated resource requirements:** Your rough estimate of the amount of staff effort and money that would be needed to run the project, if it were to go ahead.

❏ **Decision:** Space for a manager to record whether or not more work is authorised to investigate the proposal further and produce a Recommendation. The manager making the decision should also record here any information on the nature of the Recommendation, such as that it should be in the form of a business presentation rather than a document.

The Recommendation

In the Recommendation you record the results of your deeper investigation into the project idea, usually after talking with other people such as subject specialists. You will often have looked at different options for running the project, and if so you should briefly explain those options in the Recommendation along with, obviously enough, your recommendation for which one should form the project itself.

Just occasionally your further investigation may have shown you that the project isn't worth running after all. In that case your recommendation will be to stop here. Don't worry if that's the case. Even the Recommendation is quite short so you won't have wasted that much time. Indeed, the whole point of keeping things short at the beginning is not to waste time.

A Recommendation can be up to 20 pages long, but often will be around 10. It should take two or three days to produce.

❏ **Summary:** A short summary of the key points so that managers reading the Recommendation can focus, see the context and more quickly take on board the remaining sections.

❏ **Background:** How the project idea came into being.

❏ **Options (if applicable):** In preparing the Recommendation you may have looked at different options for the project. In this section briefly explain the options you investigated.

❑ **Recommended project:** The option you recommend, and why.

❑ **Reasons:** Why the project should be run; the justification, such as that it's a mandatory project or is entirely justi-fied by benefits.

❑ **Benefits:** Brief information on any benefits, such as that the project should save money or increase market share. A project may have benefits even when it is justified by something else, like being a mandatory project to comply with the law.

❑ **Likely time, cost and staffing:** Estimates of time, cost and staff resource levels based on your own judgment, but perhaps having checked out the details with others too, such as people who have run similar projects in the past.

❑ **Impacts:** Any known implications of the project, such as the need to make changes in other business areas.

❑ **Decision:** the outcome and what is to happen next. Managers may, for example, agree that the work should be done but not as a project.

Outline Charter

The Outline Charter, or just 'Outline' is an important docu-ment and sets down the strategic aspects of the project, including what it is and the justification for it. You'll expand it later into a full Project Charter which will then be checked by the Project Steering Group (PSG) at the start of the project to ensure that the project is viable. You then keep that Charter up to date throughout the project, and it must be checked again by the PSG at every Stage Gate to be sure that the proj-ect continues to be viable.

The Outline is, then, the forerunner of the full Project Charter which you'll produce in the Planning Stage and for which you'll find a template in Chapter 11. The difference between the Outline and the full Charter is that, as its name suggests, the Outline is higher level; it's a sort of sketch. The explana-tion for each item on this template is fairly brief but should be enough for you to complete the document. However, if you'd like a bit more detail even now then flip forward in the book to have a look at explanations for the full Project Charter template in Chapter 11.

Of course you can adjust the template to take account of your own organisational requirements. That can be by adding things and removing others, or changing how things are grouped.

❑ **Scope Statement:** The important elements of the project including what it will cover and what it won't.

  ❑ **Background and summary:** What the project is and why it is necessary or advantageous. This information can be based on the Recommendation.

  ❑ **Project Product (and any other key deliverables):** What the project will ultimately deliver, and any other significant deliveries before the end of the project.

  ❑ **Requirements:** What is needed for the project, together with the source of each item. Some may be user requirements, for example, and others may be legal requirements.

  ❑ **Areas included:** What the project will include.

  ❑ **Areas excluded:** Things the project won't include, but which some people may assume that will be part of the project unless you clearly inform them otherwise.

❑ **Objectives:** What the project is to achieve. It's important that everyone understands the objectives and agrees to them.

❑ **Business Case** (high level): The justification for the project, including an assessment of the benefits.

❑ **Showstoppers:** Things that you've already identified that will mean the project will be shut down early. That could be something like reaching a maximum cost threshold, or a competitor beating you in the race to market with a new product.

❑ **Project environment:**

❑ **Technical environment:** Any technical impact of the project, or limitation such as it must only install machines from a particular manufacturer's range so as to stay in line with existing maintenance arrangements.

❑ **Business environment:** The impact that the project will have in other areas of the business.

❑ **Project Profile:** this is PRIME's diagram to show the characteristics of the project, such as time sensitivity, risk level, quality level etc. It gives an at-a-glance view of the nature of the project and indicates the sort of control that will be needed. You might like to use a diagram to show key characteristics, even if you are not planning to use the PRIME method.

❑ **Proposed Organisation Chart:** If the Outline is approved, the next thing to happen will be the start of the project and work getting under way on the full planning. So who will take the project roles such as Sponsor and Project Manager? The Proposed Organisation Chart in the Outline sets down who should be appointed, having established that the people involved are available. The roles will be confirmed if the decision is to go ahead with the project.

Part III
Checklists for Planning

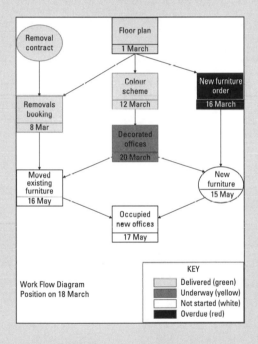

Work Flow Diagram
Position on 18 March

KEY
- Delivered (green)
- Underway (yellow)
- Not started (white)
- Overdue (red)

The Work Flow Diagram is a hugely powerful planning technique. Simple in concept, it shows the products that must be created (deliverables) in the order in which they must be produced. The diagram is also very effective for progress control. You can date and colour code the product boxes to show when products are delivered and if they were on time.

In this part . . .

✔ Understand the importance of proper planning.

✔ Think the project through and develop good plans, helping you to keep everything on track.

✔ Set up good controls so that if something goes wrong (which it inevitably will) you can deal with it.

Chapter 8

Creating the Plans

In This Chapter

▶ Planning as a foundation

▶ Solving problems on the plan, not in the project

▶ The levels of planning

▶ Checklists to help you get the plans right

*F*ail to plan: Plan to fail

It's an old saying but it's true. Like many people, you may be under pressure to 'get on with the real work' of the project and so be in danger of cutting back on planning. However, planning is real work. With a good plan you'll be in control, you'll avoid firefighting problems that were avoidable and you may even deliver earlier. The plans give you a clear view of what you need to produce, how and when. Then you can check that everything fits together and that you really can deliver. The idea is to find and solve problems on the plan, not hit them in the project. A major cause of failure in projects is poor planning, or not planning at all. Now the answer to under-planning isn't over-planning, but good, well thought-through plans for the level of control that you'll need this time around.

You'll often need to work at two levels of planning and sometimes three. You do the project level planning in the Planning Stage where you create the full Project Charter and the Project Management Plan (PMP), and the PMP in turn contains other plans such as the Risk Plan. Have a look at Chapter 2 if you're not familiar with these key documents. Usually you'll then want to create a lower level plan for each stage as you approach it, and even at the third level of team assignments (Work Packages) if those assignments are complex.

You'll find this chapter useful at all of the levels, but you'll use it most intensively in the Planning Stage.

Business Case Checklist

The Business Case is an essential part of the Charter and includes the justification for the project. Make sure that your Business Case is sound and that you have thought it through.

You'll need to revisit the Business Case as you carry out other parts of the planning, and then throughout the project. Make sure that you keep it up to date with the very latest information.

❑ **Justification:** Check that the justification is clear, accurate and fair. Have a look at Chapter 5 for more on the justification types; it isn't just about business benefits.

❑ **Complete benefits:** Are you confident that you're not understating the project's value by missing any key benefits? Check for benefits even if your project is mostly justified by something else. You'll find a checklist in Chapter 5 to help you think through the areas.

❑ **Accurate benefits:** Have you explained the benefits clearly and categorised them correctly? Where other people have set down benefits, make sure that they're real and not just wishful thinking. Again, Chapter 5 will help you check out this aspect.

❑ **Uncontaminated benefits:** Check that each benefit will be a direct result of the project, not something else. Beware of 'benefits contamination' where something other than the project could have led to the benefit, such as where the benefit will occur anyway whether the project goes ahead or not.

❑ **Prudent benefits projections:** Ensure that you have erred on the side of understating rather than overstating benefits following the accountancy principle to be prudent. Overstating the benefits can be very damaging.

❑ **Specific benefits measures:** Where benefits are quantifiable, make sure that for each one you've stated clearly how it will be measured and when it will come on stream so that it can be measured.

❑ **Realistic costings:** Hand-on-heart, are you sure that your project cost estimate is realistic, even if you can't be one hundred per cent sure at this point? And if you can't be completely sure of the cost, simply explain that.

❑ **Realistic resource estimates:** So many projects are late because there was more work than people realised. Check carefully to ensure that your staff resource estimates are realistic. Check it with others if necessary, perhaps including those who will be doing the work.

❑ **Realistic timing estimates:** Is your estimate of the duration of the project realistic in the context of the resource levels you have in mind? If you haven't already, check it out with people who have done this sort of work before.

❑ **Evidenced content:** Have you got good evidence to back up the Business Case entries such as the project cost and timescale, or are they just guesses? Depending on the time you are doing this some rough estimating may be inevitable, but if so then explain that.

❑ **Complete document:** Make sure that all of the relevant sections of the Business Case are properly completed. Have a look at the template in Chapter 11 for a default list of contents.

❑ **Clear and understandable text:** Make sure that the Business Case will be easy for others to understand, including people not familiar with the detail of the project such as senior organisational managers.

The Business Case may be seen as a stand-alone document. A Projects or Finance Committee may treat it that way to approve the funds. For that reason you should usually include things like cost, timescale and major risks. That's not mere duplication of information stored elsewhere, such as in the plans, but rather it reflects how the Business Case will be used.

The Business Case checklist includes a check for being prudent. Overstating benefits can be damaging in two ways:

✔ Your organisation may run the project when it's not really justified. That may result in another project not going ahead when actually it would have been a better choice.

✔ When the project fails to deliver on the overstated benefits it will probably be seen as a failure – and perhaps you
will too. Had the Business Case been realistic and more
prudent at the start, the project would have been seen as
a success and, who knows, you might have got that promotion after all.

Product Planning Checklist

The *product-based* or *product-led* approach to planning is
hugely powerful as well as being very logical. One of the
advantages of the approach is in flushing out hidden bits
of the project to give you a more complete view of what's
involved. Good product plans lead to complete activity plans,
realistic resource plans and more accurate costings; all of
these are really helpful for project control. If you're not familiar with the product-based approach, have a look at the UK
edition of *Project Management for Dummies* (Wiley) or hire
in Inspirandum to deliver a training course for you to really
unpack the power!

The Work Flow Diagram is a particularly powerful in product
planning. If you're not familiar with this type of diagram, have
a look at the title page of this part of the book, Part III, and
you'll find an example.

As you check your products, think about these areas.

❑ **Risk:** Check that you have included risk-related products,
such as assessments of technology developments in
competitor companies.

❑ **Inter-project dependencies:** These occur where you
can't start to build a product in your project until you
have received something from someone else's project,
such as a copy of a design specification.

❑ **Communications:** Internal project communications
don't need to be put on the plan, but there may be other
important communications products that do, such as
briefings for business staff, a website and publicity
materials.

❏ **Training:** A lot of project planners forget user training. Check that you have included relevant products such as training materials, room bookings and staff attendance schedules.

❏ **Orders:** These are important where you have external products coming in from outside the project, many will need an 'order' product; they won't arrive by magic.

❏ **Installation:** Where you have an external product, such as a Pink Widget bought from a supplier, check if you need an 'Installed Pink Widget' product which may be something that your project will create.

❏ **Legal issues:** This covers items such as licences. If you need them then include them on the product diagrams but also your applications for the licences because they're products too.

❏ **Inspections and approvals:** This includes such requirements as building inspections and electrical safety certification. The approval certificates are products, but so too are applications to ask for them.

❏ **Logic:** Check the flow of products on your Work Flow Diagram. Ensure that the dependencies are complete, necessary and logical.

❏ **Completeness:** Check that all of the products identified on any list or Work Breakdown Structure have been carried forward to the Work Flow Diagram, then that you have done the 'bottom-up checks' to ensure that nothing has been left out. See the Remember point below for more on the bottom up checks.

❏ **Management products:** Although your main product diagrams will only show team products, list the products you need to manage the project separately, such as progress reports and Stage Plans. Don't overlook them; they'll need time and resource to produce.

Workshops are great for planning and particularly for producing the Work Flow Diagram. If you have people in the workshop who are experienced and who represent all the areas involved – such as both business and technical staff – you can get the initial diagram drawn up and checked rapidly, often in two or three hours.

The two 'bottom-up checks' are essential to check the accuracy of your Work Flow Diagram. Starting at the bottom of the diagram, work up to check each product. For each one ensure that every dependency arrow feeding into it is correct. Then, for that same product, check that you don't need any other products in place to build it, only the ones already shown feeding into it with an arrow. It's the second of these checks that often shows up essential bits of the project that you hadn't realised were there.

Activity Planning Checklist

For activity planning most people use an activity network (usually a Precedence Network) followed by a Gantt Chart since this is what is provided by the mainstream project scheduling software. Use the product names as headings, then under each one list the activities you'll need to build that product. When you come to check your activity plans, run down this checklist.

❑ **Completeness:** Have you copied every product onto the activity plan as a heading? Except for the external products, make sure that you have at least one activity listed for each productto cover the work required to build it.

❑ **External products:** Check to see if you need any activity for something coming in from outside. Although your project isn't responsible for creating that item, you may need an activity to check it or install it.

❑ **Quality:** Ensure that you've included the the necessary quality activities, such as testing each individual product and then project-wide quality activity such as quality audits.

❑ **Correct dependencies:** Be sure to check every activity dependency to be confident that it's accurate and also that it's in line with the dependencies you identified on your Work Flow Diagram.

❑ **Overlaps:** Make sure that you haven't missed any overlaps where a second activity can be started before the first is completely finished.

❑ **Lags:** Check for lags where a second activity can't start immediately after a first one is complete. For example, you can't start the induction training of new staff the day after the employment contracts have been sent out. Most people will have to work a period of notice with their current employer before joining your organisation so you may have to allow for a four week lag, and probably even more.

As an alternative to entering a lag into a following activity, I usually prefer to show [waiting time] as an activity, and I use square brackets to make it clear that it isn't project work but rather a 'null' activity. The null activity avoids mysterious gaps on the Gantt Chart. I do the same for [contingency] time so that it's visible on the plan, but with square brackets again to show that there's no work involved.

- ❏ **Inter-project dependencies (inbound):** Note any inter-project dependencies on your product plans. Then make sure that the timing of your activity is consistent with the availability of the necessary input from the other project(s).

- ❏ **Inter-project dependencies (outbound):** Where another project needs stuff from your project, make sure that you will be producing it in time. Can the other project live with a pause while it waits for the product to be ready, or will you need to adjust your project to create the product earlier?

- ❏ **Holidays:** Check that all of the scheduled activity is on working days and avoids public holidays. If you are using a computer tool, it should have warned you of any problem, but even so make sure that any national holidays are correctly shown in the project calendar.

- ❏ **Staff availability:** Ensure that staff are scheduled for project work only when they will be available. Check that you've taken into account things like booked personal holidays and work on other projects.

- ❏ **Staff capacity:** Check that the work scheduled for project staff is in line with their capacity. If someone is only available to your project for ten per cent of their time, make sure that their activity reflects that with a one-day job taking ten elapsed days.

Think flexibly about staff capacity and be prepared to negotiate. Suppose that someone is available to your project for 50 per cent of their time and to another project for the other 50 per cent. You might be able to have them for 100 per cent of their time in Week 27 to get that time-critical five day job done, and then not at all in Week 28 to make up for it. You can return the favour when the other project has something time-sensitive to do. Think about that in the context of the Critical Path where you need to keep things moving along.

❑ **Lead times on supply:** Make sure that you have sufficient lead times on things like supply. A supplier won't deliver goods to the front desk one second after you have emailed an order.

❑ **Lead times on approvals:** Check that you have a realistic turnaround time on approvals. This check applies both to internal approvals (such as agreeing design specifications) and external ones (such as planning permission for building extensions).

❑ **Critical Path:** Be clear about which activities are on the Critical Path, and also watch out for those that are near critical. Your activity network will be especially useful here as the chains of activities don't show up very well on a Gantt.

❑ **Contingency:** Have you got sufficient time contingency in the plan, and is it visible? Something is bound to go wrong, and having no contingency is simply asking for problems at best, and project failure at worst. Make sure that you have contingency to protect the Critical Path, or the Critical Chain if you are using that technique.

❑ **'Crashable' activitites:** Identify which activities could be 'crashed' if you come under time pressure. Crashing an activity means reducing its duration by putting more resource on the job. Some activities are suitable for crashing, but others aren't.

❑ **Management products:** Check that you have activities and brutally realistic timing for creating and updating management products, such as producing Stage Plans, keeping the Business Case up to date and creating regular progress reports.

❑ **Control:** Don't forget your project management time for checking progress, risk, quality and the other aspects of control. And be realistic about how much time you need for it too or you'll face unnecessary pressures and bigger problems because you missed things and didn't take corrective action in time.

❑ **Project memos and change:** Make sure that you've built in and resourced continuous management activities for things such as problem investigation, investigating newly identified risks, dealing with change requests and simply visiting team members to encourage them.

Estimating activity durations is distinctly tricky. For some help have a look at Chapter 23, Ten Tips for Estimating.

Resources - Staff Checklist

'Projects are about people' my old boss used to say, and quite right too. Getting the right people in the right place at the right time takes careful planning; it's all too easy to overlook things and to make mistakes. Have a look at this checklist to help dodge avoidable staffing problems on your project.

❑ **Completeness:** Check that you've allocated resource to every activity. At first that may be a skill (Broadcast Engineer) rather than a named individual (Ann), but you should have individuals clearly identified before the plan is completed.

❑ **Staff availability:** Check that the named specialist staff are actually available when your plan shows that they'll be required.

❑ **Staff flexibility:** Are the named specialist staff available either side of the planned time, in case the project is slightly ahead of schedule at that point or slightly behind?

❑ **Manager availability:** Confirm that the members of the Project Steering Group have the availability to perform their role. That means being available to make key decisions when something comes up, not just available for the pre-planned meetings.

❑ **Staff selection:** Have you got the best staff for the project from within your organisation, or just who happens to be available? Making an effort now to get the right people will have a big impact on project performance and delivery.

❑ **Supplier availability:** Check that suppliers have staff available at the time that the plan shows that they'll be needed. This check may be part of any contract negotiations.

Don't rely simply on the terms of a contract for supplier staff availability. As with staff from within your own organisation, you want the right staff, not just any staff. It has been known for suppliers under resource pressure to send in whoever happens to be available, such as trainees. It's often better to adjust the project around the availability of good supplier staff rather than get unsuitable people sent in who then take longer to do the work anyway – or who start cutting corners to meet contract deadlines.

❑ **Reserves:** If there's a risk that key project staff could be called away to other work (such as operational emergencies) have you identified reserves? If so, check also that the reserves have the availability to step in, perhaps at very short notice.

❑ **Preparation of reserves:** If you do have reserves, have you included things in the Communications Plan to keep them 'in the loop' of what's going on? That way they can get up to speed more quickly if they are called upon.

❑ **Resource levelling:** Check that the resourcing is correct and achievable. Watch out for, and resolve, any conflicts such as a staff member being allocated for five full days of work in a week when they are only available to the project for two days each week.

❑ **Project Memos and change:** You'll need to put in an allowance for project management resource to deal with things such as problems and changes. You'll probably need to make a similar allowance for team specialists to help too, so don't schedule them to full capacity on the planned work.

Resources –Equipment Checklist

In the pressure and high profile of planning your use of staff resource, it's easy to overlook the resourcing of equipment. Look through your product plans and think whether you need any particular equipment.

❑ **Product creation:** Check whether your staff will need specialised tools or equipment that the project must provide.

❑ **Office equipment:** It's easy to overlook the everyday items. Think through what your teams will need, such as large whiteboards, flip charts, extra wide printers and desk lamps.

❑ **Testing:** Check whether special equipment is needed for testing. That might include electrical instruments, test jigs or computerised test equipment.

❑ **Scheduling:** Check when equipment will be needed and confirm that it is available at that time. You may need to book it from the area of your organisation which is supplying it, or put in an advance booking with a hire company.

❑ **Backup:** Consider what you will do if necessary equipment is not available when you need it. That unavailability may be because of breakdown or another project being delayed and using it for longer than expected.

❑ **Compatibility:** If you are using bits of equipment that must work together, check that they are technically compatible, including having the right connecting leads.

❑ **Safety:** Think about any safety precautions for dangerous work or kit, such as barriers, warning signs and protective clothing.

❑ **Buy or hire:** Would it be better to buy new equipment and sell it on afterwards rather than risk not being able to get it, or old worn equipment breaking down? That can also help if you are not exactly sure when you'll need the kit or for how long.

❑ **Maintenance:** Where you are using equipment from within your own organisation, think about how essential it is to the smooth running of the project. Would it be advantageous to have it checked out and serviced in advance (preventative maintenance)?

Compatibility and cables can be important. A company working on a deep sea survey project got a survey ship into position ready to send down a mini-submarine – a remotely operated vehicle (ROV). Then the operators found that they had not brought the correct cable to connect two essential pieces of recording equipment. The vessel had to return to port to collect the right cable, but by the time it had returned to the survey location the weather had deteriorated. The ship had to wait two weeks on station for the weather to moderate enough to send the ROV down. Two weeks lost because of one short length of cable with the wrong connectors.

Resources – Facilities Checklist

You may think that this section only affects projects that need things like specialised engineering facilities. However, read on because the need for facilities is usually wider than that, and that might just affect you.

❏ **Team rooms:** Do your teams already have suitable accommodation, or is that needed especially for the project?

❏ **Meeting space:** Staff need to come together occasionally when they are working mostly from home, and for that you need meeting space. Think also about meeting facilities at the start of the project for things like planning and risk workshops. Think whether you need meeting rooms for stakeholder briefings during the project and towards the end of it.

❏ **Security:** If staff need access to secure areas for some or all of the work and they don't already have it. Check whether existing team rooms need to be made secure.

❏ **Tests environments:** Check whether you need special environments, or facilities that are equipped with a range of different devices to test things on, such as with some new software.

❏ **Laboratories:** Check for the need for labs or 'clean environments' for any aspect of the work.

❏ **Training:** Lots of projects involve user training. Your project may need facilities for that, even if it's just meeting rooms in your HQ building. A lot of organisations are short of meeting space and rooms need to be booked a long time in advance, particularly big rooms.

❏ **Additional sites:** Consider whether you need additional sites or accommodation for the duration of the project or for parts of it. For example, if you are extending a building as part of the project do you have storage space for the building materials?

The training aspects of projects are often underestimated or overlooked altogether. A major public organisation in the UK implemented an expensive new information system. Extensive user training was an essential part of the project but nobody had thought about the facilities that would be needed to train the large number of staff involved. The delivery of the whole project was threatened when it was realised, very late in the project, that training facilities were needed and that no suitable rooms were now available. It caused big problems, but ones that could have been avoided with more careful thought and planning at the outset.

Budget Checklist

It's not just about what money you need, but when you need it. Cash flow can be important to your finance department. Check this list out to help ensure that you've considered all the cost areas, and distinguish clearly between purchases and ongoing overheads such as organisational staff time. A useful framework for the budget is to use your product plans. For each product, show what it will cost to build it in terms of staff time and materials. Then don't forget to add into the budget the cost of the project management and control.

❑ **Equipment:** What you need to buy or hire and when.

❑ **Supplies:** Consider things such as laser printer toner, stationery and raw materials to test new machines.

❑ **Supplier staff:** The cost of supplier staff time. Supplier staff costs will be a capital expense, not an ongoing 'revenue' cost where staff are employed by your own organisation anyway.

❑ **Organisational staff:** Yes, it may be an ongoing cost for your organisation, but you still need to say what their time will cost. Your staff have to be paid for and staff time is often the biggest project expense.

❑ **Structure:** Talk to your finance department about how the budget should be structured. For example, it will nearly always be necessary to show what money will be committed in which financial year.

❑ **Procurement plan:** Cross-check your budget with your Procurement Plan, if you need one, to ensure that they are consistent.

The Four Dogs Checklist

Intrigued? Well, perhaps not if you have read the UK edition of *Project Management for Dummies* or hired me in to give a project management or project governance course! There are four factors to keep in mind while you're planning. The four factors are like four dogs pulling on a piece of project canvas, each with a corner of the canvas in its teeth. Have a look at the illustration at the front of Part I if you haven't already noticed it. Make sure that the canvas is in the right tension and that the plan is achievable. The dogs are:

❑ **Scope**

❑ **Time**

❑ **Cost**

❑ **Quality**

Using the four dogs illustration, check that the canvas is in the right tension by asking 'Can we deliver that scope, by then, with that resource (cost and staff) to that quality level? Is it do-able?' If, you don't believe it to be realistic – 'do-able' – stop now and work with your Project Steering Group to get the project in balance.

If the project isn't balanced across the four key factors then it will be extremely difficult or, often, impossible to deliver successfully. If the plan is telling you 'This isn't going to work' then listen up. In his *100 Rules for NASA Project Managers* Jerry Madden notes 'The review of most failed projects or project problems indicate the disasters were well planned to happen from the start.'

The Four Dogs model is great for control as well as the initial planning. If a dog pulls a corner of the canvas, something has to give way because the project 'canvas' is very strong – it won't stretch and it won't tear – so don't imagine for a moment that one factor can change with no impact on the others. So, if the project is suddenly wanted earlier, think which other dogs get pulled by this 'Time dog'. Perhaps you'll reduce the scope and do less. Perhaps you'll put more staff onto the project to do things faster and meet the new deadline. Perhaps you'll save time by reducing the testing (although that's not usually a good option). You may do things in combination and move more than one of the other dogs, such as reducing scope slightly but also adding more resource.

Risk Category Checklist

Risk management is an essential part of any project. Very many projects fail or are badly damaged because of things that were foreseeable, controllable and even preventable. Most risk management in projects is about the negative, downside risk – spotting threats in advance and then working to control them. Some may be about positive, upside, risk to take advantage of opportunities. You should record all identified risks in a Risk Log, and you'll find a template for Risk Log entries in Chapter 16, Templates for Control.

Risk categories can be really helpful to give structure to your risk identification. You can work through the categories one at a time and think what risks there may be in that area. You can also use the categories as an indicator of who should take responsibility for a particular risk. For example, the Sponsor might take responsibility for the business related risks.

The next checklist is a full set of risk categories. You almost certainly won't want to use all of them, so take out the ones you don't need. For the ones you do need, you may even want to go into more detail for some. For example, if you work on government projects then you may prefer to have two categories. One category for political risk to discriminate between organisational politics such as the relationships between departments and another for national politics such as a change of government. As always, adapt the checklist to make it as relevant as possible to your project types.

❑ **Political:** Things like changes of government. These will affect public sector projects but others too, with changes of national policy or availability of funding.

❑ **Economic:** Changes in the national economy that can affect the project, such as an increase in consumer spending making the project to develop a new product more urgent.

❑ **Legal:** Risks related to likely changes in the law, regulations and codes of practice.

❑ **Market:** Shifts in demand or the appearance of new competitors or collapse of existing ones. That could affect projects such as those involving new product development and rebranding.

❑ **Technology:** Risks where technology developments elsewhere could impact on your project to make it even more viable, or perhaps making it not worth continuing.

❑ **Business:** Such as organisational changes in strategy or priority that would affect the project.

❑ **Operations:** Risks that could affect the running of the organisation, such as additional downtime for upgrading the production line, and which could lead to the temporary reduction of production capacity.

❑ **Reputation:** Things that could affect the image of the organisation, for example to the public or potential investors.

❑ **Environment:** Risks related to things such as waste disposal, 'Green policies' and chemical hazards.

❑ **Supplier:** Risk where you are dependent on your supplier. That is likely to be greater where the supplier is external but it could affect supply from within your organisation too.

❑ **Technical:** Technical risk occurs when the project involves doing something unusual or complicated with equipment, where things could go wrong or take much longer than expected.

❑ **Resource:** Risks concerning the availability and skills of project staff. That includes staff sickness, but also delays in staff being made available to your project because of over-running of other projects.

❑ **Schedule:** Risks affecting the project timeline, such as work being more complicated than expected, or a large proportion of the activities being on the Critical Path or near critical.

❑ **Finance:** The availability of funding and it being there at the right time

❑ **Facilities and equipment:** Risks to do with the availability of special equipment and facilities needed for the project, such as test rigs or laboratories.

When you're identifying risks discriminate between risks and impacts. Overspending isn't a risk but rather it's the result of a risk happening; it's an impact. Being late isn't a risk either but another impact. Think what the risks are which could lead to that impact, such as unreliable suppliers causing delay.

Risk Action Checklist

All of the major project methods and approaches suggest categories of risk action. The headings in this checklist are suggested by the Project Management Institute (PMI) – an American based organisation but now with chapters world-wide. There are two subsets of risk actions.

The first subset is for negative, downside, risk – the things that could go wrong. Downside risks are often referred to as 'threats'.

❑ **Avoid:** Stop the risk happening. If you have floor sockets for power in your office, people won't be at risk of tripping over trailing leads from wall sockets because there won't be any trailing leads.

❑ **Transfer:** Where you can give the negative impact, or at least some of it, to someone else. So, taking out insurance would transfer the financial part of the risk impact.

❑ **Mitigate:** Reduce the chances of the risk occurring and/ or the impact if it does. Giving all of the project staff a big pay bonus (especially you of course) might reduce the chances of someone leaving. After that, having a replacement staff member on standby ready to step in if someone does leave would reduce the impact of the loss. The replacement person would still need time to get up to speed in the project though, so you wouldn't have eliminated the impact, just reduced it by minimising the time needed to get a new person in place.

❑ **Accept:** This means accepting the risk without taking any action, often because the work or cost would be disproportionate to the impact if the risk does occur. You should still record the risk though and that's for two reasons. First to record the considered decision not to take action, and second so that the risk will be monitored during the project. It may be that if circumstances change, action will be justified after all.

The second subset is for positive, upside, risk – the things that could go really well in your project. Upside risks are often referred to as 'opportunities'.

❑ **Exploit:** The upside risk, or opportunity, might happen. To exploit it is to try and make sure that it does happen.

❑ **Share:** It can take money and effort to pursue an upside risk. It may be worth getting someone else to help fund the opportunity, perhaps in exchange for a share of the benefit.

❑ **Enhance:** The opportunity, if it happens, will be really good. Can you take action to make it even better?

❑ **Accept:** This is the same acceptance action as for a threat, you won't take any action. If the positive risk is realised you'll be happy, but it's not worth extra effort and money to chase after it. It's a conscious, recorded decision not to take action.

If you're already a career Project Manager, or are thinking of heading that way, do consider joining one of the professional organisations. The PMI has a very large international membership, and in the UK there's the APM – the Association for Project Managers. Such organisations are widely respected and have lots to help you, such as events and seminars. Do a web search to check them out.

Risk Plan Checklist

As part of your Project Management Plan (PMP) you should include a Risk Plan. You won't always need all of the elements of the PMP, but you'll always need a Risk Plan. In the plan you set down how you will manage risk in this particular project. Check your plan against this checklist.

❑ **Review:** Explain whether the frequency of risk review will be according to a factor such as probability, or at the end of each stage or at set regular intervals during each stage.

You can have a rolling review to spread out the work of risk review. If every risk is to be checked every four weeks, you could look at 25 per cent of the risks each week rather than have a huge monthly task. Have a 'Last reviewed' item on each Risk Log entry where you can enter the date to prevent any confusion.

❑ **Reporting:** Make clear exactly how project staff should report new risks that they've spotted or changes in status of existing risks, or if a risk actually happens. The reporting mechanism doesn't have to be difficult – perhaps just a phone call to the Project Manager – but it must be crystal clear.

❑ **Practicality:** The risk reporting mechanism should be simple and fast. Some risks happen very quickly and the last thing you want is some long-winded procedure with undue documentation. 'No Bloggins, I won't pass on this risk because it isn't properly recorded, in triplicate, on a form RK/113/Rev6.'

❑ **Interfaces:** Make sure that it's clear how risks will be passed to other affected projects, up to programme level if your project is part of a programme of projects, and into your organisational risk management system if it has organisational implications.

❑ **Risk Log access:** Normally everyone should have 'read only' access to the Risk Log so that they can be aware of all of the risks and be vigilant in watching them. If there are any restrictions because of security or genuine confidentiality, then check to make sure that you've explained that in the plan.

❑ **Authority trigger points:** The plan must be absolutely clear on where the Project Manager must inform the Project Steering Group immediately of a new risk – or a status change in an existing one – and where this can be left to the next progress review or report.

❑ **Communication:** Don't repeat the detail of the Communication Plan, but do explain how risk information will be communicated, such as in team briefings at the start of each stage.

❑ **Clarity:** Check that the Risk Plan is written simply and clearly so that everyone involved in the management of the project will be able to understand it – from Sponsor to Team Leader.

❑ **Checked:** The details of the plan should be checked out with the Project Steering Group before being finalised. Although the Project Manager is responsible for the plan, the Steering Group must be happy that the controls are sufficient since it is that group which is responsible for project governance.

Quality Plan Checklist

"Project Management is about delivering on time and within budget." So say many people, but they're wrong. What's the point in delivering a heap of unusable garbage on time and within budget? Delivering to the right level of quality is vital in any project, and in the Quality Plan you sets down how you're going to do that in this project. Have a look at the checklist to help make sure that your plan is a good one.

❑ **Quality level:** The level of quality you need to achieve in this project. Make sure that it's both correct and realistic. Delivering too low a level will cause operational problems later, or could even mean a failed project. Delivering an unnecessarily high level just drives up project overheads for no reason.

❑ **Standards:** Check that you have listed all of the standards that will apply to the project. That means organisational standards, such as for technical work and safety, not just external ones – important though they are. You may need to get input from subject specialists.

❑ **Mechanisms:** Individual tests of project products will be set down on their Product Definitions. Overall though, what mechanisms will you use for checking things? Your thinking here will help make the resource plans and budget realistic.

❑ **Audit:** It's one thing talking about quality, but it's another actually delivering it. The plan should set down how auditing will be done to make quite sure that tests and checks have been carried out, and by the right people too.

❑ **Clarity:** Make sure that the plan is clear, simple and understandable.

❑ **Checked:** As with the Risk Plan on the last checklist, ensure that the members of the Project Steering Group are happy with the plan before it is finalised.

Watch out for the quality box ticking trap. Quality audit that only checks to see that documents have been signed is superficial and completely ineffective. The audit shouldn't be checking that bits of paper have been signed, but that the tests were actually done. An awful lot of people approve an awful lot of things without looking at them properly, or even at all. And that includes you . . . doesn't it? No? So you never click a box on a computer or phone app installation then to say you have read and agreed with the terms and conditions when you haven't even opened the link to look at them? Don't let your project quality slide into the abyss with people just 'going through the motions'. You'll find a few ideas for quality cross checks in Chapter 9.

Stakeholder Log Checklist

The checklist after this one, for the Stakeholder Plan, includes an item to check that the plan is complete and covers all of the stakeholders. This checklist is to help you think about all the possible stakeholders for entry in your Stakeholder Log if you are using one. As always, you can adapt it for your own organisation so that it's useful for successive projects. This checklist focuses on people who are not working in the project itself, but you may prefer to extend it to project staff such as the Steering Group and team members.

❑ **Senior managers:** Relevant top managers who may be affected by the project or need to be consulted about it. This category can include a management board.

❑ **Directors:** Directors may be stakeholders not just because of their personal interest in the outcome of the project, but because they may be questioned about it by others and so need regular information.

❑ **Shareholders:** For private sector organisations.

❑ **Donors:** In the charity sector, it may be important to keep regular donors in the loop. You may even use the project as a means of boosting enthusiasm for your organisation's work and so increasing the level of donations.

❑ **Organisational managers:** Managers in the Finance Department and the HR Department might be involved in redeploying your project staff when the project is complete.

❏ **Affected managers:** Managers of business units such as other departments who may be affected by what the project will deliver, the work of the project while it is underway (such as disruption), or both.

❏ **User staff:** Those who will actually use what the project is delivering.

❏ **Staff associations:** You may want to include staff associations both for consultation and information reasons. At the least they may need to know what the project is doing, but they may also be able to make a valuable contribution.

❏ **Customers:** Including potential customers. If the project is to change the customers' dealings with the organisation, they may need to be informed or some even consulted. That consultation is common, for example, in some public sector organisations such as hospitals.

❏ **Partner organisations:** Do you need to inform partner organisations about the project? That will obviously be very important if it directly affects shared work.

❏ **Suppliers:** Often overlooked, suppliers may also be affected and may need to be informed or consulted, such as with a project affecting the way payments are made.

❏ **Government and legal:** Agencies that must be made aware or consulted about your project, or where one or more permissions must be asked for.

❏ **The public:** In terms of interest in your organisation, or being affected such as with a project to extend your HQ building.

Stakeholder Plan Checklist

The Stakeholder Plan is part of the PMP and useful if stakeholder management will be a significant part of your project – and in many cases it will. Check that your plan is a good one by working through this checklist.

❏ **Definition:** The plan should define what 'stakeholder' means if this term is not well established in your organisation. Some view stakeholders as only being those outside the project, while others take it to mean that it includes people inside the project.

❑ **Completeness:** Check that the plan covers the management of every known stakeholder. You can cross check with your Stakeholder Log if you have decided to use one.

❑ **Groupings:** Are the stakeholders set down in sensible groups according to the management actions you will need to take?

❑ **Sensitive:** Check that the plan is suitably worded so that it won't be problematical when others see it. For example, you are likely to make opposition greater if you have listed someone who has genuine concerns about the project under a heading of 'Determined troublemakers' . . . or worse.

❑ **Specific actions:** Check that the management actions for each group are specific and clear, not vague. It's no good making an entry such as 'Needs to be kept informed'. Informed of what?

❑ **Timing:** Have you made the timings of actions clear? For example some things such as progress updates may be on a regular basis while other actions may be at set points, such as just before the project completes.

❑ **Communications:** Check that the actions in the Stakeholder Plan that involve communications are reflected by entries in the Communications Plan, covered by the next checklist. The two plans must be consistent.

 When thinking about stakeholder management, watch out for stakeholders who are very much in favour of the project and who are highly influential. Your first reaction may be to think that no action is needed since they are already strongly in support of the project. However, think again – you need to keep them that way.

Communications Plan Checklist

Communications problems are an ongoing and major source of project problems leading to failure. The 'Comms Plan' is a very practical plan to think through what communications are needed and the best way of carrying them out. The plan should be structured with repeating blocks of information, one for each communication saying what it is, who prepares it, who is to receive it, what is in it and how it will be communicated. It's hard to think of everything, but think of everything you must or something or someone is going to get missed and that could have huge implications. Here's a checklist to help, divided into three communication areas.

Inbound communications

This first subset of the checklist is for communications coming in over the project boundary from outside.

❑ **Organisational risk:** Information from the organisational risk system about new risks, or changes in risk status, that could affect your project

❑ **Interdependent projects:** The state of other projects and changes in them that could impact your project, such as a change to a specification or a project delay which means that you'll be getting your copy of the spec later than expected.

❑ **Business change:** Notification of changes to organisational policy, strategy or priorities that could impact the project.

❑ **Change:** How someone outside the project should communicate a change request. It can be chaotic, for example, to allow anyone and everyone to bombard the Project Manager with change requests. You may then set down that changes have to come through the Project User manager on the Steering Group. Having to go through one of their own managers can be a disincentive to business staff to make trivial requests.

❑ **Finance:** Information from financial systems to report project spending, and changes to the availability of finance if that is a factor for your project.

Comms within the project

The next subset is for communications between the people actually taking part in the project.

❑ **Risk:** Information about new risks, changes to existing risks or risks actually occurring. This will be based on the requirements set down in the Risk Plan.

❑ **Quality:** Information on quality work, such as that a test has been performed and the product involved has passed that test. You can use a simple mechanism such as a Quality Checklist, but you'll need something in place so you can keep track of quality activity. You'll find an example of a Quality Checklist in Chapter 16.

❑ **Stage progress:** Reporting progress to the Project Steering Group at regular intervals, such as with a monthly meeting or report. The Comms Plan must specify the frequency and the content of such reports or meetings.

❑ **Team progress:** The Project Manager should set down exact requirements for team level reporting in the individual Work Packages (the work assignments given to teams). However it's sensible to have default information in the Comms Plan so 'normal' Work Packages can just say 'as Comms Plan default' rather than keep repeating the same information over and over. The reporting may be by email, or something like a regular meeting where the Project Manager meets with all the Team Leaders once a week.

❑ **Project memos:** The range of memos to be used and who can send them. For example, can any team member send a memo to the Project Manager or must they go through their Team Leader? Think carefully about this, there are pros and cons for both options.

In some methods and project standards, Project Memos are known as 'Issues'.

❑ **Warning and crisis:** The PRIME method uses two levels of escalation of something to the Project Steering Group if something is going wrong and it is outside the authority of the Project Manager to deal with it. Whatever mechanism you use, make sure that you have spelled out how such warnings will be communicated, for example by a phone call to the Sponsor.

Outbound communications

This final subset is for communications going out of the project to the organisation beyond.

- ❑ **Progress:** How the project will inform others of progress made, such as organisational managers and other stakeholders with an interest in progress.

- ❑ **Interdependent projects:** Progress and change information that will affect projects that have inter-project dependencies with this one.

- ❑ **Risk:** New risks and change in existing risk status that could affect other projects or organisational risk management.

- ❑ **Finance:** Information on money committed and spent in the project.

- ❑ **Stakeholders:** Stakeholder Management normally involves significant communications, such as to maintain interest. This section should be consistent with the comms requirements set down in your Stakeholder Plan if you are using one.

- ❑ **Public and media:** Communications such as public announcements, press releases and other media related information. These communications should normally be reflected in the products of the project itself, but referenced in the Comms Plan to show that they are covered. If the requirement is covered in the Stakeholder section above you won't need a separate entry. However, if public and media communications are high profile in your project, perhaps involving specialist staff such as an organisational Press Relations Department, you may prefer to keep this specialised section.

Types of Project Memo

The previous checklist on the whole of the Comms Plan noted that you should specify the types of Project Memo to be used in the project. As an example, here's a set used in the PRIME project method, but as always you should adapt the list to meet your exact project needs.

❏ **Issue:** An idea, problem or anything else not covered by the other memo types.

❏ **Question:** Where someone in the project needs guidance from the Project Manager. It may be easier to get this verbally, but in projects covering different time zones the question might be sent by email.

❏ **Change Request:** To ask for a change to a product that has already been completed, or where the definition of it has already been agreed and signed off. This is part of the change control and is highly effective in helping to avoid the problem of scope creep.

❏ **Non-compliance:** If a product fails test then normally it's put right and will successfully pass test the second time around. If there is some significant reason why it can't or won't meet its quality criteria, though, it's reported to the Project Manager as a non-compliance. The Project Manager will take control to ensure that the non-compliance is resolved.

❏ **Warning:** A communication from the Project Manager to the Sponsor that something is off track and it requires action beyond the Project Manager's delegated authority to deal with it.

❏ **Crisis:** A communication from the Project Manager to the Sponsor to say that a key project objective will now not be achieved or that an identified 'showstopper' has been encountered (such as your development being overtaken by a competitor). A crisis will often result in the project being closed down.

Communication Media Checklist

How you communicate is important if those communications are to be effective on the one hand and economic on the other. Here's a checklist of some things to consider.

❏ **Phone calls:** Don't forget them. With such poor email discipline in many organisations, phone calls can be particularly effective; they're fast and they build a personal relationship too. The best way for the Project Manager to report a serious problem to the Sponsor may well be a phone call.

❏ **Teleconference:** Group phone calls which can be useful where one team needs to discuss something with another.

❏ **Video conference:** Not as good as a face-to-face meeting for project staff, but usually much better than a phone call or teleconference.

❏ **Interactive development:** Office software increasingly has the functionality for people in different locations to develop a diagram or document interactively – a sort of web based workshop.

❏ **Meetings:** Another communications medium that is often underestimated. Poorly run meetings are a well-known waste of time and effort. However a concise and well run meeting can be a fast and effective way of transferring information.

❏ **Presentations:** Some reports might be better in the form of a business presentation with brief notes for people to take away afterwards. This medium can work well for regular project progress meetings with the Project Steering Group.

❏ **Road shows:** Taking a display and presentation onto different sites can be a whole lot better than brochures or long text documents. You might want to consider roadshows to pass on project information to each regional office or to major customers.

❏ **On-line presentations and demos:** An effective medium if done well, but it can reflect badly on your project if it is done poorly. The advantage is that people can look at the presentation when they want to, and more than once if they want to see it again.

❏ **Dashboard reporting:** Long and wordy reports are a pain in the rear end and few people read them properly. For progress reports from Team Leaders to the Project Manager, and from the Project Manager to the Project Steering Group, dashboards work really well. You can have 'petrol gauges' showing stage and project spending for example. A really powerful element is the Work Flow Diagram, colour coded to show delivery. Have a look at the UK edition of *Project Management for Dummies* for much more on product planning as a means of highly effective progress control.

❏ **Email:** Okay, you'll need it, but try to minimise it and then use it well. The advantage is that an email does provide a written record of something. The disadvantage is that an important email may be hidden amongst a mass of other emails in the recipient's in-box and go unnoticed for some time.

❏ **News sheet:** For communications to everyone in a large project, or to keep in touch with stakeholders, consider a news sheet. It can be an electronic one. Used imaginatively to circulate information when it's needed, a news sheet can reduce the number of inbound enquiries and so the resource needed to deal with them.

❏ **Websites:** Having a project website can save a lot of email. People can just come and look if they want information about the project rather than, for example, getting unwanted information emailed to them 'in case they want to know'. It can also be a good way to keep stakeholders informed.

Think carefully about how much really needs to be written down. Over-documentation is a real problem in many projects, particularly those using project methods which seem to be more concerned about documentation than delivery. You want a successful project, not a well-documented failure.

Procurement Plan Checklist

You'll have procurement information in your plans and in the budget. However, if you have significant procurement in your project then you may also want a Procurement Plan to give a clear view on what procurement actions are needed and when. Use this checklist to help make sure that your plan is right.

Under your organisation's contracting procedures, you may need action to start and progress procurement long before the item and the service is actually needed in the project. The Procurement Plan will include the various actions.

❏ **Contract cross check:** For every contract that you know about, make sure that all the actions are set down in the plan with dates. Those actions may include things such as Invitation to Tender (ITT), contract negotiation and final selection.

❏ **Lead times:** Check that there is sufficient time for the procurement process to happen before the item or service is needed in the project.

❏ **Involvement of specialists:** Ensure that you've noted the need for specialist input, such as lawyers and contract staff. If any of the procurement even looks like it might be problematical, ensure that you have recorded the need to involve legal specialists at the outset. Lawyers would rather be consulted at the start so as to avoid problems than be called in later because of a crisis where something has gone badly wrong.

❏ **Project staff resource:** Ensure that you have noted the need to involve project staff. Lawyers and contract staff aren't mind readers and need input from those who understand the projects and its needs.

❏ **External products:** Check the external products on the Work Flow Diagram. For those that involve procurement (and not all will) check that you have the details in the Procurement Plan.

❏ **Budget and plans:** Check the Procurement Plan and the project budget against each other, then against the Project Plan and Stage Plans to be sure that they are all consistent.

Chapter 9

Establishing Controls

●●●

●●●

*I*t's one thing getting a project up and running, but it's another keeping it in control so that you can move smoothly through to delivery. You'll have to think through and plan the controls before you get caught up in the busyness of the project, and that's why this chapter comes in the Planning section of the book.

A key message for any project is *get it in control – keep it in control*. It would be nice if this chapter could just give you a 'how to' checklist to achieve that control but, of course, it isn't quite as easy as that. The nature and degree of control you'll need depends on the project, any standards in your organisation and, perhaps surprisingly, you; there's room here for your own preferred way of running projects.

As you come to think about control, the point to remember is that it's all about balance; the control needs against the overheads of those controls. A highly complex, high-risk project with dozens of people involved will need much more in the way of control than a simple, low-risk project that only involves you and one other person to help.

 Watch out if your organisation, or Project Management Office, is one that tries to apply a one-size-fits-all approach to projects. That leads to even small, straightforward projects being swamped in excessive controls and heaps of paper designed with much bigger and more complex projects in mind. The result is excessive work and unnecessary overheads, which are in nobody's best interest. It's certainly not in your best interest if it's you that ends up having to do all the unnecessary work! You may need to work with your Project Steering Group to challenge unnecessary controls and get exemption from irrelevant ones.

This chapter is to help you think through what you need by way of control . . . and also what you don't.

Another warning? Well yes, because organisations make a lot of mistakes around the area of control. Where they have tried to take a more flexible approach it's common to fall into a different trap. They adjust the degree of control required according to the size of the project such as large, medium and small projects, and that's wrong. For example, a very big project may actually be very low risk and need little in the way of controls for risk, while a much smaller project may be extremely high risk and need very sophisticated risk management. So, think about the whole range of characteristics of your project, not just its size.

Project Characteristics Checklist

When you're thinking about the degree of control you'll need for your current project, consider these characteristics.

❑ **Size:** The size of the project isn't the be-all-and-end-all when it comes to thinking about control, but it's still a factor. A very big project with a lot of people and money involved will usually need more control than a very small project with just two or three people and a small budget. Please note the 'usually' in the last sentence though because there are exceptions arising from the other characteristics.

❑ **Geography:** If your project is to be run across several sites, or perhaps even in different countries, you'll need more control than you would if everyone were in one place.

❑ **Business criticality:** If the project is extremely important to the business – perhaps a new product launch or re-branding – then it justifies more careful control than if it won't have a lot of impact if it fails.

❑ **Complexity:** Complex projects need greater control than simple ones.

❑ **Inter-project dependency:** You'll need less control if your project is stand-alone than if there are a lot of inter-project dependencies where your project will affect the running of other projects and their work will affect yours.

❑ **Business impact:** You'll need more control if the project will affect other parts of the organisation rather than just the area where the project is running. There will certainly be more in the way of communications but you may also need to co-ordinate the integration and include things like pilot installations.

❑ **Organisational experience:** If your organisation has run lots of projects like this before, the project will need less control than if this is the first project of this type that's ever been done. Experience pays since project staff have a better idea of what's involved and how to avoid the known problem areas.

❑ **Project Manager experience:** If the Project Manager is very familiar with this sort of project, then controls can be lighter than if this is the first time that he or she has ever run a project like this.

❑ **Timescale:** If the project must deliver to a tight timescale, and particularly where the end date is fixed as well (such as the end of a financial year) then you'll need more control than if delay would be regrettable rather than devastating.

❑ **Visibility:** If the project will be highly visible, such as to customers, donors (for a charity), government or shareholders, you'll need to exercise more control to be quite sure that things go right. Reputation damage from the failure of a high-visibility project can be very severe and is often underestimated.

❑ **Risk:** A high-risk project needs more control than a low-risk one. Have a look at the overall risk level, as well as other items in this checklist that are risk-related, such as the last one about visibility.

❑ **Quality:** If your project requires extremely high-quality delivery, such as with safety-critical systems, it will need more control than if the project is genuinely 'quick and dirty'.

❑ **Teams:** Will you have a single team, a few teams or many? A single team working through the project is much more intimate and you'll be more aware of what's going on, so your controls can be simpler.

Your assessment of the different project characteristics will affect the nature of the controls, but then also the plans of how you will set up and operate them. Plans such as the Risk Plan, the Quality Plan and the Communications Plan go into the 'folder' known as the PMP – the Project Management Plan. You'll find more about the PMP in Chapter 2.

Stage Decision Checklist

The big control in projects is the Delivery Stages. It's a Project Steering Group (PSG) decision on how many there should be in the project. If the PSG wants to authorise less at a time and check the project more frequently, its members will specify shorter stages and that will mean more Stage Gates (the review at the end of a stage). However, while the PSG's control is greater with more stages, so are the overheads. More stages mean more Stage Plans and more Stage Gates, and they cost time and money. If the PSG wants fewer Delivery Stages, even down to just one where it authorises all the work to be done in one go, the overheads are reduced . . . but then so too is the PSG control.

So what factors should a PSG and the Project Manager bear in mind when thinking about stages and stage boundaries? You might even think a checklist would come in handy here.

❑ **Finance:** The maximum that the PSG is willing to authorise at a time. If the limit is $1 million, and a block of work is estimated to cost $1.6 million, it will have to be done in two Delivery Stages with a Stage Gate between them.

❑ **The timing of major spends:** Have a stage end just before, not just after, a major spend. The PSG can check the project, then authorise the project continuing into the next stage and making the big investment. That's much better than spending a whole heap of money on something really expensive, then having a Stage Gate and deciding that the project is no longer viable and that it should be stopped early.

❑ **Major deliverables:** Sometimes in projects there are one or two really significant deliveries during the project and not just a big one at the end. Often these interim deliveries make a good stage boundary as a natural break point at which to pause and take stock.

❑ **Major resource change:** A small change of resource, such as one supplier team leaving and another one arriving, is not a reason to have a stage boundary. However a big shift, perhaps from one major supplier company who did most of the work in the first part of the project to another major supplier who will do most of it in the last part, is a good stage boundary. In that case you'll probably want to change the Project Supplier on the PSG too.

❑ **Supplier payment points:** Small suppliers in particular can't wait until the end of a long project to be paid. They will have gone bust long before then because of their need to pay staff. Often, then, you will have to set up 'staged payments'. You can adjust the project stages accordingly to check the supplier's work at the end of each Delivery Stage and then pay them.

❑ **Time:** This factor is rather like the finance in the first point on this list. The PSG may have a maximum time that the members are willing to go without having a thorough review at a Stage Gate. Stages will be different lengths, but the PSG may specify that no stage is ever to be longer than 12 weeks, for example.

❑ **Risk:** In a low-risk project, the PSG will normally be happy for stages to be longer than in a high-risk project.

❑ **Key decision points:** A point in the project where an important decision is made can be a good stage end. The PSG may not be involved in making that decision but if it could affect the running of the rest of the project, or even determine whether there is to be a 'rest of the project', then it's another good point at which to take stock.

❑ **Planning horizons:** Sometimes you can't see clearly to the end of the project. However, you can see the first bit clearly, and you know that when you reach the end of that you will be able to see the next bit, and at the end of that you should be able to see to the end of the project. I think of it as being like driving down a foggy road. You can use these 'planning' horizons – or at least one or two of them – as a factor in the stage length decisions.

Progress Report Checklist

Everyone calls them 'Progress Reports' but usually Progress Reports report more than just progress. They actually report the state of the current stage. Dashboard reporting with diagrams such as 'petrol gauges' can be particularly effective for the reports. You may deliver the report verbally in the form of a business presentation instead of a paper-based or emailed one.

Whichever form of report you use, here's a checklist of information so you can think through what your project will need and what it won't.

- ❑ **Delivery:** The products which have been delivered (quality checked and signed off) compared with what was planned to do by this point.

- ❑ **Stage spend:** The stage spend to date compared to the budget for this point, and the projected spend for the rest of the stage compared to the plan.

- ❑ **Project spend:** Your current projection of the final project cost compared to the original estimate.

- ❑ **Time:** If your projections show that the stage will finish on time, or early, or late. If it's early or late, by how much will it vary from the plan.

- ❑ **Change:** The amount of change budget used in the stage so far and the extra staff time used to carry out approved changes.

 It makes sense to have a separate change budget. The stage budget is for work that is planned but changes, by definition, are not planned. It's logical to fund changes separately, but the spend is conditional. If nobody asks for any changes, the Project Manager cannot use the change budget for other things. Otherwise the important warning sign of overspending in the stage could be disguised and so missed.

- ❑ **Team performance:** The degree to which teams are exceeding, achieving or falling below the expected performance. That has implications for the delivery of the rest of the products in the project. It may be, for example, that products are consistently being built with less effort than expected and so the whole project may come in early. In turn, that could affected scheduled resources (people and equipment) that will now be needed earlier than originally planned.

❑ **Quality:** The degree to which the required quality is being met. You might use a measure such as the number of products passing test first time, or the ratio of re-work time (correcting errors) to original build time.

❑ **Risk:** The current overall status of risk, such that it is falling across the project or increasing, as well as comments on the status of individual key risks and reporting of any new ones.

Problem Solving Checklist

Even in the best-run projects, things are going to go off track. When something does go wrong, use this checklist to help understand the problem and to decide what you'll do about it. This checklist is broken down into three areas to make it easier to zoom in on the things you'll need; timing problems, resourcing problems and spending problems.

Timing problems

If things are taking longer than expected, have a look at these causes and things you might consider to help get things back on course.

❑ **Team availability:** If things are taking longer than expected, check whether the team working time to build products is greater than you estimated or whether your staff have less available time to work on the project than expected. If the team's availability is reduced, try to free them up to get the resource levels back to what was planned for. You will usually need to involve the members of the Project Steering Group who agreed that resource in the first place.

❑ **Unexpected work:** Is the delay to work that was already planned for, or has extra but necessary work been discovered? If known work is off track, look at the next bullet point. If extra, but essential, work has been identified, review your plans. Talk to your team members to see whether they can see anything else that's missing. It's better to get all of the bad news now rather than have this instance as merely the start of a whole string of similar problems.

❑ **Extent:** If products are taking longer to build than planned because of unexpected complexity, check whether the delay is likely to just affect those products, or whether this is the start of something bigger, and you have underestimated the work needed for all products.

❑ **Supplier delay:** Check to see if the teams are waiting on suppliers who have missed deadlines. If so contact the suppliers. If the supply is subject to contract, work with your contract staff.

❑ **Inter-project dependency:** If your teams are waiting on a product being sent in from another project, contact the other Project Manager to get an update and to remind him or her of the impact on your project. Also review your controls for getting early warning of delays on interfacing projects.

❑ **Quality:** Check to see whether products are failing test, and the delay is because of the need for re-work and re-testing. If quality is the cause, look at why products are failing. Is the quality set incorrectly? In that case you may need to revisit your quality plan and individual product requirements.

❑ **Early completion:** This might look strange on a list of problems, but check it out because early completion can indicate a problem. Are teams finishing early because products are not being built to the right standard or because vital quality checks are being missed out? If the work is proving less complex than expected, assess the remaining products to see whether it is likely that the whole project can be delivered earlier.

Resourcing problems

It's not uncommon that the major problems in a project arise not from the work itself but from the staffing, whether in the suitability of your people or their availability. Use this checklist if you are hitting difficulties in this key area.

❏ **Quality:** no, this isn't a mistake and a repeat from the earlier list. This time it's where you have a lot of problems with achieving the required quality level, but the specification is correct. You should now look at why staff are stuggling to meet the quality levels. Have you got the right staff or suppliers, and do they have the right facilities and equipment needed to achieve the standard you require?

❏ **Non-conformity:** If supplier products are being delivered below standard, contact the supplier quickly to try and find the reason and if it's just a glitch. If it isn't a one-off glitch and you have a poor supplier (so that's why they were so much cheaper) you have a real problem. You may need to terminate the contract and quickly look for another supplier. Contact your legal or contracts people now to discuss the problem and don't wait until it has got bigger.

❏ **Staff change:** you need staff stability in the project, and if staff are being taken off unexpectedly then you have a resource reduction. Even if the replacement staff are just as skilled, it will normally take time to get up to speed on your project. If a lot of unexpected staff changes are happening, talk to your PSG and spell out the impact.

Spending problems

If the spending pattern is different to what you planned for this point in the stage, check out this list.

❏ **Delivery:** How does the spending compare with delivery? If your teams are ahead of schedule, the spending may be on track even though they have spent more than was planned for this point.

❏ **Early spending:** There's a world of difference between early spending and over-spending. For example, if equipment is being bought early because it's on special offer at the moment, the eventual spend may be below budget.

❑ **Increasing costs:** If things like equipment and facilities are costing more than was budgeted, an overspend may be unavoidable. However, you may need to warn the Sponsor if you think the overspending will continue beyond any flexibility within the stage budget.

❑ **Changes:** If approved changes being carried out by suppliers are proving very expensive, you may need to change your change control approach to minimise changes. That could have a negative impact on your project, but not as negative as running up huge unforeseen bills.

A lot, or even most, suppliers are very good. However, you have to be streetwise and on the lookout for those suppliers who aren't as ethical – and that can be big companies as well as smaller ones. If suppliers are putting in huge bills for even minor changes, you have a problem. It's a bit late for this project but an important lesson for future ones. Some suppliers will put in a very low bid, and even understate the work involved, in order to win the contract. Then, hidden away in the small print of the agreement is a huge charge for extra work, and that's how they make their money. Be very careful to check the charges for additional work when you work with your contracts staff to set up the contracts. And don't fall into the trap of thinking that it doesn't matter too much because you can't see that you'll want anything added in.

Change Checklist

You must have change control in your project if you are to avoid *scope creep*, the big project killer. Just in case you're not familiar with the term, scope creep is the gradual and uncontrolled inclusion of a large number of very small changes in the project, but with no extra time or resource to do them. Each change is so small that the project is just supposed to absorb the extra work; it's only a ten-minute job after all and what's that on a $50 million, two-year project with 60 staff? Cumulatively the small changes add up to a huge total, and occur frequently enough to kill the project, which now can't deliver to the required time or within budget.

Change control is not to prevent change, but to consider whether the change should be made. If it should, you'll usually need additional time, money and staff resource to do it.

When you get a change request, have a look at this checklist to see if you think it should be done.

❏ **Essential:** You may stop immediately on reading this point. The change is essential and must be done, perhaps for legal compliance or because it involves the correction of a serious error. It's a no-brainer.

❏ **Benefits boost:** Assess whether the change would increase project benefits.

❏ **Benefits reduction:** Check whether the change would reduce benefits in any area. Be especially careful with shared projects where several organisations are taking part. If a change eliminates all the benefits for one of those partners, they will pull out and that could bring the whole project down.

❏ **Time impact:** Check how long it would take to implement the change and whether you have that time available. Clearly this point will be more significant if you have a fixed delivery date for your project.

❏ **Resource impact:** Check what staff resource would be needed to perform the change and whether you have that resource available or could get extra.

❏ **Cost impact:** Check what the change would cost, and whether sufficient change budget is available, or whether extra funds could be obtained.

❏ **Risk:** Check the impact on risk. The change might increase or reduce negative risk, or help you take advantage of an opportunity (upside risk).

Change Options Checklist

A lot of people asking for a change want it done right away, and of the rest most want it done yesterday or preferably the day before. You have some options with your final decision on whether or not to carry out a change; it's not simply 'yes' or 'no'. Even if it's 'yes' it doesn't always have to be right now. This checklist sets out the possibilities.

❏ **More information:** In some instances you may need to ask for more information to make an informed decision. Don't make a poor decision based on inadequate information when with a bit more detail you could make a good decision.

❏ **Yes:** Okay, you'll carry out the change right now. You have the time, change budget and authority to commit to it.

❏ **No:** You don't think that the requested change is advantageous, so you turn it down. It helps if you explain your reasons to the person who asked for the change.

❏ **Refer:** The requested change is worthwhile, but big. The time, cost, impact or any combination exceeds your delegated authority so you refer it to the Project Steering Group for a decision.

❏ **Perhaps, but later in the stage:** It's a good change, but minor. You don't want to use up all of your change budget on trivial stuff at the start of the stage and then have nothing left for something important later. So you tell the person asking for the change that you'll do it towards the end of the stage if you still have budget left but if you don't, you won't.

❏ **Perhaps, but later in the project:** A good change again, but too big to accommodate in this stage. You'll talk to the PSG about having the work added to a later stage in the project.

❏ **Perhaps, but not in this project:** Again the change may be a really good one with substantial business benefits, but you don't have time to carry it out in this project. You may be up against a fixed deadline and carrying out this change would mean missing the deadline and the whole project failing. However the change will be recommended back into the organisation for adding into a future project or doing as a stand-alone job. That recommendation will normally be made through the PSG and often by the Sponsor.

Communication Pattern Checklist

Part of your control decision making is on how staff can communicate. Communications can be sensitive, particularly where you have teams in different departments reporting to different managers who want to be kept in the loop, or even in control of what is happening. The communication pattern may already be fixed as an organisational norm, but you think that for the project to run well you'll need to change it. Here are some options, with a few diagrams this time.

❏ **The star:** This option is where the Project Manager is in absolute control and all communications must be through him. It means that the Project Manager knows exactly what is going on all the time, but it has high overheads and can lead to the project staff feeling disempowered. Figure 9-1 shows the star.

Figure 9-1: The star.

❏ **The hierarchy:** This allows some communication at lower levels, but referral through higher level managers for communication across teams. It can lead to delays and misunderstandings ('chinese whispers'), but it does put the managers in control. Figure 9-2 shows the structure of a typical hierarchy.

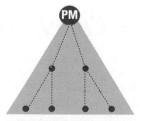

Figure 9-2: The hierarchy.

❑ **The bridge:** If you are stuck with hierarchical communications in your organisational environment, you may be able to set up some 'bridges' to allow specialists in different teams or parts of the organisation to communicate directly on particular aspects of the project. Figure 9-3 shows a hierarchy with a bridge.

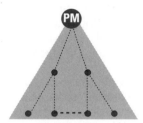

Figure 9-3: The hierarchy with a bridge.

❑ **The network:** where project staff can communicate freely with each other, no matter what team they are in, and the Project Manager and Team Leaders will never even know about some of the discussions. This works well with experienced teams . . . and very secure Project Managers and Team Leaders. Figure 9-4 shows the structure of a network.

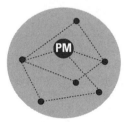

Figure 9-4: The network.

Quality Crosscheck Checklist

The last thing you want in a project is quality games, where on the surface everything appears to be okay, but actually important tasks haven't been done properly. The last chapter included a warning about poor Quality Audit, that merely checks that test documents have been signed. What it should be doing is checking that the quality has actually been achieved, not merely that someone signed something.

You may trust your staff, and that's great, but be aware that even good people will sometimes cut corners if they are under pressure. An installation in one of my projects went wrong once because of something that had been tested and signed off as okay. When I challenged the member of staff involved he said 'I didn't test it.' He was a very good guy, but he was under more pressure than I'd realised and he hadn't told me. I simply said 'Don't *ever* do that again.' and he never did. The matter was put right and the installation went ahead, but it taught me to double check on essential areas of quality.

So how do you crosscheck to ensure that the right quality is actually achieved? Here are a few ideas to help.

❑ **Set a realistic level:** If you set the quality level of the project at an unrealistically high level, everyone will see that it's nonsensical and they won't take any of the quality seriously. Get the level right at the outset.

❑ **Emphasise quality:** Talk to your project staff about quality at the start of the project and at the start of each new stage. Tell them to tell you if they come under pressure, not start cutting corners.

❑ **Brief your quality auditors:** If you have quality auditors on your project, talk to them about what checks are to be done. That will help prevent merely superficial checks.

❑ **Carry out spot checks:** Say at the start of the project that you will be calling in on some of the quality checking to see how it is going, but don't say on what products or when. Then go along at a time that a check is supposed to be being done and make sure that it is, and by the right people too.

❑ **Follow up on failures:** If something does fail that has already passed test on that point, go and find out why. See whether someone is signing things off without checking them (as in the example just before this checklist).

❑ **Re-test:** Test a random sample a second time using different people. If you find faults in the second test, you'll know that the first one wasn't done properly.

❑ **Suppliers and your staff:** Where suppliers are building a product, involve your own specialist staff in at least some of the testing rather than the supplier doing the build and then all of the testing.

❑ **Suppliers and right of access:** If something is being built for your project, but on the supplier's site, get a clause put into the contract so you have right of access and can see your stuff being built, not just take delivery at the end. For some products it won't matter how it's built provided that it works, but for others it might matter very much.

❑ **Look for unlikely success:** If all products are passing test first time, or only have trivial errors, make sure that they are being properly tested.

Some suppliers have learned that saying everything was perfect the first time around just leads to suspicion and investigation. However, if they say that minor stuff was wrong and has been corrected, they can get away with missing out tests without being detected. I'm not out to run down external supplier companies, and in my experience most of them are pretty good. However, be aware that some unethical ones are out there, and even large and supposedly professional companies can stoop to such behaviour on occasions. So, when looking for 'unlikely success' (the last point in the checklist above), include checks where a range of products only had trivial errors, not just those that had none.

Risk Review Checklist

Many risks change during the life of the project, and even the project itself may change over time. A downside risk or threat that didn't seem too significant early on in the project may have become much more significant later on and so justify a change of action.

You might review risks at set points, such as towards the end of each stage, or on a regular basis, such as every four weeks. You'll have set down your choice of review pattern in the project Risk Plan and agreed it with the PSG. As you review the risks during the project, watch out for the following; for some you may need to get input from other people.

❏ **Project change:** Consider whether any significant changes have occurred in the project since your last review, and if so, whether they are likely to affect risk. For example, if the project end date has been brought forward because delivery is now needed earlier, risks that have delay as an impact are now likely to be more sensitive.

❏ **Environment change:** Has anything changed in the marketplace or business environment in which the project is taking place that could affect some risks? Perhaps you hear that your company made more profit than expected last year, so risks concerning funding availability will be reduced.

❏ **Probability:** For each risk, is it more likely to happen, or less likely, or has the probability stayed the same since the last review?

❏ **Impact:** If the risk were to occur, would the impact be the same as before, or do you think it would be greater or less?

❏ **Management actions:** If risk management actions are being taken to control a risk, are they working?

❏ **Near misses:** For threats in particular, even if there have been no instances of the risk happening, have there been 'near misses' which indicate that the management actions need changing?

❏ **Overall risk level:** Look at the overall risk level across your project. It may be that none of the downside risks has increased significantly in severity, but just about all of them have increased slightly. You need to check on the cumulative effect then, not just shifts in individual risks.

'Near misses' can be very significant for some risks and the international ISO standard for risk recommends watching out for them. For example your project staff may be at risk of injury when using the powerful machines needed for some of the work. At the start of the project you arranged for safety training and you supplied warning signs. If there have been no reports of anyone being injured, you may think that your risk management is working well and there's no need to do anything more. However, if there have been lots of near misses where someone was almost injured but a colleague just managed to pull them clear in time, then you need to take further action after all, and you need to take it quickly.

Project Log Checklist

The Project Log is a really useful document, and all the more so because it's extremely simple. You can usually have it as a word processor document or a spreadsheet. It functions as the Project Manager's diary and journal during the project. In thinking about the sort of things you should record in it during the project, consider this checklist.

❑ **Reminders:** Just like in a diary, write in reminders of things that you need to check. For example, you had to use a particular supplier because your organisation has fixed up a three year call-off contract. However, you hear that on an earlier project there were problems with supplier staff not turning up at the times they were needed, and that it caused several delays. So you make a note in your Project Log to check on the day that the supplier staff are supposed to arrive that they actually have.

❑ **Actions:** Picking up on the example in the Quality Crosscheck Checklist earlier in the chapter, you may have decided to attend some of the tests. Put them in your Project Log 'diary' then so that you don't forget, along with any other actions that you have planned.

❑ **Authorities:** You can use the Project Log to record authorities and so avoid more formal documentation. For example, the Sponsor said in a conversation today that he approved an extra spend of $500 because an extra bit of specialised equipment will speed up the work and make up some lost time.

❑ **Records of conversations:** It's helpful to record important details of conversations, such as phone calls to suppliers. Note the name of the person you spoke to, the date and time of the call, and briefly what was said and agreed to. If there is any disagreement afterwards, it's very impressive if you can list the dates and times of your phone calls, say who you spoke to on each occasion and what they agreed to.

❑ **Points to remember:** Some project standards include having a Lessons Learned Log, but that's often unnecessary and you can just note things down in your Project Log – good and bad – that will be helpful for future projects, or even for later in this one.

Lessons Checklist

Following on from the last point in the Project Log Checklist, lessons learned in this project can be extraordinarily valuable for future projects. If your organisation doesn't keep track of lessons, then you can do it personally for your own projects. The problem is that you always think that you'll never forget a particular incident or lesson but then, 15 months later, you're scratching your head and saying to yourself 'I know that there was something important in that project that I said I'd never forget'.

In considering what sort of experience to pass on to future projects have a look at this checklist. You can make notes as things happen, but there are also key times to think about lessons you've learned, usually at the end of each stage and then again at the end of the project.

❑ **Problems and 'why?':** When investigating a problem, find out why it happened. Then think whether the difficulty could have been foreseen and even prevented. If you could have done something, that may be a useful lesson which could help a future project avoid the same problem.

❑ **Warning signs:** If you did hit a serious problem, were there any warning signs that went unnoticed? Perhaps if you had been looking and picked up on them, it would have prevented the problem becoming so serious. That early warning information may be a real help a future project.

❑ **What went right?:** Think what worked particularly well and, again, why. Would this work just as well on similar projects in the future, or perhaps it would even work well across all types of project.

❑ **Improvements:** You may have done well, but could you have done things even better? Perhaps something could have been done more simply or faster.

❑ **Project management:** Did you find a better way of managing part of the project?

❑ **Next time around:** At the end of each stage and at the end of the project, think 'If I had to do this again, what would I do differently next time?'

Sometimes experience from a project should be passed back into the organisation immediately, rather than waiting for the Project Completion Report. Think about it like this: Suppose another project hits a serious but avoidable problem but doesn't warn you, and you then fall into the same hole a few weeks later. What would you say to that Project Manager next time you see him in the staff restaurant? 'Thanks a lot Fred. You knew I was running a similar project – you might just have warned me.'

Chapter 10

Managing the People

● ●

In This Chapter
▶ People matter
▶ Three key areas to watch out for
▶ Motivation and performance

● ●

I'm a huge fan of practical project techniques and powerful methods that really help get the job done. However,
although things like good methods are genuinely valuable,
you're probably every bit as aware as I am that without the
right people these things aren't going to make your project
successful. Methods are like any tool. The tool is valuable and
helpful for sure, but without the right pair of hands holding it,
it isn't going to get the job done well. In fact some tools in the
wrong hands are downright dangerous; and I'm talking projects here, not 1200 watt power saws.

Even where you have got the right people, it's all too easy to
overlook their needs by focusing solely on the job in hand. In
turn, failing to manage your staff well is almost bound to lead
on to motivation and performance problems which, in turn,
will affect the delivery of the job in hand. The one you were
bothered about in the first place. And on that point about
performance, don't ever think that getting the best out of your
team members is exploiting them. Most people on projects
want to do a really good job. Just think of yourself here, and
when you are the happiest and the most satisfied. Is it when
you can see that you're doing really well or when you know
you're not working at your best?

One kind of Project Manager focuses on the hard skills such
as planning and financial control and says that she's not 'a
people person'. Such a viewpoint simply isn't workable for

effective project management and your people are the most valuable asset you have.

The international standard for project quality management systems emphasises the importance of staff too. It says:

> *The quality and success of a project will depend on the participating personnel. Therefore, special attention should be given to the activities in the personnel-related processes.*

> *ISO 10006:2003(E) 6.2 Personnel-related processes*

The checklists in this chapter are to help you make sure that you are keeping up to speed on the staff management side of the project.

Three Areas to Watch

Along with some others Professor John Adair, a widely respected consultant and author on teams and team performance, has pointed out that there are three areas to watch for when managing people in teams, and that's obviously very applicable to projects. The three areas interact and are often illustrated as a Venn diagram, like the one in Figure 10-1

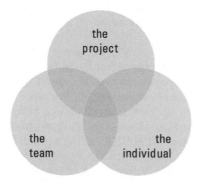

Figure 10-1: The Three Staff Management Areas.

Make sure that you balance your management across the three areas, and think about them when you do your project resourcing and you're deciding who should do what.

❑ **The project:** You have to get the job done and the project delivered. That's your primary objective, though it doesn't mean you should neglect the other two areas.

❑ **The team:** You need to bear in mind the needs of the team. Unless the project circumstances are very unusual, you don't have room for mavericks who will disrupt the team and drag the overall performance down.

❑ **The individual:** Your people matter, and wherever you can you should give them work that will interest them, challenge them and develop them. However, you must balance this area against the other two. It's no good developing a member of your staff if the project then fails as a direct result.

Performance Levels

One of the sad things about buzzwords is that good concepts get forgotten when the buzzwords finally go out of fashion. One buzzword that used to be bandied about a lot was *synergy*, but now nobody ever seems to talk about it. That's a shame because synergy is something extremely valuable. Individuals and teams can progress in the ways that they interact, and the more that they progress, the more effective they become. You may have experienced finally achieving synergy. I have, and the effect is mind-blowing. Here's one variant of the progression, with four levels.

❑ **Dependence:** A team member can't do much by themselves without asking lots of questions. She's dependent on others to achieve anything. You may remember how it was for you when you first started a new job in a new organisation and everything was strange. You couldn't even find your way to the stationery cupboard without asking someone.

❑ **Independence:** Now the team member knows what to do. She can work alone and achieve things within her own capacity and skill levels.

❑ **Interdependence:** This is the start of effective teamwork. Team members can help achieve things well beyond their own capabilities because of the mix of skills across a team. One person's expertise in some areas is matched by the expertise of others in different areas. Together they also have much more capacity and can tackle bigger things.

❏ **Synergy:** Where team members just 'click' somehow and work extraordinarily well together, achieving considerably more than just their total work hours would indicate. Achieving synergy on a team has been compared to a fighter jet switching to afterburner and shooting forward with enormous power. Look out for people who work unusually well together, and team them up wherever you can.

 At the start of the chapter I mentioned that getting the best performance isn't exploiting people. That's true when you look out for people who work exceptionally well together and achieve synergy. Although it's exhausting working at that pace – so be sure that you give them space to wind down occasionally – it's extremely enjoyable and rewarding.

The Motivation Checklist

Are your people well motivated? Highly motivated team members will help drive your project forwards, whilst demotivated staff can drag it down. Check out this list to help think through what you need to include in your management of the project in this key area.

❏ **Their last project:** Look at what the team, or individual, did last. If it was a failure you'll need to build staff up and motivate them much more at the beginning of their work on this project than if the last thing they did was an outstanding success.

❏ **Is the team a team?:** If the team members haven't worked together before, put in some effort to build them into a team from being just work colleagues. That includes motivating the team.

❏ **Explain the benefit:** Children will work at just about anything enthusiastically, with the possible exception of tidying up their bedrooms, but adults need a reason to get fully engaged. Explain what the project is about and why the contribution your staff will make is important; that's motivating.

❏ **Recognise the down side:** Explain to your team members where work will be mundane and boring, but how it fits in and why it's important. When your staff know that you know some stuff is boring it will make that work more bearable and team members will be more motivated to do it and do it well.

❏ **Motivation points:** Look for key points in the project where you can see that you'll need to add in extra motivation. There's more on this in the next checklist.

❏ **Personal development:** Check the distribution of activities within the project to ensure that, wherever possible, staff members have the opportunity to work on things that will stretch and develop them.

❏ **Targeted development:** Provided that team members are suitable for the work, give them tasks in areas where they've expressed an interest in working and extending their skills. When they see that you have a real interest in their development, they will be all the more dedicated to you and the project.

❏ **'We not me':** The UK military makes frequent use of the phrase 'we not me'. Those words emphasise that success is the something the team will achieve, not individuals putting their own wants first (such as the Project Manager claiming all of the credit for success). This 'group' identity is motivating and builds team spirit.

Motivation Points Checklist

You have to watch motivation levels throughout your project if you want your staff to perform well. However there are particular points where you can see in advance that you should step in to motivate people. Here are a few of them.

❏ **On joining the project:** When staff join the project it's a key time for motivating them. In a lot of projects that will be a frequent process as new staff join at different points according to the work to be done.

❏ **Starting a stage:** A project meeting at the start of a new stage is a great time for encouraging staff and spelling out again the value of the project. This focus and re-energising can be powerful indeed.

❏ **Flat times:** In some projects there are times where a lot of work is being done but there isn't too much to show for it yet in the way of product delivery. The flat times are points to visit the staff involved to give some encouragement and show your appreciation of the work they're doing.

❑ **On the completion of a significant task:** When staff have finished a major task, perhaps the delivery of major product on the project, that's a good time to express gratitude and show recognition for their work, the more so if they've really pulled out all the stops to achieve it.

 Don't undermine your recognition and thanks for a job well done with thoughtless, throw-away remarks about the next bit of work. 'Well, you've done really well on that job so now I'll be expecting equally high performance on the next one too.' Comments like that just make people wish they hadn't worked so hard and made a rod for their own backs. So focus on the completed job, say 'Thank you' and leave it at that.

❑ **On leaving the project:** It's only fair to thank staff for a job well done. However, if you 'motivate' staff as they leave the project, just think how they'll arrive on your next one.

❑ **At the end of the project:** If the project is a success, which I'm sure it will be, share that success. Make sure that organisational managers know who the team members were and try to get those managers involved in thanking people for their work. If it's possible to reward your people then do so. If you can't do that financially, with a bonus, you can at least have some sort of celebration to recognise the success. If you do have a celebration, don't forget to invite those staff who were only involved in the early part of the project, contract staff and support staff.

Performance Problems Checklist

If your people are not performing on the project as well as you expected, find out why and work hard to correct it. You must monitor performance all the time to pick up on any problems. If you don't you'll find yourself missing targets and the longer the performance has been below par, the longer it will take to catch up. In fact you may never catch up because the future performance will have to be much better than planned in order to make up the lost ground.

Here are a number of things to check if the staff performance levels are lower than you expected.

❑ **Complexity and difficulty:** Are the project products proving much harder to build than anticipated? That might mean you'll need more people and perhaps with more skills and experience.

❑ **Lack of skill:** Have you got the wrong team members? Perhaps this is an instance where you were given the staff who happened to be available rather than who were suitable for the project. If so work with renewed energy to change that position; and now you have some performance data to back up your case.

❑ **Demotivation:** You know yourself that you work well below your capacity when you are demotivated. Check if this is a factor and revise your pattern of visiting and encouragement if it is. See the previous checklist on Motivation Points.

❑ **Excessive specification change:** Review the amount of change taking place in the project. If it's excessive and the goalposts are constantly moving, productivity and delivery will suffer.

❑ **Staff change:** Look at the amount of staff change. If it is more than you'd expected, that may explain the productivity loss for two reasons. First, replacement staff take time to get up to normal speed, so you have a loss of productivity until they do. Second, the team dynamic is disrupted. That can be incredibly damaging in a high performance team.

❑ **Multi-tasking:** Where team members are working on other projects as well as yours, check the degree of multi-tasking. If they're trying to do too many things at once, all of the work will slow up dramatically. A five-day job will take six weeks if someone is working the same amount on four other projects at the same time. And no, the six weeks is not an arithmetical error. You know yourself that if you put a job down and pick it up again a week later, it takes you a while to get back up to speed, and you make more mistakes too.

❑ **Communications and documentation:** Check whether the documentation and communications are sensible. Are people spending too much time reading and writing emails instead of making a quick phone call? Are they bogged down in unnecessary paperwork when they could be moving the project forward?

❑ **Personal use of social media:** Are younger team members in particular (though not just younger ones) spending a lot of time keeping in touch with friends on social media or with sending and receiving texts? You may need to set down some rules here, for example that personal stuff be left for lunchtimes. One survey has found that a significant number of staff now spend up to an hour of working time each day on personal use of social media.

❑ **Support:** Ensure that you have sufficient support in place, especially for junior team members. If staff feel unsure of the work, don't know what to do and don't have anyone they can ask about it, they'll slow up.

❑ **Relationships and disputes:** Check for friction within the team. If people aren't working well together, even to the point of not being on speaking terms, then productivity is obviously going to suffer. Try to resolve any disputes and if that doesn't work, change the team membership. See the first checklist in this chapter on The Three Areas to Watch.

❑ **Bad management:** Check how your Team Leaders are managing their teams. If they are bullying staff for example (regrettably, it happens) then productivity will suffer as people do the minimum possible in the hope of avoiding criticism on what they have done. Move in very quickly on this one for the sake of the staff as well as the project, but be sure to gather facts first to support your actions. Also be extremely careful to follow your organisational rules for disciplinary action.

❑ **Environment:** Check the working environment of your teams. Poor working environments are known to bring down performance. If this is the problem, get the team moved to somewhere better or at least take steps to improve the surroundings.

❑ **Disturbance:** Check to see whether team members are being disturbed. Disturbance might be because of hustle and bustle in a busy open plan office where they can't concentrate, or because they're repeatedly called on to do other work alongside their project work, such as operational support.

❑ **Equipment:** check that the teams have the equipment and tools they need to perform well.

❑ **Concern at the future:** make sure that your team members know what they'll be doing after the project – succession planning is important. If team members think that they'll be made redundant at the end of the project because their job in their home department has now been permanently filled by someone else, they're going to be focusing more on finding a new job than getting your project finished.

Motivator and Hygiene Checklist

My favourite management guru has to be Fred Herzberg, sadly no longer with us. He put forward a *Two Factor Theory* of motivators and what he called *hygiene factors*. In brief, his theory (which incidentally has never been disputed) is that things like good pay and company cars don't motivate people. He was misquoted as meaning that you don't have to pay people well, but he didn't say that. He said that if you neglect these hygiene factors you'll reduce performance below the norm. He called the norm the *Potter line* where people potter along doing a fair day's work for a fair day's pay. However the hygiene factors won't boost performance above the Potter Line; for that you need motivators.

Have a look through this checklist of Fred Herzberg's 'motivators' and see how you can build them into your project to maximise motivation and commitment. To validate the list, think how important these things are to you in your own work.

❑ **Achievement:** To produce something worthwhile and do it well.

❑ **Recognition:** You've worked hard and someone notices what you've done.

❑ **Meaningful interesting work:** Doing work that's deadly boring, and of which, what's more, you can't see the point anyway, is inherently demotivating and a recipe for poor performance. So strive for the opposite and design the Work Packages (work assignments) keeping in mind those who will do the work. But see the advice in the Motivation checklist earlier in this chapter because not all project work can be interesting.

❑ **Increased responsibility:** People respond to responsibility and rise to the occasion. That's reasonable responsibility, though. Don't put someone in charge of something on the project where they're in over their head or they'll just freeze.

❑ **Growth and advancement:** Offer the opportunity to develop, alongside delivering the project.

If you want to know more about Fred Herzberg, search on the internet for 'Jumping for the Jelly Beans'. The material is a bit dated in terms of presentation quality, but entirely current in terms of content.

Stage Briefing Checklist

Use this checklist to help prepare your staff briefing at the beginning of each stage. The briefing is to encourage and motivate staff, and also to be sure that they're clear on project controls and communications.

❑ **Welcome:** If new staff are joining the project to help with the work of the stage, this is a natural point to publicly welcome them.

❑ **The work of the stage:** An explanation of what's involved in the stage and how it fits into the project. This will be less significant where a single team is working right through and the staff are already fully aware of all the project work.

❑ **Key risks:** List and explain the key risks affecting the work in the stage ahead. Some may be ongoing risks while others may be localised to this stage alone.

❑ **Risk responsibility:** Include a reminder that everyone in the project should be watching out for risks. Check that everyone knows how to report risk-related information (usually a Project Memo).

❑ **Quality:** Keep in mind the ISO emphasis to maintain 'a culture of quality' in the project, and emphasise the need for everyone to take quality seriously. However taking quality seriously means delivering at the specified level, not 'gold plating' with excessive and unnecessary levels of quality.

❑ **Quality openness:** Particularly where you have junior team members, encourage staff to be open about errors found in product tests. If testing never found errors, there wouldn't be any need for testing. The important thing is to find and correct errors, not cover them up so that they just cause bigger problems later.

 It's a learned behaviour to be grateful when someone finds an error in your work. Junior team members in particular tend to be too proud of their work. If someone finds an error then an inexperienced person will try to rush the rest of the test or review through before anyone else finds something wrong with their precious product.

❑ **Time recording:** Explain why you need time recording on project activities and emphasise that team members should complete time sheets accurately. Explain how you need the information for project management and control and it's not to 'snoop' on staff or criticise performance.

❑ **Problem reporting:** To remind staff that there will be problems. If anyone encounters one that they can't deal with then there's no shame in reporting it. Remind the teams of 'we not me' and if someone hits a problem everyone will work together constructively to help resolve it.

Supplier Staff Checklist

If you'll have supplier teams working on your project, don't forget them or imagine that they don't need anything. If they're going to work effectively and help you deliver, they need support too. The supplier staff are on your side; they're not the enemy. Have a look at this checklist to help think what you need to do to help them perform well.

❑ **Induction:** Supplier staff may be technically expert, but they won't necessarily understand your organisation. To help prevent misunderstandings and mistakes, include some induction briefing. That may mean bringing supplier staff on site for a day or so, perhaps a couple of weeks ahead of the project work.

❑ **Support:** Supplier staff will have questions about the project; they can't work in a vacuum. Unless the supplier staff are working alongside your own people, have someone available to answer questions, and be sure that everyone knows who that person is.

❑ **Project controls:** Make sure that your supplier staff understand the project controls that you'll be using. Your own staff may be very familiar with the controls because of past projects, but supplier staff work in many different organisations with many different ways of doing things.

❑ **Cut them some slack:** Supplier teams that are well established may have their own way of working that's every bit as effective as yours, just different. Don't make them work your way just for the sake of it. It will lead to misunderstandings and slow things down. When setting up the controls (notably the Work Packages or work assignments) discriminate between what's important, in order to fit in with the rest of the project, and what isn't.

❑ **Facilities:** The working environment affects performance; we know that. So don't put supplier staff in the broom cupboard under the stairs then.

❑ **Inclusion:** Supplier staff are part of your project, so include them in any team events during the project. You might need to get financial approval to spend organisational funds on supplier staff as well as your own organisational staff but it's worth it. The last thing you want is a 'them and us' divide in your project.

❑ **Handover:** The trouble with suppliers and consultants is that they walk out of the door at the end of the job and take a lot of knowledge with them. Think if you need to record any useful information before they leave, or even build in a handover briefing for the staff who will take on responsibility for the operational use of project products.

Don't overlook supplier support. In his *100 Rules for NASA Project Managers* Jerry Madden observes that NASA staff

> *. . . should be making every effort possible to make sure the contractor gets a high score (i.e. be on schedule and produce good work). Contractors don't fail, NASA does and that is why one must be proactive in support.*

To repeat the point from just before the last checklist, remember that the supplier staff are not the enemy. They're part of your project and if they succeed then that will help ensure that you do too.

Chapter 11

Templates for Planning

● ●

In This Chapter

▶ A template for the Project Charter

▶ A template for the PMP – the Project Management Plan

▶ Templates for major plans within the PMP

● ●

*T*his chapter has a number of templates aimed at saving you time and effort as you plan your project. As with all other templates in this book, you may need to adapt them a bit to fit the exact needs of your organisation and then, if necessary, your current project. If you're new to projects and not completely sure what you need, it's best to leave most of the headings in and do a bit too much rather than a bit too little when it comes to the Project Charter and the Project Management Plan (PMP). You want to be sure that you've thought everything through, and it shouldn't take that long to do anyway.

This chapter contains templates for the Project Charter and Project Management Plan which in turn contain other things. If you're unfamiliar with the Charter and PMP, have a look at Chapter 2. In short, though, they are the two key project-level planning documents that you produce in the first stage of the project, the Planning Stage. The Charter contains strategic elements such as the scope (what the project covers and also what it doesn't) while the PMP contains the more tactical elements such as the Project Plan and the Risk Plan.

Header Block

For each document you'll need a header block with standard information. This first section of the chapter lists the sort of information you should include. The individual templates will then just have a section called 'header block' to save repeating the same stuff over and over.

Try to keep the header block simple. Instead of a simple header block, some templates that are available (both free and paid for) have a big cover page for every document. This page has all sorts of detailed information but nearly always you simply don't need all of that.

❑ **Document name:** Such as 'Project Charter'.

❑ **Project name:** A short project name.

❑ **Version number:** This is very important. You need this number so that you know whether a particular copy is the latest one or not.

❑ **Date:** The date on which this document, or version of it, was created.

❑ **Author:** The person who created the document and who can be asked about it. For many documents the author will be the Project Manager.

The Project Charter

This important document sets down the strategic aspects of the project, including what it is and the justification for it. The Charter will be checked by the Project Steering Group (PSG) at the start of the project to ensure that the project is viable, but then you keep it up-to-date throughout the project. It must be checked again by the PSG at every Stage Gate to be sure that the project continues to be viable.

❑ **Header block:** Project and document information.

❑ **Background and summary:** Very briefly explain the background to the project and how it came about (such as an HQ instruction or the need to solve an operational problem) and then describe the project.

❏ **Scope statement:** Explain here exactly what the project will cover. Unless your project is very simple, it's best to use some subsections.

  ❏ **Project product:** What the project will deliver at the end. It's surprising that people can use similar words but still have a misunderstanding of what the project will actually produce.

  ❏ **Areas included:** What the project will cover. You might define that by geography such as regions within your organisation, or functions.

  ❏ **Areas excluded:** What the project won't cover. The exclusions aren't the whole world outside the project, but rather things that could be misunderstood and where somebody might assume that they are included. Although the project is a perfectly good one, that person will be disappointed when the project finally delivers. Making things clear at the beginning is powerful in managing expectations.

It pays to include the section on 'Project Product'. It won't take long to write and it adds great clarity. In the National Health Service in the UK, a major project document similar to the Charter was approved by senior managers and signed off. Parts of the document described how the project would investigate a problem, design new procedures and stop there. In other places the text referred to implementing the procedures and the wording at those points indicated that the implementation was part of the project. So what project had the managers agreed to when they signed the document?

❏ **Requirements:** A list of requirements for the project, such as from users, senior managers and perhaps including legal requirements, and then a note against each one of where that requirement came from.

❏ **Objectives:** Set down here what the project is trying to achieve. It's important that everyone is clear on the objectives and agrees with them. Otherwise you may have people thinking different things and bringing the project under pressure later. For example, the Production Manager thinks that the new production line project is about increasing quality and product reliability, even if the cost of manufacture goes up slightly. However the Finance Manager thinks it is about reducing the production costs with new, low-maintenance machines and making more money, even if quality is reduced. We're in for problems then when it comes to specifying and ordering the new production line equipment later in the project.

❑ **Business Case:** State the justification for running the project, along with details of the business benefits. Although part of the Project Charter, the Business Case is a major document and you'll find a separate template for it in this chapter.

❑ **Organisation:** Specify the roles and responsibilities. You can have a text list but it's usually best as a chart showing who is doing what, such as who the Sponsor and Project Manager are. You'll find checklists on roles in Chapter 6.

❑ **Business Impact Statement:** This item is high profile in the PRIME project method, but I've yet to see it anywhere near so clearly in any other approach. It's important information, though, and here you say how the project will impact business areas outside the immediate area where the project is taking place. That impact might be in other departments which must change their procedures to fit, or perhaps with central computer systems where modifications will be needed to some databases. If no external impact occurs, you just say so. PRIME says that the Sponsor must personally sign this section to confirm the extent of the business impact. It's an important element of the strategic view embodied in the Charter.

❑ **Constraints and acceptance criteria:** In this section put in any constraints that will affect the project. That might be things like a fixed delivery date, or a limit on funding or constraints on which specialist staff can be used. Then specify the acceptance criteria for the project. The reason that both of these items are in a single section is that they are often related. So an acceptance criterion is that the project product must be ready to hand over on or before 1 December, but that fixed deadline is also a constraint on the project. Failing to reach one or more of the acceptance criteria doesn't necessarily mean that the project will be refused, but it won't be seen as an outright success.

❑ **Assumptions:** Record in this section any assumptions affecting the project and any other elements of the Charter. For example, in setting a particular delivery deadline in the 'Constraints and acceptance criteria' section, that may assume that other projects ahead of this one will finish no more than four weeks late. If those projects are late finishing and don't release the specialist project staff until six weeks after they were supposed to start work on this one, everyone will then understand why you were late, because you stated the assumption clearly up front.

❑ **Acceptance arrangements:** How the project team will hand over the project product(s) at the end of the project. Don't ignore this section because it won't take long to agree and record, but could save huge confusion later. You may also want to record who is responsible within the organisation for taking delivery of the product(s). The acceptance may be fairly informal, with just verbal agreement, or might be legally binding, such as with the handover of a new building from the developers to the new owners.

Business Case

The Business Case forms part of the Project Charter and is a seriously important document. It's the justification for the project. The contents are wider in scope than you might expect, but that's because the Business Case may sometimes be seen on its own, such as by senior organisational managers who want to know what the project is all about and why you are doing it, or perhaps because their authority is needed for funding it. If you're sure that the Business Case will only ever be seen as part of the Charter and alongside the PMP, then you can take out information that is in other places, such as in the Project Plan (time and cost).

You must keep the Business Case up-to-date throughout the project. It will be used by the Project Steering Group at Stage Gates (as mentioned earlier in the chapter) to ensure that the project is still viable, but also when dealing with change or problems during the stages. Some changes, for example, may have a significant impact on the Business Case such as to increase benefits.

❏ **Header block:** Project and document information.

❏ **Project summary:** A short description of the project so someone can quickly get to grips with what the project is all about.

❏ **Justification:** Why the project should be run.

❏ **Benefits:** A list of benefits and for each quantifiable benefit, how it will be measured and when. Have a look at Chapter 5 for a checklist on the three different types of benefit.

❏ **Cost:** The latest estimated cost of the project, including staff costs. You should normally separate out *capital costs* – which are one-off expenses – from *revenue costs*, which are ongoing running costs in the organisation such as for project staff. And don't leave out the staff costs; they're a genuine project expense and probably quite a big one.

❏ **Time:** The latest estimated time that the project will take to deliver.

❏ **Risk:** Detail of the major risks involved in the project. It's important for any senior managers reading the Business Case to see what risk the organisation is exposed to in order to achieve the project result, such as business benefits.

The Project Management Plan

The Project Management Plan (PMP) is primarily the Project Manager's plan to say how he will control the project. However the Project Steering Group (PSG) has an interest too, since the PSG members, with their 'project governance' hats on, must make sure that the project will be properly managed and controlled. It can be really productive for the Project Manager to work in 'workshop mode' with the members of the Steering Group to at least sketch out the main parts of the PMP and so incorporate the right PSG controls from the start. That workshop will also pay off for the PSG since the members will have a much better feel for the project which will help them as it progresses.

The PMP is a bundle of other plans and you can think of it as being a bit like a folder. As with the Project Charter, you must keep the PMP up-to-date throughout the project.

❏ **Header block:** Add the project and document information.

❏ **Project Plan:** Put together the product plans, activity plans, resource plan and budget. You can find a number of checklists to help you in Chapter 8, including the 'Four Dogs' to help you check that the plan is achievable.

❏ **Procurement Plan:** In projects that involve a lot of procurement, use this plan to record the details of what has to be bought and when. This plan should also include the elements involved in the procurement and the timing. For example, major purchases may have to go through your Procurement Department and there is a six week lead time. You'll find a separate template to help where your project justifies having a Procurement Plan.

❏ **Quality Plan:** Specify the level of quality you need to deliver in this project, and exactly how you are going to achieve it. The plan also sets down the checking mechanisms such as Quality Audit. There's a separate template for the Quality Plan later in this chapter.

❏ **Risk Plan:** State how you are going to manage risk in the project. Don't confuse this with information on individual risks; that's all in the Risk Log. Again you'll find a separate template in this chapter for the Risk Plan.

❏ **Stakeholder Plan:** Include information on how you will handle different groups of stakeholders. There's a separate template in this chapter for the Stakeholder Plan too.

❏ **Communications Plan:** Specify what communications will take place and how they will be carried out. Your objective here is to achieve good communications and to avoid over-communication where people are bombarded with information that they don't want. You may be very aware of the over-communication problem as you plough through all those unwanted emails in your in-box. In Chapter 8 you'll find a checklist to help you think this through.

❏ **Version control:** You have to keep track of versions. That applies to management products such as the Risk Plan as well as to technical products such as the floor plan for a new building or the system specification document. Your version control may be very simple, with just a central record of what the latest version is for each document, or something much more sophisticated. As with so much else in project management, the degree of sophistication you go to will depend on the needs of the project.

❑ **Project controls:** This is the section where you set down controls that aren't in other plans in the PMP. For example, situations may arise where the Project Manager must refer something to the PMP immediately, even if it doesn't affect the time and cost of running the project.

Look carefully at what version control you need, because you'll just about always need it, even in very small projects and even if it's just the management products. Figure 11-1 illustrates two management documents, and they're different. Which one are we supposed to be using then? You'll find a template for a Version Record in Chapter 16, Templates for Control.

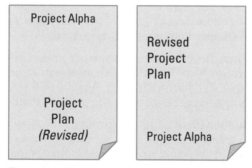

Figure 11-1: The need for version control.

You may hear version control referred to as *versioning* and, more confusingly if you're not an engineer or IT specialist, *Configuration Management*. Strictly speaking Configuration Management is a bit more than just version control, but that isn't a concern for the vast majority of projects.

Procurement Plan

Not all projects need a Procurement Plan. However, if you have a lot of procurement involving a lot of steps, such as with setting up contracts, the plan can be really helpful. The Procurement Plan brings together information from other places, such as the Project Plan, Stage Plans and budget. It gives you a clear view of what procurement actions are to be carried out and when, and when money will be spent.

The simplest way of structuring the plan is to set down the procurements one at a time with a block of repeating information for each procurement. Have the normal project header block first, then the individual procurement information blocks.

- ❏ **Item or service:** A brief description of what is to be bought.

    - ❏ **Contract/internal procurement:** Say whether a contract is to be set up as part of the project, or whether the item is to be procured through your organisation's normal purchase procedure and doesn't need a contract.

    - ❏ **Cost:** Insert here the total cost of the procurement and when the money will be committed and then spent. Or, if the cost is to be split up with something like staged payments, put in the detail of that split as well as the total.

    - ❏ **Date required:** Specify the date when the item or service will be needed in the project.

    - ❏ **Procurement steps:** List the steps in the procurement, with the target date for each. For example, Invitation to Tender (ITT), shortlisting, presentations and then award of contract. Or it might be a single step for an internal procurement which is putting in a procurement form to the Procurement Department seven weeks before the item is needed.

    - ❏ **Authority:** Say whether any particular authority is needed to make the procurement. For example a very large purchase may have to be approved by the Finance Director.

- ❏ **Item or service:** The next block of information for the next procurement. Continue for as many blocks as you have procurements in the project.

You'll usually commit money before you spend it so the procurement steps can be very significant for your project budget. When you place an order, the money to cover that procurement is committed and can't be used for anything else. However the invoice won't usually be sent in by the supplier until after an item or service has been delivered, and the bill will be paid about four weeks after that. The timing of the steps can be important. You may place an order in one financial year, but the actual payment is made in the next one. In some cases your finance people will want to put money from the first year on hold so that the purchase falls into that year's accounts, even if the money is spent in the following year. Clear? Well if not, then ask your finance guys to explain how they record finances and about *accruals*.

Quality Plan

You won't deliver the required project quality by accident. It needs careful thought and then a considered plan on how you will achieve it. 'Considered' doesn't mean long and complicated though. Your Quality Plan may be short and straightforward, and actually it's an advantage if it is.

The Quality Plan forms part of the PMP. To help you get the plan right, you'll find a checklist in Chapter 8.

❑ **Header block:** Project and document information.

❑ **Quality level:** The overall level of quality you need to achieve in this project. You might have an organisational scale here or you may write in a description of the quality level, such as 'safety-critical' or 'low-quality'.

❑ **Standards:** List here any standards with which you must comply. You may immediately think of external standards such as electrical, data protection and safety. However don't forget any relevant internal standards required by your organisation.

❑ **Testing:** A generic description of the sort of tests and checks that you will do in the project to ensure that the quality is right. It's not the detail of the individual tests on products; that goes onto your Product Definitions. For example, you may say that you will use informal, 'peer level' review to check out some documents, but major designs will go through full formal review.

❑ **Quality records:** If you need to, specify the nature and content of quality documentation, such as test reports.

❑ **Audit:** A crucial section where you set down how you will check that the required testing and checking has actually been done, not merely talked about and then quietly forgotten.

Specifying an excessive quality level isn't a good thing. It will drive up project overheads unnecessarily both in money and staff effort. Good project quality is *appropriate* project quality. Remarkably few of your projects will need to achieve a 'safety of life' level, unless your career is building air traffic control systems or nuclear reactors, that is.

Risk Plan

As with the Quality Plan not covering individual tests, the Risk Plan isn't there to say how you will manage individual risks, but rather how you are going to control risk across the whole project.

❑ **Header block:** Project and document information.

❑ **Overall risk levels:** An overview of the nature of the risk in the project and if it is high risk, medium or low risk. In your description specify the level for the positive as well as the negative risk. The project may be rich in 'opportunities' (upside, positive risk) to increase benefits for example.

❑ **Risk measures:** Specify the risk measures for impact, probability and proximity. Depending on the size of your organisation, a $1 million negative risk exposure may be threatening to your whole organisation, a minor inconvenience, or something in between. For *proximity* (how soon the risk can occur) you might specify project stages, project week numbers or calendar dates.

❑ **Risk procedures:** How people in the project will report new risks, changes to risks already identified and risks actually happening. Also explain how the project risk management will interface with organisational risk management and the procedures for passing information between the two.

❑ **Risk review:** the pattern for reviewing risks in the project to look for changes and to see whether the risk management actions are working. For example, you might review all risks at the end of each Delivery Stage, or the very high- and high-probability risks every two weeks and the rest every six weeks.

❑ **Risk documentation:** If you need it, the format and content of risk documentation. Don't bother with this section if you're only going to specify the content of the Risk Log because that's self-evident from the Risk Log itself.

 Keep the risk procedures very simple and easy to understand. Don't have too many people in the reporting chain either. When advising clients on risk management I always suggest a *one-bounce* approach. That means that there is never more than one person between the person making the report and the one empowered to take action. If there's more than one person, there are two dangers. First, it will take too long for the information to reach the person who needs to take action. Second, that information dilution will take place where a 'serious crisis' is transformed into 'a minor inconvenience' by the time it has gone through six levels.

Stakeholder Plan

Stakeholders can often make or break a project. If you have a lot of stakeholders then you can set up a Stakeholder Log. If the management of those stakeholders will be a significant part of your project, which often it is, you can then develop a Stakeholder Plan in which you group stakeholders together and specify the management action that you'll need during the project. Then make sure that you build the actions into your Project and Stage Plans.

❑ **Header block:** Project and document information.

❑ **Summary:** In this section explain the significance and pattern of stakeholders in the project. For example that most of the management action will be needed at the front end of the project to consult stakeholders, or perhaps that the most significant ones are actually outside the organisation, such as shareholders or customers.

❑ **Stakeholder group:** Replace the title 'Stakeholder group' with the actual name of the group, such as 'voluntary organisations' in a hospital project or 'major donors' in a charity.

> ❑ **Description:** In this section describe the characteristics of the group. In other words, why have you grouped these stakeholders together?
>
> ❑ **Stakeholders:** list the stakeholders who are in the group. Cross check with your Stakeholder Log that you have got everyone in a group somewhere, even if one or two 'groups' are just an individual stakeholder who needs individual management.
>
> ❑ **Specific project concerns:** List the specific interests that the group has in the project. You can also include the overall stance of the group as to whether it is in favour of the project or opposed to it. Note the warning below though.
>
> ❑ **Management actions:** List the actions needed to manage the stakeholder group, each with a date (or frequency if it is ongoing) and say who is responsible for taking the action.

❑ **Stakeholder group:** The next stakeholder group with the subsections as before.

Be careful how you record the stance of a stakeholder group. For example if you note that a group is opposed to the project and you use derogatory terms, that's not only unprofessional but you'll also increase the opposition if those stakeholders then get to know what you've written about them.

Communication Plan

The Communication Plan records those communications that you expect to take place within the project, to come in from outside and be sent out of the project. For each, you record how the communication will take place, such as by email, meeting or phone call.

The Communications Plan forms part of the PMP. When you have completed it, make sure that the related activity is reflected in your Project and Stage Plans. For example, don't forget to plan for the Project Manager's time to produce a progress report each month.

❑ **Header block:** Project and document information.

❑ **Communication:** A short name for the communication such as 'Stage Progress Report' or 'Stakeholder briefing'. Then include further information in subsections.

> ❑ **Created by:** Who generates the communication, which could be someone outside the project if the communication is inbound.
>
> ❑ **Received by:** Who receives the communication. It may be a single person or a group; a distribution list.
>
> ❑ **Frequency:** The frequency with which the communication is made. It could be a progress report sent out monthly, or an event-driven communication, such as when a team member notices and reports a new risk.
>
> ❑ **Media:** The way in which the communication takes place, such as by email or written report.
>
> ❑ **Content and format:** What the communication will actually contain and any requirement for the way that it is formatted. For example, a report may contain financial information on spending, and you should present that financial information in the form of a table. In many cases it helps to attach an example so people can immediately see what you mean rather than struggle while they try to interpret a text description.

❑ **Communication:** The next communication with subsections.

If you have a lot of expected communications in the project, you may find it easier to break the plan into three sections to cover inbound communications, internal project communications and then outbound communications. The Word template available to accompany this book has got those sections on it, so just remove them if your comms will be simpler and you don't need the sections.

Part IV
Checklists for Project Control

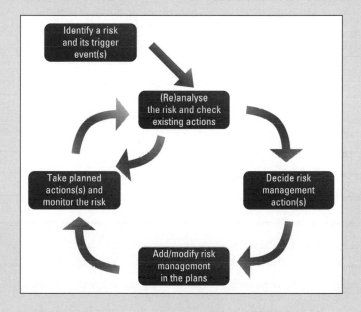

Risk management isn't just something you do at the start of the project. You must keep monitoring the risks and change things if the control actions aren't working. Then you may notice new risks as you work through the project and, of course, they'll need managing too.

This example of a risk cycle is from the PRIME project method and it's unusual because the model allows for action and monitoring to continue if review shows that everything is okay. The model helps you keep a clear picture of what you are doing when managing risks during the project.

In this part . . .

✔ Get in control and stay in control.

✔ Learn how to manage risk.

✔ Find out how to check each stage and conduct Stage Gates.

✔ Review the completed project.

Chapter 12

Checking Each Stage

● ●

● ●

*P*lanning a project thoroughly is essential, but if you have any knowledge of project management at all you'll know that the trick then is to keep it on track, monitoring it against the plan. One thing's for sure, your project isn't going to go exactly to plan but, strangely perhaps, that makes the plan even more important. It forms a baseline that you correct to.

You must keep the plan up to date if it's going to be any use to you for control. Checking the stage must begin then with updating your Stage Plan from the information and actuals (time sheet information and spending information) that comes in with the Team Progress Reports.

Your stage checks should be in three areas:

✔ **Team progress:** To assess the position of each team as you look at the Team Progress Reports.

✔ **Whole stage position:** Having got all of that progress information in, take a wider look to see how the whole stage is progressing, including some forward projections to see where it's going and if it will finish on target.

✔ **Periodic checks:** At some of your assessment points you'll probably want to do periodic checks, notably on the risk position and the viability of the Business Case but perhaps on other things too such as supplier management and stakeholder management.

This chapter has checklists to help you in each of the three areas of checking. As always, adapt the list to the needs of your project. On the one hand you don't want to perform unnecessary checks that just waste time. On the other hand, many projects get into trouble, and even fail, because the checks are inadequate and fail to pick up on warning signs in time to take action to deal with a project-threatening problem.

Team Progress Checklist

When it comes to teamwork you really need to check in two ways:

➤ Look at factual progress information given in progress reports or in regular meetings with Team Leaders.

➤ Visit personally to see how each team is getting on.

This first checklist focuses on examining progress-related information; the second one tackles the team visits.

❑ **Production:** If the Work Package is to deliver multiple products, are any products that are due to be complete by now actually complete?

❑ **Quality timing:** Are all the scheduled tests being done at the right time, or are any getting delayed or missed?

❑ **Quality responsibilities:** Are tests being done by the right people?

❑ **Spend:** Check that any team spending or commitment of funds is according to plan.

❑ **Outlook:** Look at the Team Leader's forecast for the rest of the Work Package, and consider if anything could affect the running of the stage.

If the reports from teams show everything going exactly to plan, go check that out. Make sure that the team is not merely feeding back the information that was on your plan in the first place; 'At the end of Week 3 on this job we're supposed to be 50 per cent complete and it's the end of Week 3 so that means we should report 50 per cent complete.' If you confirm that a team really is exactly on target then that's great . . . just unusual.

Team Visit Checklist

Getting out-and-about is important for you as a Project Manager. It's been said that you can't project manage from behind your desk and that's something I very much agree with. Actually talking to team members will give you information that you simply can't get in other ways. Part of that information is picking up on non-verbal clues. When you're talking to different people take careful note of their expression and attitude. Also listen out for *how* they say things, not merely *what* they say.

❑ **Equipment and facilities:** Check that the team has what it needs to do the work.

❑ **Environment:** Is the work environment proving suitable for optimum performance?

❑ **Atmosphere:** Check whether the atmosphere in the team room is purposeful and upbeat. Look out for people who don't seem to be engaged and for messy work areas that indicate lack of organisation.

❑ **Motivation:** Assess whether the team members seem well motivated and enthusiastic.

❑ **Cooperation:** If the team members have to be in touch with people in other teams, does that interaction seem to be working well, or are there signs of a lack of co-operation or signs of friction?

❑ **Encouragement:** Take the opportunity to encourage team members and express appreciation for their work (if they're doing a good job, that is).

I started working in projects with computer systems analysis and design. I was taught that when I went to visit people in their offices the first thing I should do on entering the room was to take a quick and unobtrusive scan round. It's a habit that's stuck with me and it pays off in project management too. You can take in a surprising amount of information in just a three-second sweep around the room with your eyes as you enter. For example, are people looking purposeful or bored, and does the room look well organised, or cluttered and disorganised?

Another lesson from my systems analysis days is to beware of *snapshot syndrome*, where you see something in a 'snapshot' at a particular moment and then wrongly assume that it's happening all the time. A senior manager tried to put me on the spot once. He had walked past a room and, glancing in through the glass panel in the door, saw some of my staff talking together. I was summoned to his office to explain why my staff spent all their time chit-chatting and not working. He was a bit taken aback when I pointed out that at that moment he and I were talking, not sitting silently at our desks. He didn't like it either when I went on to challenge his assumption that the staff talking was continuous, and then his other assumption that they weren't talking about the work. I gave him a clear example of where those staff would need to discuss something. The reality was that the staff performed very well and were very professional. So, use your eyes, but check things out and beware of snapshot syndrome.

Stage Check Checklist

To get early warning of any problems and keep on track, you must carry out regular checks. So build a regular check into your routine. The sooner you detect any problem, the earlier you can do something about it and the less damaging it is likely to be. Finding problems isn't a problem ∅ you can now do something about them – but problems going unnoticed is a major problem.

A common question is about how often you should check the project. There's no definitive answer to the question because it will depend on the nature of the project, your own management style and the people you are working with. Personally I prefer weekly as a default because if everything is okay the check doesn't take very long to do . . . and I always prefer to find any problems sooner rather than later.

❑ **Update the plan:** Put the 'actuals' from timesheets and spending information into your project plan, although if you have a project administrator then he or she can do that for you. If you haven't kept the product plans up-to-date with product deliveries during the last period, do it now.

❏ **Progress:** Check what products have been delivered in the stage by the team(s) compared to the plan.

❏ **ETC:** Check the 'estimated time to complete' for current Work Packages against the plan. If anything is too far off the plan or exactly on plan, check it out.

❏ **Performance:** Check whether teams are performing at the level that you expected or if performance is significant above or below what you had anticipated.

❏ **Staff availability:** Check the timesheets to see whether the work hours reported by teams and team members are in line with the work hours that they are scheduled for. If staff are not sufficiently available to the project (perhaps they are being called out to do other work) then take action now before you start missing important deadlines.

❏ **Spending:** Check what has been committed in the last period, compared with the budget (and Procurement Plan if you are using one).

❏ **Quality:** Look at your Quality Checklist, or log. Check that tests and checks that are supposed to have been completed by this point have been. Also check the signoffs to ensure that the tests were carried out by the correct people.

❏ **Rework:** Look at the level of rework after quality checks to correct faulty products. See if the amount of rework is reasonable or if it reveals a quality problem with significant errors in things going for test.

❏ **Risk review:** Check that you've taken any planned risk reviews in the last period. If you've overlooked one, schedule it for priority action now.

❏ **Project Memos:** Look through your Project Log for outstanding action points. Make sure that anything unresolved is genuinely 'on hold' while you are waiting for something such as additional information and it's not that you've simply forgotten about the matter.

❏ **Morale:** Assess the morale of your staff. You might schedule a walk-about just before your stage assessment or you can think about project staff you have met recently to talk about the work. Were they upbeat and enthusiastic, or downbeat and subdued?

❑ **Relationships:** Think about how teams are working together. Think back to see if you have seen any signs of friction or frustration. Check particularly on relationships between your own organisation's staff and any supplier staff working on the project.

❑ **Forward projection:** Using the information you've assembled for the previous points, do a forward projection to make sure that you will finish the stage within any limits set by the Project Steering Group (PSG). If not, consider if you can alter things so that you will hit the target or, if you can't get things back on track, then report the matter to the Sponsor using a Project Memo – Warning.

❑ **Forward view:** Check what lies ahead in the period up to your next check. Make sure that you're aware of action such as major spends, checks on suppliers and action on risks. If you're using a Project Log for reminders, then cross check with that log to be sure that you've noted everything in there.

Most computer tools for project scheduling allow you to monitor progress using the measure of *percentage complete*. Remember that this measure is unreliable. Instead, focus primarily on the products, which are about delivery, and are much better for progress monitoring. Progress reporting based on delivery is fact based and verifiable. A team that has finished a product so that it now 'only' has to pass test may well report it as 95 per cent complete. However if the product fails test and needs substantial re-work it could be considerably more than five percent away from completion. You only know for sure where you are when the product is delivered.

Risk Check Checklist

From time-to-time during a stage you may want to check the overall position on risk. This check isn't the same as the regular reviews on individual risks but rather a global view.

❑ **Overall risk:** Check to see whether the overall risk level is still within the limits set down by the PSG. If not, report it to the PSG (or just the Sponsor) in the way set down in the project controls.

❑ **High severity risk:** Look at the high-severity risks to see whether any significant change could cause a problem for the whole project.

❑ **Risk mechanisms:** Review the risk mechanisms to make sure that they are working. You usually do this check more in the early part of the project than later, when you have more confidence that everything is working well.

Business Case Check Checklist

This checklist is for a high-level checks of the Business Case, where you need them, at intervals during each Delivery Stage. You'll be doing a more thorough check towards the end of each Delivery Stage to update the Project Charter in preparation for the Stage Gate.

❑ **Benefits projections:** Do the projections still look right in the light of any new information or circumstances that have emerged in the stage to date?

❑ **New benefits:** As you get more certain of the project and its impact, check to see whether there are any new areas of benefit that weren't apparent at the start.

❑ **Changes:** Check the effects of any changes to the project and make sure that you've picked up on any knock-on effect on the Business Case. There may be additional benefits, or perhaps reduced benefits, as a consequence of the change.

❑ **Cost and time:** See whether any changes in the forecast cost and time of the project are likely to affect the viability of the project.

❑ **Viability:** Following on from the last point, assess the ongoing viability of the project across all of the elements, including the latest risk assessment.

❑ **Stakeholder impact:** Check whether you need to inform particular stakeholders of any changes to the Business Case. Perhaps the latest projections of benefits in a particular business area are now reduced and you need to warn the PSG or the relevant organisational manager about that.

When assessing the impact of any proposed change in the project, you should include any impact on the Business Case. If a change then goes ahead, you should update the Business Case if it was affected. The Business Case check in the list above is to be quite sure that you remembered to make any necessary adjustments.

Supplier Check Checklist

Where your project involves contracts, monitoring the contracts has to be part of the work of your stage checking. You must make sure that the work is being done in line with the contract, that the supplier is performing well and also that supplier staff are supported.

Remember that supplier staff can't work in a vacuum. In his '100 Rules for NASA Project Managers', Jerry Madden estimates that NASA needs to allocate one of their employees to work alongside every contractor. Unless you're involved in That may seem a high ratio where you're not involved in aerospace engineering, but it nevertheless demonstrates the need for supplier support and sometimes to a surprising degree.

❏ **Correct delivery:** Make sure that you are getting what you want and not what a supplier assumes you want. Particularly in the early part of the project make sure that suppliers are following the Product Definitions, not 'what we usually do'.

❏ **Progress:** Check on progress, especially if the supplier's staff are working on their own premises rather than yours and are out of your direct view. Are you being told actual progress or what a supplier thinks you want to hear?

Watch for defensive and even angry reactions from supplier managers when you check things. I once uncovered a major problem. I asked to see some records when visiting the supplier's premises and when I checked them I found very significant discrepancies. The supplier manager involved showed no regret at all about this major error, but instead was very angry with the member of their own staff who had let me get sight of the records.

❑ **Formal monitoring:** Check to see whether a formal contract monitoring point is imminent. If so, part of your check should be to cover the points set down in the contract. You should have these points recorded in your Procurement Plan if you are using one.

❑ **The right people:** If the supplier's staff have recently arrived on site, check that the right people have come. Be sure that it's the experts you agreed, for example, not trainees.

❑ **The right people retained:** If it's later on in the supplier's involvement, make sure that the right people have stayed on. Some suppliers have been known to send in good people at the start, but then those staff get mysteriously called away because 'something urgent has cropped up' and are gradually replaced with less experienced people.

❑ **Quality:** Are the right tests being done or is the supplier cutting corners and hoping that the staff get products right first time?

❑ **Involvement:** Are organisational staff being involved as required, such as with testing, and not being sidelined?

❑ **Support:** Check that supplier staff are getting the support they need from your organisation's staff.

❑ **Relationships:** Check to be sure that a good working relationship exists between supplier staff and your own organisation's project staff, and between the staff from different suppliers. If there are problems, address them quickly, including involving supplier managers.

❑ **Integration:** Make sure that supplier staff are sufficiently integrated into the project. They won't usually be regarded in quite the same way as full time employees, but check that a 'them and us' divide isn't forming that will threaten effective working.

❑ **Payment:** check that any payments due to suppliers have actually been made.

Working with suppliers is a two-way street. You have a responsibility to the supplier as well as the supplier having one to you. In particular make sure that payments are made in a timely way. It's unfair anyway to delay payment to a supplier who has supplied the agreed items or service. But then you may want to use good suppliers again so it's in your own best interest to maintain a good reputation. Small companies in particular may not want to work with your organisation in the future if they have to chase payment repeatedly to get what they are owed. Be aware too that you could face legally enforced surcharges if you don't pay within a reasonable period.

Stakeholder Check Checklist

Stakeholder management is often talked about, but mostly at the start of a project. Clearly, if you need to manage stakeholders that's an ongoing action. Stakeholders can often make or break a project, so it will pay you to keep on the ball during the stages. This checklist is to help make sure that you're keeping tabs on your planned management actions and to spot where you might need new ones.

❑ **Comms:** Where communications were planned to keep stakeholders informed, were those communications made?

❑ **Feedback:** Check with one or two stakeholders to make sure that they're getting the information that they need or want. If you talk to one or two each time you do a stakeholder check, then over the course of a stage you'll keep in personal touch with all of them. That contact will create a good impression and to get, or keep, stakeholders on side.

❑ **Involvement:** If stakeholders were to be consulted, for example in the design of particular products, check that they were actually consulted.

❑ **Current state:** Check to see whether stakeholders are happy with the project or if they are getting disaffected. If you are trying to bring opposed stakeholders on side to support the project, are you making the progress you hoped for or do you need to modify your stakeholder management?

❑ **Management actions:** Where you were planning particular stakeholder management activity has it been done or has it been overlooked in the busyness of the main project work?

❑ **Planned actions:** Check to see whether any planned stakeholder management actions are due in the coming week (or your selected period between stage checks)

Readiness Check Checklist

If other projects or areas of the organisation have to make changes to accommodate what your project is going to deliver, you need to keep tabs on progress with that related work. You won't be in direct control of that related work since if you were it would be part of your project. What you want is confirmation that everything else is on track, or to get early warning if it isn't.

❏ **Plans:** Check that plans are in place for the other areas of work and that the delivery dates are correctly coordinated with your project.

❏ **Progress:** Check progress on the related work. As with project progress try to get factual information not estimates such as 'We're about half way there, more or less.' or 'Well we *should* be ready in time.'

❏ **Priority:** Ensure that other managers have given the right degree of priority to the work. If the work needed to accommodate your project is just a low priority inconvenience compared to the important day-to-day work of the department then it's likely to get put off if that area comes under pressure. In turn that could threaten the successful delivery of your whole project.

Your project is important to you and in the front of your mind most of the time. Remember that to people doing associated work, their bit is probably just another task in a long list of things that they've got to do in their already busy jobs.

Lessons Checklist

Taking note of lessons being learned in a project is hugely important, but something that you can so easily put off when facing day-to-day pressures in the project. You'll be tempted to think 'Oh I won't forget that, I'll make a note later.' Then, later, you've forgotten about it completely.

The good news is that it doesn't take long to think through if you need to note down any valuable lessons when you include it as a routine part of a stage check. Neither does it take long to make a few brief notes – so don't leave the job out because it will be of enormous value to future projects.

Keep the lessons notes brief. That way you won't feel it's a huge job to write them and people reading them in the future will have a couple of pages to read through, not a thick book.

❑ **Warning signs:** Starting with the bad stuff, think about anything that's gone wrong and, importantly, whether you missed any warning signs which could have helped you take action earlier.

❑ **Pressures:** Sometimes you won't have had a problem, but you did come under pressure. Think if you could have avoided the pressure.

❑ **Corrections:** If you had a problem and took action to correct it, assess how well your solution worked and consider it for your lessons notes. That way if a future Project Manager hits the same problem, she'll have some advice on how to deal with it effectively.

❑ **Different approach:** A really helpful check when thinking about lessons is to ask 'With the benefit of hindsight, if I had to do part of the project again would I do it differently the next time around?'

❑ **Novel stuff:** Think whether you have tried anything new in your project control that's worked really well. If so, note it to help future Project Managers.

Chapter 13

Stage Reporting

● ●

In This Chapter

▶ Team level reporting

▶ Reporting to the Project Steering Group

▶ Specialised reports

● ●

*R*eporting during a stage provides control to the management level 'above'. In the case of reports prepared by the Project Manager, that level above will mostly be the Project Steering Group (PSG). In the case of reports produced by a Team Leader, well they'll normally go to the Project Manager.

Reporting is simple on the one hand, but needs careful thought on the other. You want to include enough information for effective control but over-reporting merely drives up overheads . . . or worse. Every bit of redundant information is written by someone, wasting time and effort. But then the recipients of the reports then have to scan through the redundant information to find the bits they really do want, and that wastes more time still. The 'worse' is that reports become so unwieldy that those who should be reading them simply don't bother to look at them at all.

There's inevitably a bit of overlap between this chapter and others in that it covers some of the same information. During a stage you are going to check progress, obviously enough. And during the stage you will also report progress so there's an inherent information overlap with the checks. However this chapter has a different objective from other parts of the book and that is to help you decide on what should be reported, and then how.

The KISS Principle: 'Keep it simple, stupid!'

Team Progress Report Checklist

If you're the Project Manager, you'll set down your requirements for the Team Progress Reports in the relevant Work Package, but you may base that on a default report format that you've set down in the Communications Plan. As with all reports, the content must be balanced. In the case of the Team Progress Report you'll strike that balance depending on the amount of autonomy you give to the team and the characteristics of the work, such as whether it's very high risk, or low risk, or something in between. The Team Progress Report will be prepared by the Team Leader, or by an individual team member if the 'team' consists of people working on their own (effectively as a team of one).

❑ **Progress:** this item is a no-brainer. However think exactly what information will be best in terms of being the most accurate and the most helpful.

❑ **Productivity:** Team productivity information is generally very helpful, but strangely absent on standard reports in most methods and approaches. The information is very helpful for forward projections though, such as that the team is performing better than expected and getting through work 15 per cent faster than set down in the plan.

❑ **Problem updates:** A Team Leader should report problems that have stage level implications using a Project Memo or equivalent. However the progress report is a useful place to update the Project Manager on what is happening with a reported problem at the moment, such as that it has now been resolved.

❑ **Quality:** Beware of quality reporting, even though it's a no-brainer that quality is important. However, the information will probably be readily available elsewhere, such as on a Quality Checklist, so you may not need to include it in the Team Progress Report. The item is mentioned here because it's in many project standards.

❑ **Work in hand and forecast:** Again, beware of this item even though it looms large in one leading project method. The work in hand and to be tackled next is already set down on the plan so again this information is already available. Including the same data all over again in a report is usually just wasteful.

❑ **Comments:** This section of the report can be very brief, but at the same time it's enormously helpful. It is space for the Team Leader to comment on any aspect of the work of which he thinks the Project Manager needs to be aware. If there is nothing relevant to say, the Team Leader can leave this section blank on a particular report.

As also mentioned in Chapter 12, the progress measuring information in most computer tools is the percentage of the various activities which is complete. However, this is a guide at best and unreliable at worst. For team reporting, try to get facts not estimates. For example, that fact could be the completion of lower-level components of the products being created.

Stage Progress Report Checklist

As with other reporting, be careful to design the Stage Progress Report to include information that is both necessary and wanted by the PSG. There's no point in having huge reports crammed with detail if nobody is ever going to read them. The Project Manager will prepare the report at the frequency that the PSG wants it and that's often monthly or two-weekly.

Make the progress report 'digestible' for the PSG managers that it's primarily designed for. That might be with 'dashboard' reporting with diagrams and graphs or giving the report as a brief presentation with a short handout rather than a formal written document. The Work Flow Diagram, colour-coded to show delivery, is especially effective.

When I'm invited to give project governance briefings to senior managers I recommend that they implement standard reporting across seven main areas, then with an addition item for any comments the Project Manager wants to include.

The information can be fitted easily on a very easy-to-read, three-page report making use of dashboard style graphs and diagrams, so it's very fast for managers to absorb the information. This checklist reflects the governance advice.

- ❑ **Progress:** This might be at stage level or project level or both. Having approved a Stage Plan, some PSG's then like to focus on the project level to keep the 'big picture'. Either way report progress with fact, notably product delivery.

- ❑ **Cost:** Spending on the stage compared to plan, and possibly overall spending on the whole project compared to plan.

- ❑ **Time:** An assessment of if the stage will finish at the planned time, early or late.

- ❑ **Benefits:** Comments if needed on anything in the last reporting period that has an impact on the level of benefits and the viability of the project.

- ❑ **Performance:** The performance of the teams against what was expected. Performance information clearly has implications for whether or not the project will stay on track and deliver to target.

- ❑ **Quality:** Measures to show the achievement of quality. This is often neglected in project governance and oversight but it's a vital element.

- ❑ **Risk:** A statement on the current overall position on risk and any particular ones that the PSG should know about. However, you can leave this item out if you are also preparing a dedicated Risk Report – see the next checklist in this chapter.

- ❑ **Comments:** Space for the Project Manager to comment on any aspect of the running of the stage so far and the next reporting period.

Be wary of organisational standard project reports that have been designed by over-zealous administrators. They may have little real experience of project management and no understanding at all of the control needs of your specific project. If a standard report format is unsuitable but mandatory, the Sponsor and Project Manager should work together to challenge it or at least get exemption for this project on the grounds that it will lead to unnecessary overheads.

Getting people to read your reports

I had the privilege of writing the PRIME project method with my friend and colleague Philipp Straehl. Philipp has run some seriously big projects in his time and worked for many years in a huge multi-national company. In one project he had a very senior finance manager on his Project Steering Group and Philipp was talking to him one day. The manager complimented Philipp on his concise reports which used a dashboard format with 'petrol gauges' and other visual indicators. The manager said 'Philipp, I receive many reports from many people and I don't have time to read them all. I just ask the people giving me the reports if they are okay, and if they say that they are I sign them. But your reports Philipp, I read.' What a fantastic accolade, and it's an example that you can follow with careful thinking on the content of your reports and then the format you use to present the information.

Risk Report Checklist

Depending on the level of risk in the project, you might include the risk information in the normal Stage Progress Report or have a separate, dedicated Risk Report. Another reason for having a separate Risk Report is if it has a wider circulation than progress information, such as to your organisation's Risk Manager.

❏ **Overall status:** The Project Manager's assessment of the overall risk position in the project. For example, is it increasing, decreasing or is it stable at the moment? Depending on the nature of the project it may be worth having separate reporting sections for upside risk (opportunities) and downside risk (threats).

❏ **High severity risks:** Specific information on the status of each high severity risk.

❏ **PI Matrix:** You can show the position of each risk in terms of probability and impact (PI) on a matrix. This is a good visual summary.

❏ **New risks:** A summary of new risks that have been identified since the last Risk Report.

Financial Report Checklist

You may just report project spending to the Sponsor, but often it's necessary to keep the organisation informed too. That might be by making entries in a financial computer system or with a dedicated report. If you will use a report, consider what information should be included using this checklist.

❑ **Spend:** The money spent in the reporting period.

❑ **Commitment:** Money that has been committed, such as by placing an order on a supplier, even though there has been no spend yet.

❑ **Variation:** The difference between the actual spend and what you expected to pay for those same things.

❑ **Changes:** Information, where necessary, for instances where the spending pattern is different from that which you planned and which finance staff therefore expected. For example, something may have been purchased earlier than planned to take advantage of a short-term special offer from the supplier. Although the project looks overspent at the moment, actually it isn't. Early spending is, of course, very different from overspending.

If you'll have to submit financial reports to your Finance Department during the project, be sure to find out how the finance people want the information presented. For example as a simple list of items with totals against them on a sheet of paper, or in a spreadsheet, or by entering it directly into their financial computer system. If you supply data in the wrong format just through ignorance, you'll be making work for someone to 'translate' that into the format that your finance staff need. Instead, find the preferred form and then use it. If there's some reason why your data won't fit the normal financial format, talk to the finance staff to find out how they would like you to deal with it.

Chapter 14

Conducting a Stage Gate

A Stage Gate is a meeting of the Project Steering Group members with the Project Manager at the end of a Delivery Stage. Typically the meeting will be between 45 and 90 minutes long, but erring towards the 45 minutes. The meeting is to check back on the stage just finished, a check on the current state of the whole project and then a look forward to the next stage and check its plan. Figure 14-1 shows the three views of the Stage Gate.

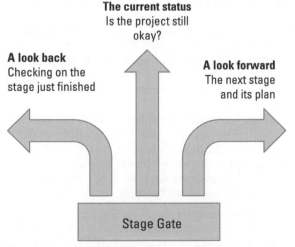

The current status
Is the project still okay?

A look back
Checking on the stage just finished

A look forward
The next stage and its plan

Stage Gate

Figure 14-1: The three views at a Stage Gate.

Stage Gates are important, they really are. But along with all other responsibilities of Steering Groups (sometimes known as Project Boards) this has to be one of the worst managed areas in projects. It would be a great kindness to say that Stage Gates are generally done badly because the truth is that they aren't often done at all – except superficially to make things look good.

The fact is that the work of the Project Steering Group (PSG) is absolutely vital, just like the work of senior managers in a department is absolutely vital if that department is to succeed. It's the PSG that has overall responsibility for project governance – that the project is set up properly and then is being run well. A key element of this is the Stage Gates which are extremely important, though not necessarily difficult, control points in the project.

If you're reading this as a PSG member that's great because clearly you want to get the Stage Gates right rather than play project games. The next three checklists are to help you do exactly that.

 You'll find a sample agenda for a Stage Gate meeting in Chapter 16 along with other, hopefully helpful, templates.

The 'Look Back' Checklist

Here's a list of things to help check on the Delivery Stage that's just finished. You may do some of the checking in advance of the meeting or have checks done by Project Audit. If there has been an audit, you should review the findings before the Stage Gate, not during it.

❑ **Stage Completion Report:** Review the report provided by the Project Manager. You may have asked her to do this as a business presentation with notes of the details; that requirement will be set down in the Communications Plan. The review may take in at least some of the remaining points on this checklist.

❑ **Product completion:** Make sure that everything that the project has delivered everything it was supposed to have during the stage. Also check that any necessary acceptances or sign offshave been obtained.

❑ **Quality:** Check to ensure that the required quality was delivered and that all necessary tests and checks were performed.

❑ **Timing and performance:** Review the use of staff hours in comparison with the original plan, and also check team performance. If the teams performed better or worse than expected, ask questions to find out why and then consider action and implications for the rest of the project.

❑ **Budgets:** Review the spending for the stage and how close the final figure was to the planned amount. Also check on the use of the Change Budget and Risk Budget. If you're not too clear about the different budgets then have a look at the side panel on the next page.

❑ **Projections:** Look to see whether the experience of the stage just finishing, together with any before that, has implications for the remainder of the project.

❑ **Lessons:** If useful things were learned in the stage (good stuff as well as bad stuff) that would be of immediate help to other projects, get the details from the Project Manager in order to forward them to others in the organisation.

The three stage budgets

Just in case you're new to being a PSG member, it may help to clarify the three budgets where you will authorise the Project Manager to spend money in each stage.

• **Stage Budget:** The money for the planned work of the stage

• **Change Budget:** Money set aside to cover changes. Changes, by definition, aren't part of the planned work. The budget is conditional. If nobody asks for any changes, the money can't be spent. It isn't a 'slush fund' for the Project Manager to cover overruns in planned work.

• **Risk Budget:** Money set aside for any financial impacts of particular risks. The money is pre-approved by the PSG and should a risk occur, the Project Manager can take action and spend the allocated money without further reference to the PSG. Like the Change Budget, the Risk Budget is conditional. If a particular risk doesn't occur then the proportion of the Risk Budget set aside to cover its financial impact can't be spent by the Project Manager on anything else, even on handling another risk.

If the change and risk spending was significantly different to what was anticipated in the budgets, try to establish why. If the budgets were over-generous, you might consider reducing the amounts for future stages. However, think carefully because the future stages may run differently to the one just finishing.

The 'Current State' Checklist

This part of the Stage Gate is to assess the current state of the project and also to establish if authorising the next stage is actually the right thing to do. If the project is out of control or is no longer viable, the correct management decision is to stop the project, not let it roll on and so waste money and staff resources.

Make it easy for the Project Manager to tell you the facts including, importantly, any bad news. Don't even think of resorting to silly and damaging management catch phrases such as 'Don't bring me problems, bring me solutions' or 'We don't have problems in this organisation, we have opportunities' which merely prevent people from telling you what's really going on. Get the truth, warts-and-all, and then be on-side and totally supportive in helping resolve any problems. If the Project Manager has messed up on something and that's the cause of some of the problems, help her to say so and move forward. Everyone makes mistakes, even me . . . even you.

❑ **Project Manager's assessment:** check out the Project Manager's view on the project, both the positive and the negative.

❑ **Business Case:** Review the Business Case carefully and think about the implications of any changes. For example, the projection of benefits may have changed (in either direction) and that could affect the viability of the project.

❑ **Scope:** Check the Scope Statement to ensure that it remains both accurate and sensible. If any new requirements have emerged in the last stage, check that they've been recorded, together with the source, and that the Scope Statement or any other documents reflect them.

❏ **The rest of the Charter:** Review the rest of the Project Charter to be sure that it accurately reflects the current position of the project.

❏ **PMP controls:** Review the controls in the project as set down in the latest version of the Project Management Plan (PMP). Check things such as referrals to the PSG and progress reporting and ensure that they have been working satisfactorily. If there have been any problems, then make sure that the necessary adjustments have been made or make them now.

❏ **PSG:** Following on from checks on the overall controls, honestly review whether the PSG itself has functioned well in the last stage. If not, make changes.

❏ **Roles:** Review how well people have been functioning in the project roles. In other words, have you got the right people and are they doing their jobs well? If necessary, make changes – and that includes changes to the PSG roles.

❏ **Risk:** Review the overall project risk position as it is now, based on the Project Manager's recent update of the Risk Log. Also check the risk management mechanisms to ensure that they're working.

❏ **Viability:** Based on the knowledge you have gained from the previous items on this checklist, especially the Business Case, assess whether the project is still viable and should continue. If not, instruct the Project Manager to begin the work to close it down.

 The PRIME project method stresses the importance of Stage Gates and being totally objective in deciding whether or not to continue with the project. PRIME suggests that PSG members shouldn't be asking 'Should we stop this project?' but rather 'Why should we continue with this project?' There must be a clear and ongoing justification if you decide that the project should move on into the next stage.

The 'Look Forward' Checklist

If the PSG has decided that the project should continue, you must now turn to the detailed plan that the Project Manager has compiled for the next stage. If you're a PSG member then the Project Manager should have consulted you during the preparation of this plan so nothing in it should come as a surprise. However, you still need to be sure that you're happy with it before you approve it and authorise work to begin on the next stage.

Don't authorise the start of the next stage unless you are convinced that the plan for it is realistic and achievable. As a PSG member you're responsible for the good governance of this project. If you sign a plan that you don't think is achievable then you completely undermine the good governance that you're supposed to be ensuring.

Many organisational managers think that planning is basically a waste of time and merely delays the start of the project work. Planning isn't a waste of time. A good plan means that the stage will run more smoothly, and it will actually save time. What wastes both time and energy is hitting unnecessary problems because things weren't thought through properly at the start. Some projects lurch from crisis to crisis with constant firefighting of one problem after another after another. Don't let your project be one of them.

❏ **Accuracy:** Check that the Stage Plan is accurate and correctly reflects the Project Plan for this part of the project.

❏ **Contingency:** Make sure that there is sufficient contingency in the plan to cover things that will go wrong, because something surely will. The amount of contingency will partly reflect the degree of identified risk in the stage, but contingency is also needed for unforeseen problems.

Murphy's Law: If it can go wrong, it will go wrong. O'Connor's Corollary: Murphy was an optimist.

❏ **Controls:** Make sure that you are happy with the controls for this stage. The controls may be slightly different from the previous stage perhaps, for example, because this stage is higher risk.

❏ **Quality:** Check that there will be sufficient control over quality to ensure that the right level will be delivered. This check may be fast to do if the stage will continue with the controls used earlier in the project and they have already proved to be effective.

❑ **Resource:** Look at the resource allocation and check that the resource is available. This will mean the Project Supplier and Project User on the PSG confirming that the resource shown on the plan will be available.

❑ **Funding:** Confirm that the finance is available for the stage, and that includes the Change and Risk Budgets. Check that the budgets are sensible and reflect the work on the one hand, and the assessment of risk and likely change on the other.

❑ **Realistic and achievable:** Stand back from the plan and assess whether, overall, you are confident that the plan is realistic (such as the estimates for activity durations) and achievable.

Go for effectiveness, not speed

I vividly remember my first Stage Gate meeting. I wasn't yet a Project Manager but rather a recently qualified Systems Analyst responsible for the design and build of my first new computer system. I had been brought along to the Project Board meeting by the Project Manager to answer any questions that she couldn't. The person chairing the meeting and in overall charge of the Project Board was a senior manager who had chaired the board for the previous project and the one before that and . . . you get the picture. I will never forget his opening statement because it's burned into my memory.

"Well, our previous record for a Project Board meeting is 23 minutes. Let's see if we can beat that today!"

What was the primary objective of that Stage Gate then? Perhaps to check that the project was set up properly as it was about to get underway? What about checking that the risks had been identified and were going to be managed effectively? Or maybe that the project plans were well thought through and realistic? No, no and no. The primary objective was to get out of the room as fast as possible and preferably in under 23 minutes so as to set a new record.

PM's Stage Gate Checklist

If you're the Project Manager, you'll be preparing information for the Stage Gate. Here's a checklist to help you make sure that you've got everything ready in advance of the Stage Gate. A lot of the ground is covered in the Stage Completion Report but the checklist adds a few bits that you'll need along with it.

❏ **Stage Completion Report:** Starting with the most obvious, you'll need to provide copies of the report for the PSG members – and don't forget one for yourself.

❏ **Charter and PMP:** Provide copies of the updated Project Charter and PMP (Project Management Plan) for the PSG members, with a copy of each for yourself too.

❏ **Equipment:** If you're giving the report in the form of a business presentation, don't forget to check out the kit beforehand to make sure that it's in place and working, and be sure that you have the presentation slides loaded on the computer and ready to roll.

❏ **Supporting information:** Have information to hand to answer any questions of detail, including your source calculations for things like spending and team performance.

❏ **Lessons:** If lessons have been learned in the stage just finishing that will be of immediate use to other projects, have brief notes ready in a form that the PSG can pass on into the organisation.

❏ **Notes for your points:** If you want to mention any particular points about the running of the project, prepare a list of them with brief notes so you don't forget to cover them.

❏ **Next Stage Plan:** Provide copies of the plan for the next stage for each of the PSG members, and again a copy for yourself so you don't have the embarrassment of having to ask to look over someone's shoulder at their copy if they ask a question on it.

Chapter 15

Reviewing the Project

• •

In This Chapter

▶ The importance of project evaluation

▶ Two points at which to look back on a project

▶ Measuring the project benefits, including multiple measures

▶ Checklists to help with evaluation and reporting

• •

*A*fter the main work of the project you should carry out a review and produce a report at two points. The first is when the project is completed, and that will involve producing a Project Closure Report. The closure report records an account of how the project went and records the final figures for things like spending. The report should also give details of any benefits already achieved. The second is a review which takes place some time after the end of the project with a Project Evaluation Report. The second review focuses on the achievement of benefits and the effectiveness of project products (deliverables) after an initial period of use.

Reviewing the project at the end is important. The most obvious reason is to report the return on investment. If you invest money in something like shares or a savings account you want to know the return – how well your investment has performed. So too with the project. The organisation has invested money and, perhaps even more significantly, staff time, and it should know what the return is on this investment. That return will primarily be the realisation of benefits. There are other reasons for the reviews, though, such as to report on the performance of the project as a whole and to assess the operational suitability of project products or *deliverables*.

Different approaches adopt a different pattern to closure and review, so check what your organisation requires if it has a chosen approach, or make your own mind up if it doesn't. Figure 15-1 shows the process for the end and review of a project.

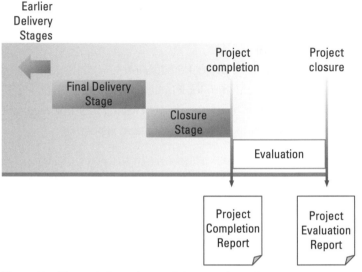

Figure 15-1: The end of a project and the reporting points

Closing and Evaluating a Project in PRINCE2 and PRIME

Two project methods with which I'm particularly familiar have rather different ways of dealing with closure and evaluation. PRINCE2 closes down when the project closes down and the Project Manager produces an 'End Project Report' (PRINCE2 isn't fully ISO compliant and sadly that includes its sometimes awkward terminology). Evaluation after the end of the project, including measurement of benefits, is left to the organisation and isn't part of the method. However, perhaps because the evaluation isn't part of the method, it's common for organisations to neglect it and either do it very superficially or not do it at all.

ISO standards in projects

The current International Standards Organisation (ISO) standard for project management is ISO 21500:2012. Like other ISO standards it's quite short but it's nevertheless solid and well thought through. There is an ISO standard for project quality (ISO 10006:2003) and also one for risk management (ISO 31000:2009) which is relevant for project risk management.

The person who chaired the PSG or Project Board is often responsible (or assumed to be responsible) for any evaluation after the project. If the project didn't turn out very well and didn't deliver anything like the benefit that he claimed so confidently and optimistically at the start, then it's rather more comfortable for him to forget all about project reviews and benefits measures. It's clearly much more important to focus on the success of the next project and deal with all the other important-stuff-I-have-to-do-that-you-wouldn't-understand.

The PRIME method keeps the project open until the evaluation is complete. It says that there's unfinished business until the evaluation is done. That makes it harder for evaluation to be quietly forgotten. PRIME has a Project Completion Report (the method has been built to be fully ISO compliant and so uses the ISO report name) at the end of the closure stage. Then it has an Evaluation Report after the final evaluation, which in turn may be some time after all of the delivery work has been finished. PRIME doesn't shut down until after the Evaluation Report has been presented.

If you're fairly new to projects, you may find it hard at first to get your head around the idea of a project still being 'open' after all its products have been delivered. PRIME uses the example of a shop, and you may find that helpful. When a shop closes, it isn't the end of the business day. There's still work to be done to tidy up and count the day's takings before everyone can finally go home. So too with a project.

Project Completion Checklist

There's quite a lot to do towards the end of a project so you're a long way from putting your feet up, breathing a sigh of relief and thinking it's all over. Here's a checklist to help you get organised and make sure that you don't miss anything.

❑ **Product completion:** Check to be quite sure that all project products are completed, which includes successfully passing any tests and checks. If you're doing version control you should check that too and make sure that everything has a 'complete' status.

❑ **Signoffs and handovers:** Check that all necessary products have been signed off as okay, and that any handovers to users have been done.

❑ **Handover documentation:** If there should be formal handover documentation (such as legal documents), check that it's been completed and is properly stored.

❑ **Acceptance criteria:** Check to ensure that the project acceptance criteria (set down in the Charter) have been met. Hopefully that will be all of them, but see the tip below if not.

The trouble with the term 'project acceptance criteria' is that it sounds as though the project won't be accepted unless it meets them. While that may be true for some projects, in most cases a failure to meet one or more of the criteria will be a disappointment, but not a reason to abandon the whole venture. If delivery is a bit late, for example, a supplier may have to make a compensation payment, but the customer will still accept the new computer system or building extension. The PSG should be clear at the start about which criteria really are show-stoppers while the rest, although perhaps very important, are actually negotiable if push comes to shove.

❑ **Resource release:** Finalise the release of project staff back to their home departments, or perhaps on to new projects.

❑ **Celebration:** Assuming that the project was successful, it's time to celebrate with the project staff. Although you might think this is a light-hearted point, it's actually a serious one. It's important that you mark the achievement by thanking the staff for their work and celebrating the success. And don't forget supplier staff and support staff when preparing the invitation list.

❑ **Physical resource release:** Arrange the return of equipment and the release of accommodation, such as team rooms and perhaps even whole sites.

❑ **Benefit measures:** Often, some benefits will already be visible at the end of the project, so they can be measured now and reported now.

❑ **Metrics:** Calculate the final totals for financial spending, staff hours, performance and any other figures required for the Project Completion Report.

❑ **Cost code:** Arrange for the project cost code(s) to be closed, unless it is to be kept open for any modification to products after project closure.

❑ **Assess the controls:** Think back over the project and evaluate to see whether the controls worked or whether there were problems.

❑ **Assess the plans:** Think back and assess whether the plans worked, or whether they were too detailed or not detailed enough to exercise effective project control.

❑ **Assemble lessons information:** Prepare a statement of lessons learned during the project. Check back through your Project Log to make sure that you pick up everything relevant.

❑ **Project Completion Report:** Prepare the Project Completion Report together with a business presentation, if this is required by the PSG. You'll find a template for the report in Chapter 17.

❑ **Project Completion Meeting:** Ensure that preparations are in hand for the completion meeting of the PSG (it's like a final Stage Gate), such as a room booking, presentation equipment and refreshments.

Crash Stop Checklist

Sometimes things go badly wrong with a project, or perhaps it simply isn't needed any more because of a change in the business. In that case, the project must be shut down early with a *crash stop*. That stop might be at the end of a stage if the PSG decides that it can't authorise the next stage, or it might be because something happens during a Delivery Stage.

In an early close follow the points on the last checklist for a normal close but note these variations.

❑ **Resource warnings:** Warn home departments and suppliers that staff will be released earlier than expected because of the early project close.

❑ **Review products:** Think carefully about products which are currently under construction and discuss their states with the PSG. It may be worth finishing some of the products which will still be usable and so give some benefit.

❑ **Lessons:** This item is on the list for normal completion, but in the event of a crash stop think particularly carefully about two additional areas.

• **Avoidability:** If the crash stop was because of severe project problems, think whether those problems were avoidable and whether early action could have saved the project. If so, note that for future projects.

• **Forewarning:** If the project simply wasn't needed any more or was overtaken by events, could that have been spotted earlier resulting in the saving of more staff time and expense?

Evaluation Plan Checklist

Think through what you need to do to evaluate the project, and when, and make a simple plan.

❑ **Business Case:** Review the Business Case to see what benefits are to be measured, how and when.

❑ **Plan the review points:** Group the benefits measures according to when you'll need to do them. For example, one set of benefits might need to be measured one month in and the rest three months in.

❑ **Early use:** Think what you need to do to assess the suitability of project products. For example, have they proved easier or more difficult to use than was expected?

Note down what assessment work is needed and when, and add that to your Evaluation Plan.

❏ **Resource planning:** Consider what staff resource you'll want for benefits measures and usability assessment. Think whether you need specialists, such as finance staff, to help with the evaluation.

❏ **Resource confirmation:** Check that the people you need are actually available, explain the work to them and let them know when they'll be needed.

❏ **Reporting:** Think through what you need to do to produce the Evaluation Report and make any necessary business presentation. Add this work to the plan.

Sometimes you may have to measure a benefit more than once. For example, PSG members and organisational managers may want an early, ballpark figure of staff savings at first, then a more accurate figure when things have settled down some weeks later.

Chapter 16

Templates for Control

● ●

In This Chapter

▶ Fitting the templates to your project at two levels of detail

▶ Using an overview for some logs as well as detailed entries

▶ Templates for controlling your projects

● ●

*Y*ou might be able to use the control templates in this chapter just as they are, but if not you can adapt them at two levels. First, you can adjust each template to fit the needs of the sort of projects that you normally work with. Second, when you're starting a new project, you can take a copy of your normal template and adjust again to fit your exact needs that time around. For example, if you have a particularly high risk project then you'll almost certainly want a more extensive range of information in your Risk Log than you have normally.

As with all the other templates in this book, you can download electronic versions in Microsoft Word and Excel formats from the www.dummies.com/extras/pmchecklists. Feel free to adjust the electronic templates in any way that you like to suit the needs of your projects, even if that's only to include your organisation's logo.

For a couple of the logs you'll find that there are two templates. The first is for an individual log entry and the second if for an overview. To take the example of risk again, you'll find a Risk Log template for recording information about each individual risk. However, that entry could be quite long if you've got to hold a lot of information such as on the management actions. What you'll find really useful in addition then is an overview of the whole Risk Log so you can look at all of the risks, and that's where the second template comes in.

For a Risk Log Entry, you'll almost certainly want to use a word processor app as it will be unwieldy to put lots of text into spreadsheet cells. In contrast a spreadsheet is excellent for the overview where you duplicate limited information with each risk on a single spreadsheet line. That format allows you to scroll up and down and see all the risks, and also to sort the risks according to different criteria, such as severity and review date. Of course, if you're really computer literate you can build a database in which the full information and the subsets are just different views.

Think carefully before setting up standard databases for things like the Risk Log. While your Project Office may be keen to set up a default database which each project can then copy and use for their risks, such a database can be limiting. The default database may have particular views included, such as one that allows you to see risks grouped by severity rating. However, unless you have database skills you may need help every time you want to view the data in different way. A spreadsheet, on the other hand, is usually much easier for everyone to understand and use. If you have a database then you can always export the required current data to a spreadsheet each time you want to manipulate it, but now you're just making extra work. Anyway, once again there may be too much information in each spreadsheet cell to be able to get a clear overview.

Change Log Entry

A Change Log is a great idea and the use of it I describe here is based on the PRIME project method, which has a particularly effective approach (though I'm totally biased: I helped design it). If someone puts in a change request that's not sensible, then it shouldn't get as far as the Change Log. However if the change is worth considering, then you make an entry in the Change Log and track the change from there. Having all the changes in one place means that you keep a clear view of what's going on. In a busy project that view can be extremely valuable.

❑ **Change ID:** Just a simple reference number or you could prefix it with a letter to show the type of change such as 'N' for new requirement and 'E' for the correction of a previously undetected error.

❑ **Change name:** A very short description of just three or four words if possible so that you can use it as a heading. 'Adjust order input screen' is a good example. This will help you find the change quickly if you are looking for it amongst other entries.

❑ **Status:** The current status of the change such as 'Under investigation, being implemented, on hold, referred to PSG, closed'.

❑ **Priority:** Perhaps on a scale of 1–5, or you might use a text range such as that based on the MoSCoW acronym (must have, should have, could have, won't have at this time).

TIP

The priority should be set by someone involved in the management of the project, not by the person asking for the change unless they are part of that management team. Most people, particularly junior business staff, think that the changes that they want are *all* top priority.

❑ **Source:** Where the change request or change requirement came from. The source will normally be the person who asked for it but it could be something like a new organisational policy that affects the project.

❑ **Description:** Details of the suggested change and the reason why it's being requested.

❑ **Impact:** For some changes this could be a substantial section listing all the different impacts.

❑ **Resource:** The staff resource that will be needed to carry out the change.

❑ **Estimated cost:** How much you expect the change to cost based on current information.

❑ **Decision:** Whether or not the change is to go ahead, who made the decision and when. In many cases it will be the Project Manager who decides on the change but sometimes the matter may have to go to the Project Steering Group (PSG).

❑ **Final cost:** The eventual cost of the change after the work has been done. This entry is important to calculate use of the Change Budget. There's a neat use of this entry in the next template, the Change Log Overview.

Change Log Overview

There can be a great deal of information in a Change Log entry, particularly in the 'Impact' section. An overview of the log, which you'll probably want to hold on a spreadsheet, is very useful with limited information about each change on a single line. As this is mostly a subset of the Change Log entries, only one heading needs explanation.

❑ **Change ID**

❑ **Status**

❑ **Priority**

❑ **Source**

❑ **Short description**

❑ **Estimated cost**

❑ **Decision**

❑ **Final cost:** This is the entry that gives the final cost of the change when it's done and is the 'neat use' mentioned in the earlier Change Log Entry template section. See the tip below for a steer on how to use it.

If you include a 'Final cost' item on your spreadsheet overview and put in a formula to give a total for the column, you can then see exactly how much of your Change Budget you've used so far. If you want to track committed money as well as how much you've finally spent, you could have an 'Expected cost' column as well, once it's been decided to go ahead with the change. This idea is taken from the PRIME project method which has a powerful but simple range of financial controls. Many other approaches and methods simply don't cover this aspect of control and leave you to struggle and find your own way, which is an inexcusable cop out. Financial control is obviously a vital part of project management, and that has to include your use of the Change Budget.

Product Definition

For every product on your product planning diagrams you should produce a Product Definition. Product Definitions really earn their keep – they're not bureaucratic overkill. It's so easy for someone to misunderstand what's needed and to then build the wrong thing. The Product Definition spells out exactly what's needed including, importantly, the quality criteria it must meet.

You'll produce the Product Definitions while planning, but the template is included in this chapter because once written, the definitions form part of the Work Packages (there's a template later in this chapter for those) which are an important element of control.

- ❑ **Product ID:** A number, perhaps taken from your WBS (Work Breakdown Structure).

- ❑ **Product name:** The short name, again taken from your product planning diagrams.

- ❑ **Description:** A description of what the product is, including whether it is made up of any sub-products. You should include here any information about what it should look like. For example, you could say of a report that it should be A4 size with the financial information presented in tables rather than in the main text.

- ❑ **Quality criteria and tests:** In this section record what criteria the product must satisfy in order to be accepted. For example, you could say that a report should be understandable to the target audience or that the new office layout should comply with the 11 cubic metre minimum space per person regulations. Against each of the criteria you should then specify what test(s) will be needed to confirm compliance. With the report, you might want to get two people from the target audience to read a draft and highlight anything that they don't understand.

- ❑ **Resource:** What staff resources you'll need for building the product and then testing it. Be careful to note any needs for specialists on the one hand and for completely unqualified and inexperienced people on the other.

Think hard when it comes to resources for testing. Sometimes you want people for their lack of experience and understanding. If, for example, you're installing a new computer system and have written a user guide, the last person you want to check the guide is one of the development team who already knows exactly how the system works. The ideal person is a member of the user staff who has never seen the system before. You sit them down in front of a computer with the test system loaded and say 'There's the user guide and some customer information. Please input a new customer record.' That will show you whether the guide is a good one.

Project Log

The Project Log is a practical and powerful document, which you'll usually keep on a spreadsheet or possibly in a word processor document. The log is there so you can note down reminders of things to do, Project Memos that have come in and things that have happened. Used imaginatively the Project Log can save a lot of formal and more lengthy documentation.

This template is a bit of a cheat because there isn't much in it – in terms of the headings anyway. The entries are basically a date followed by a note although, as you'll see, you can add a couple of bells and whistles to make it more useful still.

❏ **Date and number:** The date, and then the number of the entry that day. So, 20-11-20XX/3, the third log entry on 20 November 20XX. Okay, okay; if you're American you can switch the date format around if you think you really have to depart from the entirely sensible UK format. Good grief, you even drive on the wrong side of the road and misspell 'colour'.

❏ **Category:** The type of entry, such as a note, a Project Memo or a reminder.

❏ **Status:** You'll usually want to keep this very simple such as 'open, on hold and closed'.

❏ **Notes:** The details that you want to record.

Risk Log Entry

This template is for recording details of a single risk. Use further records for more risks to make up the full Risk Log.

A risk is uncertain. If something will happen for sure then it isn't a risk and should be covered in the plans.

❑ **Risk ID:** Usually the next in a number sequence running through the Risk Log.

❑ **Risk name:** A short descriptive name of the risk so you can easily understand what it is such as 'team specialist resigns' or 'extra energy savings'.

❑ **+/-:** Whether the risk is an opportunity or a threat (an upside or a downside risk).

❑ **Status:** The current status of the risk using the chosen range for the project, such as 'under review, increasing, decreasing, stable, dead'.

❑ **Category:** Using your chosen range of risk categories such as 'business, technical, environmental'.

❑ **Description:** A (preferably brief) explanation of the risk and how it is likely to behave. For example, will it come on very slowly where the danger is that it won't be noticed, or will it happen suddenly requiring a very fast reaction?

❑ **Origin:** How the risk was identified and in some instances by whom. For example, it might have been reported by a team member or it might have come from your standard risk list for this type of project.

❑ **Impact:** On the impact scale selected for the project (for example 1–5, 1–10). It's also helpful if you add some explanation on the nature of the impact, not just give a figure.

❑ **Probability:** Using your defined scale (for example, 1–5 or 1–10 or a probability percentage).

❑ **Severity:** Impact multiplied by probability – where you've used a numeric scale for those factors.

❑ **Owner:** The person responsible for the risk and who can authorise action.

❑ **Management action(s):** The actions selected to control the risk. Where this involves people, specify against each action who will take it.

❑ **Review:** When the risk should be reviewed, such as every four weeks or at the end of each Delivery Stage.

❑ **Next review date:** When the next review of this risk is due. It will give you a warning if you've missed a review because the date will be in the past.

As mentioned at the start of this chapter, you can make this template more sophisticated if you are dealing with a project with a high level of risk. For example, you might find it helpful to record the degree to which the risk is controllable. Something like bad weather is inherently uncontrollable, in the lifetime of your project anyway. Other risks may respond well to your risk management actions.

Risk Log Overview

The previous template covered the full range of detail that you might need to hold on an individual risk. If you have a large Risk Log, you can't see all the risks at once. Like the template for the Change Log Overview, this one duplicates the control entries from the log. As the headings are a subset of the Risk Log there's no need to explain them.

❑ **Risk ID**

❑ **Risk name**

❑ **+/–**

❑ **Status**

❑ **Severity**

❑ **Owner**

❑ **Next review date**

Stakeholder Log

The Stakeholder Log is another simple log which, as the name suggests, is basically a list of stakeholders. The log is important because you need to keep track of stakeholders and make sure that you've got all the necessary management thought through in your Stakeholder Plan. Have a look at Chapter 11 to see a template for the Stakeholder Plan.

- ❑ **Name:** The name of the stakeholder, obviously enough. It could be an individual or something like 'management board' or 'on-line customers'.

- ❑ **Date identified:** You won't always need this heading on the template, but sometimes it's helpful to know whether a stakeholder was identified at the outset or later on in the project.

- ❑ **Interest:** What interest the stakeholder has in the project, such as that they will use what the project is finally delivering. Use this section also to note whether the stakeholder has any concerns about the project or is generally supportive.

- ❑ **Group:** Sometimes you can group stakeholders for action. For example there may be a number of stakeholders who just need to be kept informed of progress on the project so you can handle their needs in the same way at the same time. There's more on this on the Stakeholder Plan template in Chapter 11.

Quality Checklist Template

The Quality Checklist is simply a list of tests, checks and any other quality actions (such as quality audits) that are to be done in a stage, together with a sign-off of each one when it's done. You can then see at a glance whether something has been overlooked. You compile the list of tests from the Stage Plan and the Product Definitions.

Don't be fooled by the Quality Checklist. It may be simple, but it's enormously powerful to help make sure that the required quality is delivered and tests aren't missed out. In fact, the power of the list is largely because it's simple; it's quick to build, fast to check through and extremely low overhead to maintain.

- ❏ **ID:** If you need it, and usually just a sequential number.

- ❏ **Name:** A short descriptive name, such as 'loading test'.

- ❏ **Product:** The ID and name of the product to be tested, if a product is involved. If the item relates to something else such as a quality audit then just leave this section blank.

- ❏ **Responsibility:** Who is responsible for the test or other quality action.

- ❏ **Planned date:** The date that the test is due to take place, taken from the Stage Plan.

- ❏ **Sign-off:** The signature (preferably) of the person who did the test and the date that it was done.

Version Control Record

Some things in your project will need to be version controlled. For example, you'll always need to know the latest version of a product that's been changed, such as a design, or even for some management products such as the Project Plan. To keep track of the products you'll need a central record for each one being controlled.

Some approaches, such as the UK's leading project management method, have a horrendously long and complex list of data items for version control. I once designed the control for a rather sensitive computer system where versioning was vital, but I never needed a fraction of the information set down on that method's standard form. Think through carefully to identify what you genuinely need for version control and don't get unnecessarily complicated – KISS, keep it simple, stupid.

This template gives you a basic list of headings for version control, but you can always add more if you really need to.

- ❏ **Product ID:** The reference number for the product, usually as used on its Product Definition.

❑ **Product name:** A short name for the product so you can recognise it quickly. For example, 'Floor Plan' and 'Business Case'. Stick to the short name you used for the product in your product planning.

❑ **Current version:** So people can check whether they have the latest version of a design document, for example.

❑ **Current status:** Such as whether a report is in draft or final format, or whether a machine is built, installed, tested or commissioned.

❑ **Last amended:** Particularly useful for version controlling documents, the date it was last changed.

❑ **Location:** Particularly appropriate for team products (as opposed to products you are using for project management such as the Project Plan). If a product has now been created, where is it?

❑ **Owner:** The person currently responsible for the product. For a lot of products that may be the Project Manager until they are handed over for operational use.

❑ **Knowledgeable person:** often one of the people who helped build the product, but if they've left the organisation you'll need someone else. If you're considering a change, this information is incredibly useful so you can check whether the change is sensible.

❑ **Change history:** a simple list of changes made, usually since the product first passed test. For each entry include:

- **Date:** The date on which the change was completed

- **Change:** A short summary of the change

- **Reason:** Why the change was made. This entry can be very important. For example, someone may think a change looks weird and should be reversed, until they read this section and see that it was necessary for legal compliance.

❑ **Cross references:** Useful for circumstances in which a product is made up of sub-products that are also being version controlled. It's also useful for things like engineering drawings, where a change on one might require changes on others to keep them consistent.

❑ **Related documents:** This is another cross-referencing section but this time for documents. There may be related correspondence, entries in the Change Log and entries in the Project Log.

Work Checklist Template

There aren't many headings in this template. Good, isn't it? Try and keep it that way. The Work Checklist is something that you can use to help with stage control. It's a simple list of the products to be produced in a Delivery Stage so you can track progress by delivery.

❑ **Product ID:** The ID from the product plans, such as the Work Breakdown Structure (WBS).

❑ **Product name:** The short name, again from the product plans.

❑ **Status:** The status, such as 'Not started, under construction, being tested, delivered'.

❑ **Planned delivery date:** The date, taken from the Stage Plan, when the product is due.

❑ **Actual delivery date:** The date the product was finally delivered. That means that it had successfully passed all of its tests and checks or was specifically exempted because of a problem in meeting the required quality.

'Delivery' in the context of product based planning means that the Team Leader has passed the product over into the control of the Project Manager. For a physical document that might mean hole punching it and filing it in the project records or scanning it and putting the electronic copy in a particular computer directory. However if the product is something like the central span of a suspension bridge then it isn't going to be 'delivered' in the sense of being put somewhere else such as in a filing system – for a start you can't get it through the doorway of the file store. Instead the Team Leader will notify the Project Manager that the product has been 'delivered'.

Work Package

The term 'Work Package' is used in many approaches to project management and simply means a work assignment given to a Team Leader, or just to an individual if your project is a small one. Whatever the size of the project, though, it makes sense to give the team or the person instructions on exactly how the work is to be managed. If the instructions in the Work Package are straightforward, then that's great, but still record them. And if they're straightforward it isn't going to take you long to set them down – certainly much less time than if there's a misunderstanding because of a lack of clear instructions.

❑ **Package ID:** A number, but in a bigger project particularly you might prefix it to give other information. For example, 6-I-9 might refer to a Work Package in Stage 6, given to the Implementation Team and it's their ninth assignment in the stage.

❑ **Team:** The team or individual who creates the products in the Work Package.

❑ **Product(s):** The product or products that the team is to create in this assignment. For each one you should provide a copy of its Product Definition.

❑ **Controls:** Controls such as the frequency of progress reporting and what to do if something goes significantly off track.

❑ **Time and cost:** When the products covered by the Work Package are due to be completed and delivered. You might also include a budget if the Team Leader is to control the spending too.

As with the other templates in this book, you can add in more headings if you need them. However, be careful not to get too complicated. Don't start unnecessary duplication of information that is readily available to the Team Leader elsewhere. An exception is for the target date for delivery and any budget because it only takes a moment to record those details and it makes it crystal clear what your requirements are for completion.

Stage Gate Agenda

A Stage Gate is the meeting of the Project Steering Group (PSG) with the Project Manager at the end of each project stage. The agenda is quite long and that reflects the importance of the meeting as reflected, quite rightly, in the international ISO standards and notably the project management standard ISO 12500:2015. Stage Gates don't happen very often and it's an essential element of the PSG's control in order to fulfil its responsibility for good project governance.

The template reflects the three views at a Stage Gate as explained in Chapter 14, Conducting a Stage Gate.

❑ **Stage Gate:** The name of the Stage Gate, such as End of Stage 4.

❑ **Meeting details:** The planned date, time and location of the meeting.

The Last Stage

A report and check on the stage just finishing.

❑ **Stage Completion Report:** The presentation of the completion report by the Project Manager including any matters which she wants to bring to the PSGs attention.

❑ **Stage review:** Discussion and questions on how the last stage went overall, including costs and team performance.

❑ **Quality:** Specific confirmation that the required quality was delivered for products created in the last stage.

❑ **Forward view and lessons:** Discussion on any implications from the last stage for the rest of the project, and also the collection of lessons learned (based on both good and bad experience) that need to be passed on into the organisation for the benefit of other projects.

The Present Position

A review of where the project is at the moment, a decision on whether it should continue and adjustment of any controls.

❑ **Business Case:** A check of the recently updated Business Case to see whether the project is still viable.

❑ **Risk position:** Evaluation of the current risks, again to help determine whether it's worth continuing. If the benefits have fallen from the first projections but the negative risk has increased considerably, then it may not be worth continuing.

❑ **Viability decision:** To establish whether the project should continue or be closed early. If the decision is to close it, the Sponsor should now give that instruction to the Project Manager and the rest of the agenda will be replaced with discussion of the closure arrangements.

❑ **Project Charter review:** To check that the Charter is up-to-date and relevant for the project as it is now.

❑ **Controls review:** Discussion to establish whether the project controls are working satisfactorily and review any changes proposed by the Project Manager. For example, does the Project Manager have sufficient delegated authority for change control, or is she having to refer too much to the PSG for decisions? Further adjustments should be discussed if the PSG is unhappy with the degree of control in place for the next stage.

❑ **Risk management review:** A specific check to ensure that the risk management is working effectively and to make changes if it isn't.

❑ **PSG review:** The PSG members should honestly and frankly review the working of the PSG in the project up to this point and decide whether individual members are fulfilling their roles. If not, changes should be made now.

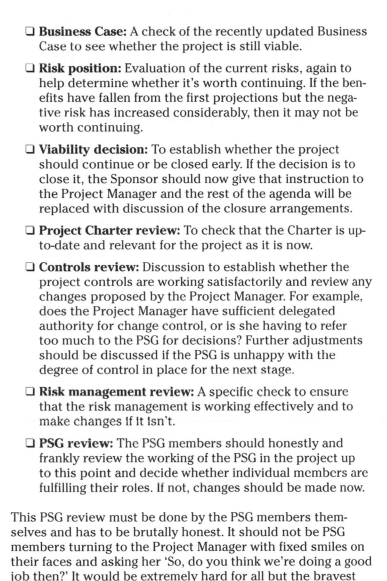

This PSG review must be done by the PSG members themselves and has to be brutally honest. It should not be PSG members turning to the Project Manager with fixed smiles on their faces and asking her 'So, do you think we're doing a good job then?' It would be extremely hard for all but the bravest Project Manager (and one who has already abandoned all hope of promotion) to say 'Well, actually no. You're less use than a chocolate teapot.'

❑ **Organisation review:** A check to ensure that all other people are functioning well and remain the right people for the project. Changes should be made if not.

❑ **PMP review:** A check of the Project Management Plan (PMP) to ensure that any changes to controls have been carried through correctly and that the PMP is sufficient for the effective day-to-day management of the next stage.

The next stage

If the PSG has decided to continue with the project, it must then authorise work to start on the next stage, provided that the PSG members are happy with the plan.

❑ **Stage Plan:** Presentation of the next Stage Plan by the Project Manager. PSG members must be convinced that the plan is realistic and achievable.

❑ **Resources:** Confirmation that funding and the required staff resources are in place.

❑ **Purchasing:** A review of any major purchases to be made in the next stage, as recorded on the plans, and any arrangements needed before the money can be spent such as final confirmation from the organisation's Finance Director if a spend is a particularly big one.

❑ **External controls:** A check on any external controls in the next stage so PSG members are aware of them. For example, building inspections or central audit checks on the adequacy of financial controls in a new computer system.

❑ **Approval:** Authorising the Project Manager to start work on the next stage. This approval should be recorded and signed, but can be done simply by the PSG members signing a panel on the Stage Plan.

Conclusion

This is to close the meeting and make sure that everyone is aware of the first progress meeting in the new stage.

❑ **Actions:** A summary of any actions agreed in the meeting that weren't carried out on the spot, such as to find a replacement Project User on the PSG if the current one said she no longer had the time to fulfil the role properly.

❑ **Next meeting:** Confirmation of the date of the first Stage Review Meeting in the next stage as set down on the Stage Plan.

Chapter 17

Templates for Reporting

In This Chapter

▶ Templates for reports made during the project

▶ Templates for reports and the end of the project and after it

*T*his chapter covers templates you can use to help you prepare reports. At the start of the project consider what reports you'll need and put the details in the Communications Plan for the project (part of the PMP – the Project Management Plan).

As with all reports, small is beautiful. Think critically about the items on each template and remove any headings that won't be relevant for your current project. Where you do need a heading you should include it in your report (obviously enough) but then be careful to put only essential information in that section. Writing huge amounts of excessive information just makes unnecessary work for you in writing the report, and wastes the time of those poor people who must now plough through it all.

Managers with any experience value concise reports and won't be at all impressed with unnecessarily lengthy ones. Provided that the report contains the required information, busy managers will be much more pleased with a short document than with a long one. If you're new to projects and project management you may have assumed that writing a lengthy report demonstrates that you're very conscientious and doing your job well, but actually it doesn't.

Team Progress Report

This first reporting template is for reports from Team Managers to the Project Manager to inform him of progress in the current Work Package (assignment). The report should be produced at regular intervals, usually weekly.

 Think carefully when setting up team progress reporting and don't ask your Team Managers to provide information that you already have. One well-known project management method is very poor in this respect and in all progress reports it has sections for information that's already readily available. That's silly and just wastes everyone's time. If you're using a particular project approach, such as a method, alongside this book, be critical as you think through what information you'll need . . . and what you won't.

❑ **Work Package ID:** The Work Package that the team is currently working on.

❑ **Date:** The date of the progress report.

❑ **Progress:** Brief information on what has been achieved, such as the completion of particular sub-products in the Work Package and whether the work is on time or ahead or behind the schedule on the Stage Plan.

❑ **Spend:** If the team is spending money, a short account of what money has been spent and what has been committed (orders placed, for example).

❑ **Staff resource:** The detail of what time has been spent on the work will be in the next section. In this section the Team Manager can make any observations on the overall use of resource, such as that the team is working 10 per cent faster than expected and with fewer errors than anticipated. This will help the Project Manager with forward projections for the stage.

❑ **Timesheets:** Usually attached to the report, the specific information from team members on how much time they have spent on the different activities as listed in the Stage Plan.

❏ **Outlook:** The Team Manager can add any comments on the outlook for the next reporting period, usually the week ahead. For example that the work rate will increase because two team members will be back from annual leave.

Stage Progress Report

This report is for the Project Manager to tell the PSG about progress, but the report may be copied to others as well such as the Programme Manager if your project is part of a programme of projects.

The Stage Progress Report is produced at regular intervals, often monthly but the Communications Plan will record the PSG's requirement for reporting. The report may be circulated before a Stage Progress Meeting, or provided in it and perhaps in the form of a business presentation with notes.

❏ **Stage and report ID:** Such as Stage 3, month 2.

❏ **Date:** The date of the report

❏ **PM comments:** The Project Manager's comments on the running of the stage in the last reporting period.

❏ **Delivery:** Delivery of products in the stage compared with the delivery set down in the plan. Product delivery is a key progress indicator and you can show this graphically on a colour coded Work Flow Diagram. You can see an example of this diagram at the start of Section 3 in this book which covers planning, with shading representing the colours.

❏ **Spending:** A brief financial report on what has been spent, again compared with the plan.

❏ **Outlook:** The Project Manager's assessment of how well work will progress in the next reporting period based on experience so far in the stage.

Dashboard reporting where you report information using graphs and things like 'petrol gauge' graphics is particularly effective for Stage Progress Reports. In my company, Inspirandum, I've devised a three page report using such things and including, importantly, the colour coded Work

Flow Diagram to show product completion. I provide this report example in my governance briefings for senior staff in organisations because the measures I use are all factual and evidence-based even though managers can take in the graphical information at a glance; fantastic for really effective project governance.

Stage Completion Report

This report is prepared for the Stage Gate, the PSG meeting held at the end of each Delivery Stage. It may be circulated by the Project Manager beforehand or presented at the Stage Gate itself.

❑ **Stage ID:** Such as 'Delivery Stage 6'.

❑ **Report date:** The date the report was compiled.

❑ **PM's comments:** the Project Manager's assessment on the stage, such as that it tracked very closely to plan or that there were many more Requests for Change than expected.

❑ **Costs:** The final cost of the stage, compared to the stage budget.

❑ **Resources:** The use of staff hours compared to those estimated in the Stage Plan.

❑ **Quality:** Confirmation that the required quality was delivered and a reminder of anything that failed to meet its quality requirements but a decision was made to accept that rather than spend more time and money.

❑ **Stage Gate decision factors:** In this section the Project manager should draw to the PSGs attention any factors that he thinks could affect the decision on whether or not to go on to the next stage. For example that the benefits projections in the Business Case are now stronger, or that the negative risk levels have risen considerably in the past stage. These factors will be included in other relevant documents, such as the Risk Log, but it's extremely helpful to the PSG if the Project Manager (who is involved in the project day-to-day) draws attention to them.

Project Completion Report

❏ **Project and date:** The project name and the date of the report.

❏ **Completion data:** Final figures on cost, delivery date against the plan, team performance and achievement of quality.

❏ **Initial benefits (if any):** A lot of benefits won't be seen clearly until after the end of the project and are then covered in the Project Evaluation Report. However if any benefits have come on stream at the end of the project, or even before the end, they can be measured now and reported now.

❏ **Lessons:** Things that may be of help to similar projects in the future.

❏ **Project Manager's comments:** The Project Manager's assessment (normally brief) on how the project went and how well it worked. He should not merely duplicate the lessons information from the previous section of the report, though.

Project Evaluation Report

This report is for after the end of the project when benefits have been assessed and measured, and you can also assess the suitability of project deliverables now that they have been in operational use for a while.

❏ **Quantifiable benefits:** A list of the benefits shown in the Business Case and for each

- Expected benefits
- Actual measured benefits

❏ **Non-quantifiable benefits:** A list of the non-measurable benefits as shown in the Business Case with an assessment for each as to whether it seems to have been achieved or not and whether that is as much as expected, the same or more. Have a look at the reminder below on non-quantifiables.

❑ **Product effectiveness:** an assessment of how well project deliverables have been in the first period of operational use.

Non-quantifiable benefits are, by definition, impossible to measure meaningfully. When reporting on them try to be as objective as possible and do your best not to either talk them up on the one hand or dismiss them on the other. It's possible that you may be able to assemble and report some evidence, even though you can't measure it reliably.

For example, you may have anecdotal evidence from a few regular customers that the new website delivered by the project is much easier to use. Perhaps a few retail outlets in the UK should take note of such evidence when they do an 'improvement' project and replace a great website with one that you can't find your way around, let alone place an order.

Part V
More Project Checklists

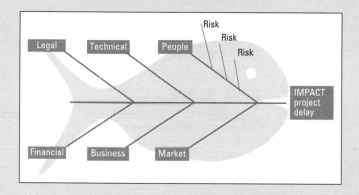

The Ishikawa (or Fishbone) Diagram is a cause and effect model. It works really well for risk management though. You put the risk impact, such as overspending, as the effect and then analyse each of your chosen risk categories as shown on the primary bones. You write in the risks in that category as the secondary bones. This technique works really well in a risk workshop.

In this part . . .

- ✔ Find out how to take over someone else's project with minimum disruption.

- ✔ Get to grips with project audit.

- ✔ Understand common and powerful project techniques to save you time and make your life a whole lot easier.

Chapter 18

Taking Over an Existing Project

....

In This Chapter

▶ Pressures on taking over a project

▶ A checklist for the Project Manager

▶ Checklists for projects in trouble

▶ Taking over as Project Sponsor

....

*T*here's no getting round it, taking over someone else's project is usually a really tough job, and that's for two reasons. First, there's only one chance in a million that the project is set up the way you would have set it up had you been in at the start. Second, you'll be under great time pressure. You have to get to understand the project and its characteristics fast, and the clock won't stop while you do.

This chapter is to help you get to grips with your newly acquired project, and to do it quickly. There's a checklist to help if you are a Project Manager taking over a project that's in decent shape, even if it's not quite as you'd have set it up. Then there are a couple of lists to help where you have been sent in as a replacement Project Manager because the project is in trouble. Finally there's a checklist to give you some advice if you are the Sponsor stepping in to take over the project.

Project Manager Checklist

If you're the Project Manager moving in to take over someone else's project, you'll be very aware that you need to get organised and to get organised quickly. This checklist is to help you think through what you need to do and in what order so you can get to grips with the project and bring it under your project management control.

❑ **Charter:** Read the Project Charter to get an understanding of the basis of the project, especially the scope and objectives. If you're not familiar with the Charter and Project Management Plan (PMP) documents mentioned in this checklist, have a look at Chapter 2.

 If the project hasn't got a Charter, go straight for the plans and any documentation you can get your hands on that shows what the project is to deliver and how. If that information isn't available either, talk to the Sponsor, key users and, if she is still around, the previous Project Manager. Don't put her on the spot by asking 'Why didn't you bother to record this essential information?' but rather take the more subtle approach of 'Can you help me get a clear view of what the project is about and what it has to achieve?' Also, be careful to leave the door open and say 'If I need to talk to you again on one or two points, will it be okay if I call you?'

❑ **Roles:** Find out who is involved from the Project Organisation Chart. Make a beeline for the Sponsor (or equivalent) to get her take on what's important in the project and how things have been going so far.

❑ **Team Leaders:** Make contact with your Team Leaders, perhaps by holding a meeting. Emphasise that you value their work and want to do everything you can to support them. Say also that you value their input as you familiarise yourself with the project.

❑ **Team members:** Go and visit the team members. You may not be too concerned about their part in the project at the moment because you're still getting your head around the high-level stuff. However, they'll be wanting to know who you are, what you're going to be like to work for and whether you're a monster with two heads or not. So go see them and build your reputation of being approachable and supportive.

❑ **Team Leader discussions:** Now talk to your Team Leaders one at a time to get their perspective on the project. Ask if anything in particular has been a problem so far. Reinforce the point that you will be looking to do all that you can to support them – and note any points so you can deliver on that support.

❑ **User and supplier:** Talk to the Project User and Project Supplier to get their views on the project.

❑ **Interfacing projects:** Check to see whether your project has interdependencies with other projects and work areas. If so, go and talk to the other managers of those projects and work areas and make sure that you fully understand the dependencies . . . in both directions.

❑ **Re-plan:** In the light of your discussions and fact-finding, review the Project Plan and re-plan if you think it's necessary; it probably will be.

❑ **PMP:** Review the project controls in the PMP or equivalent and be critical on two grounds. First, to check whether you think that the controls are suitable, based on your discussions with PSG members and Team Leaders. Second, to assess how the PMP fits in with how you think the project needs to be controlled.

❑ **Step back:** Even if the project is very busy, go and find a quiet place or work for a day at home. Reflect on the dynamics of the project from what you have learned so far and think about how you need to control the project to bring it to a successful conclusion.

❑ **Sponsor re-visit:** Go and see the Sponsor again to talk through the project in more detail now that you have a better understanding of it. Discuss with her any control changes that you think are advisable to be sure of smooth project delivery.

❑ **Hit list:** Make a hit list of what you need to do first of all. You may want to include some support work for Team Leaders alongside dealing with any immediate problems or potential problems of your own.

When revising the plans and controls, don't change more than you need to. If you don't like something in the project and it isn't your way of doing things, think whether it's really necessary to change it or whether you can live with it this time around. Don't change things for the sake of it, and especially where that would affect other people.

❑ **Visit . . . again:** In the first few days following the launch of your new plans and new controls, go and visit the teams again. You'll be able to absorb more now, and also it's important for team members to see you out and about, not just that initial 'Hello' visit followed by a disappearing act.

❑ **Review controls . . . again:** In the first few weeks following your appointment as Project Manager, check especially carefully to see whether your revised controls are adequate. If they're not, review and adjust them again.

'Problem Project' Checklist

If you've been appointed as Project Manager to take over a project because it's in trouble, you can take that as a real compliment. Clearly, someone somewhere thinks you're worth your keep. Basking in the sunshine of that happy thought is likely to be a short-lived experience, though. You'll probably be well aware that the sun will soon go behind a very dark cloud if you don't make rapid progress in sorting this project out and getting it on track.

How you deal with the project will obviously depend on the nature of the problems with it. This checklist is to help you 'feel' around the project to identify the immediate and obvious problems and, perhaps even more importantly, those tucked away under the surface.

Earlier in this chapter I talked about taking over a project that isn't in any particular difficulty, and emphasised that you should try to talk to the outgoing Project Manager. That won't be so easy in a problem project. The outgoing Project Manager has been replaced . . . by you. She's going to be pretty fed up that the project has gone wrong or she may even be clinging to the thought that things really aren't that bad.

She'll be very aware that she's now seen as having failed and the result is that she'll probably want nothing more to do with the whole sorry business and definitely nothing to do with you. You're unlikely to get much information or enthusiastic cooperation from that direction, then, and you'll have to put much more emphasis on other information-gathering options.

❑ **Sponsor:** As a first priority, go and talk to the Sponsor to find out exactly why you have been called in and what the problems are in the Sponsor's eyes.

❑ **Charter and PMP:** Quickly review the Project Charter, PMP or any other project documents to learn more about what the project is about.

❑ **Look for problems:** As you review project documents, look for and note any problems that you see and any important things that you don't see because they've been overlooked. Watch out for inadequate things too, such as a clearly understated Risk Log.

When looking at a Risk Log for a project a while ago I was both concerned and slightly amused to see only two risks listed in what was clearly a fairly risky project. 'Risk 1. The project will be late.' and 'Risk 2. We will have insufficient staff for the work.' Clearly the risk analysis hadn't been done properly, but the log also signalled another problem, which was poor project governance. Why had the PSG accepted such an inadequate log?

❑ **Team Leaders:** Talk to your Team Leaders, or team members in a smaller project, to get their take on what's going wrong and why.

❑ **Quick fix:** Now that you have a reasonable overview of the problems, decide on, plan and put into effect any immediate 'quick fix' actions to halt the slide into more difficulty.

❑ **Dig deep:** Now think through the problems that you've been told about and any others that you've uncovered for yourself. For each problem ask 'why' and trace it back to its roots. You'll need to get at the underlying causes not just deal with the surface symptoms.

❑ **Re-focus:** Make sure that the objectives of the project are clear and realistic and that the four control 'dogs' are balanced (see Chapter 8 for more on the four dogs). If the project is not in balance then talk with the PSG in general and the Sponsor in particular about adjusting the Project Charter. If the project is inherently unachievable, then you can expect to go down the same path as the outgoing Project Manager, and probably quite soon too.

❑ **Re-plan:** Re-plan the project and the controls you need. Pay particular attention to the product based plans and the 'bottom up' checks to find missing parts of the project. A lot of projects become 'problem projects' because of unforeseen but essential work which then throws everything else off course.

❑ **PSG:** Ask the Sponsor to set up a meeting of the whole PSG so that you can talk through what you have found and put forward your plan for tackling the problems and bringing the project in.

❑ **Project Meeting:** Unless your project is very big, in which case you may have to do this a bit at a time, call everyone together. Explain the problems and what you're doing about them. Re-focus and re-motivate the staff, emphasising that the project is now achievable and that success is entirely possible. Be open with your plan so that project staff can see that the project is achievable.

Listen carefully to any points anyone makes in the Project Meeting. You want to keep things positive, so if someone comes up with a stream of strong negatives take that discussion 'off-line'. Don't dismiss negative comments, because they could be valid, but take them off-line by saying that you'll talk to that person about the points later to be able to go into more depth. Then follow up on that by going straight to that person as the meeting closes to arrange a time for the discussion. In fact you might call out to the person as they are getting up 'Mary, can I just have a quick word to fix a time to talk?' That way everyone will know that you meant what you said.

'Problem Project' Actions

If you're taking over a project that's in trouble, look out for these problems. You'll find some suggestions in the checklist on actions to tackle the problems, but obviously your preferred actions will depend on the exact nature of each problem and the underlying causes.

❏ **Unclear or conflicting objectives:** Get a simple objectives statement together which is unambiguous and get PSG agreement and then commitment to it.

❏ **Unachievable project:** Get the 'four dogs' of scope, time, resource and quality into balance. See the 'Four Dogs Checklist' in Chapter 8 for more on the dogs and the 'project canvas' that they're pulling on.

❏ **Overspending:** If the project has been budgeted with unrealistic optimism, re-write the budget with realistic costs. Then work with the Sponsor in particular to re-write the Business Case and evaluate if the project is still viable.

❏ **Under-resourcing:** If staff resource hasn't been forthcoming, and that's why the project is under pressure, refer the problem to the PSG. Let the Sponsor take the lead in holding the other two PSG roles (Project Supplier and Project User) accountable for providing the resource in the plans. If the resource isn't available, question the viability of the project or at least its targets such as the delivery date.

❏ **Extra work:** If extra but essential work has been found as the project has progressed, and it's that work which has thrown things off track, make product planning a priority and check the diagrams for any further work that hasn't been identified so far. Have a look at Chapter 8 for more on product planning. If you want to know the full story of the approach, you might like to get hold of a copy of the UK edition of *Project Management for Dummies* (Wiley).

❏ **Moving goalposts:** Some projects get into trouble because everything keeps changing and completed work is invalidated. That has a secondary impact of lowered morale, mentioned again later in this list, as people see their work trashed. Bring in effective change control to limit change to what's essential. Make sure too that the project is properly thought through and that the PSG is committed to the Charter. Get the Project User on board to make sure that the requirement is clear because it sounds like people may be making things up as they go along.

If the goalposts are moving all the time, bringing in effective change control is considerably better than imposing a *change freeze* where all change is now refused. A change freeze just means that the project gets out of step with the business or operating environment. The problem with the freeze is that it's mindless and indiscriminate. The freeze rules out sensible and productive changes as well as the unnecessary and damaging ones.

❏ **Poor performance:** If teams are performing significantly below target find out why. If it's lack of capability then see whether you can replace some or all of the team members with staff who are better suited to the project work. If poor working conditions are to blame for the under-performance, including having a hassled environment with interruptions, work with the PSG to radically improve that environment.

❏ **Low morale:** Although related to the last point, low morale is worth making a checklist point in its own right, since it can be such a big problem. Find out why morale is down before you try to remedy it. If you leave an underlying cause in place, any morale boost you do manage to achieve will be short-lived.

❏ **Inter-personal problems in the team:** This problem can be extremely serious. Your action will depend on the nature of the conflicts. The best course may be to replace a Team Leader or one or two team members. Where two people are involved in a dispute it may be better to lose both rather than give the impression that one of them has 'won'. See Chapter 10, which is about Managing the People, and especially Figure 10-1 on the three areas of team management. In this instance you will usually have to put the needs of a team ahead of the interests of individuals.

Many organisational managers assume that small projects are always lower-risk than big projects. In some areas the reverse is inherently true, and the risk of inter-personal conflict is one of them. In a project involving 1,000 people, if two team members are in dispute then what is the overall impact? It will depend on the significance of the two people, of course, but you get the point. However, if two team members get into bitter dispute in a project involving only four people, what's the impact then? Small projects magnify some risks.

❑ **Inter-personal problems between teams** – This check-list point is usually even more serious than the previous one. Sadly the problem is not uncommon. For example a team made up of organisational staff may come into conflict with a team from an outside supplier. There's no easy remedy apart from trying to resolve any issues. The trouble is that the issues are probably just the superficial symptoms of deeper underlying antagonism. If the matter is project threatening, the Sponsor may need to consider radical action such as changing supplier mid-project, or closing the project down and starting all over with different resourcing.

When I started in computer systems analysis and design I narrowly avoided being assigned to design the user interfaces in a very large IT project that was in deep trouble. I argued against the assignment and to my amazement my head of department listened and then gave me a smaller project of my own to design and build a different system. While working on my own, and very nice, project I watched in awe as the problems mounted in the bigger one. There was a team from my own organisation doing user testing, a development team from an outside consultancy company, then a Project Manager from a second consultancy which was a competitor of the first consultancy company. The deliberate lack of cooperation and the open animosity that flashed around that organisational triangle was astonishing. It was one of the reasons that the 18-month project was finally delivered 24 months after its target date, long after my system was designed, built and implemented.

Sponsor Checklist

If you're a new Sponsor for a project that's already underway, here's a checklist to help you take on your new responsibilities, understand the project and work out how to be really effective in your new role.

❑ **Read up on the project:** Before you've even taken over formally, unless things have happened very quickly, get hold of the key project documents and read up on what the project is about. Look for the Project Charter in particular, but then check out the Project Management Plan (PMP) too. Check that you agree with the objectives and nature of the project. If you don't make a note of why.

❑ **Characteristics:** Take careful note of the characteristics of the project. For example, is it business critical, very visible to customers, high-risk or heavily dependent on other things? Taking the characteristics on board will help you develop a clear idea of the approach you'll need to take.

❑ **Talk to the outgoing Sponsor:** Get the outgoing Sponsor's take on the project and what she thinks the key issues are. If you disagree with what the project is currently trying to do or the way it is set up, don't say so. If pressed with 'What do you think?' just indicate that it's a bit early to take any view as you're still getting your head around everything. If you even hint at criticism, you're likely to close down the communication and so miss out on things that could help you.

❑ **Meet and greet, but briefly:** Meet up with the Project User(s) and Project Supplier(s) on the PSG individually and briefly. This is primarily a courtesy action at the moment. Be careful not to commit to anything or to start discussing detail until you have a better grasp of the project. Ask open questions about the project and the way it has been running. Get a feel for whether your fellow PSG members understand their roles and are fulfilling them properly.

In case you're unclear on question types, an open question encourages someone to talk. A closed question has a single answer and does not encourage further explanation. 'What's your name?' 'Nick Graham'. 'Do you advise organisations on good project governance?' 'Yes, I do.' Those questions are both closed questions, with a single answer. 'Tell me, what do you think about the way in which we're implementing project governance in this company?' is an open question. There isn't a short, single answer so the question encourages me to explain. When you ask open questions, people will often mention things that you wouldn't have thought to ask about with your closed questions. Closed questions come out of your existing knowledge while open ones can explore areas that you don't necessarily know about.

❑ **Project Manager:** Book a session to have a long talk to the Project Manager. You might include lunch in this to encourage more relaxed conversation. Check with the Project Manager how things are going from her perspective and ask about any problems. Say up front that you want to note down any particular points, and then do that so that you don't forget anything important. Also ask, but carefully, about how the PSG has been functioning, if she is getting enough support and if decisions are being made in a timely way.

❑ **Project audit:** If your organisation has a project audit function ask for an additional audit to be done now. The audit will give you another view on how the project is running and warn you as to whether there are problems that you need to address. Talk to your auditors first though to spell out your reasons for wanting the audit. There are references elsewhere in this book, such as in Chapter 19 on Auditing Someone Else's Project, to 'nit-picking' audits that just frustrate everyone rather than help deliver the project securely.

❑ **Formal meeting:** Fix a meeting between the PSG and the Project Manager. Talk through the project and particularly the objectives and controls. If you're thinking of making changes then get input from others at the meeting before you make any final decision.

❑ **Organisational manager(s):** If you're thinking of changing the nature of the project in some way, such as the scope, clear this with the organisational manager(s) who appointed you, and perhaps others as well.

❑ **Business impact:** Look carefully at any impact that the project will have on areas outside your immediate control. For example, will other departments need to change their procedures to fit in with the new procedure that your project will implement? Make sure that the impact is documented. Then make sure that managers in the other areas are aware of the work they need to do and that they have made arrangements (not necessarily projects) to do it.

❑ **Controls:** Review the project controls and make sure that they are in the right balance; not too much control and not too little. In particular check the amount of authority delegated to the Project Manager, and that includes how the stages and Stage Gates are set up. Also review the way that the PSG is working and make adjustments if it isn't functioning as well as it should.

❑ **Adjust:** Work through with the Project Manager and PSG members what needs to be changed, if anything. Make sure that the Charter and PMP are brought into line with that. You might put in an additional stage boundary to mark the point at which the changes will be made, unless a convenient boundary is coming up anyway.

Resist the common management temptation to make a few changes in order to stamp your authority onto the project. Making unnecessary work for people is extremely bad management in any setting, but especially so in busy projects. If you need to cause inconvenience and create needless work to make your authority clear then you weren't paying attention during your management training course. On the other hand, if you're secure in your management and with your authority then you won't feel any need to resort to such tactics, will you?

Chapter 19

Auditing Someone Else's Project

*P*roject Audit isn't important; it's vital. It's strange, isn't it, that while just about every organisation wants to be sure that its projects are running well, project audit is still undervalued? Good audit should be really positive and productive, and the case for it is a no-brainer. The good news for you if you are auditing someone else's project is that you can make a genuine and valuable contribution. Although you're independent of the project, you should approach the audit task with a 'member of the team' mindset, not as someone whose role is to put the project under pressure, cause irritation or make life even harder for the Project Manager than it already is.

Your objective as an auditor is to make sure that the project is set up properly at the start and then is running properly as it continues. When you stop to think about it, that's almost certainly what everyone else in the project wants too. Unless the project team is a bit weird (probably unlikely even in your organisation) then everyone will want it to succeed. If you spot an error or omission then it can be corrected and that will help the project run smoothly towards successful delivery.

Audit Focus Checklist

Predictably this chapter is quite detailed, so before you get into the nitty-gritty it may help you to pull back first and make sure you have a clear view of what your task is all about when auditing a project.

❏ **Completeness:** To check that documents such as the Project Charter are complete and that essential parts haven't been forgotten.

❏ **Accuracy:** Where there are calculations, such as for benefit levels, making sure that the arithmetic is correct; a simple but important check.

❏ **Appropriate control:** That the level of planning and control is appropriate to the nature of the project. Check for excessive control as well as insufficient control. For example, that there isn't a huge Project Steering Group (PSG) with 27 members to oversee the repainting of the stationery cupboard.

Okay, I admit that the 27 member PSG for a stationery cupboard is an exaggeration in a weak attempt at humour. However I once saw a project that wasn't too important but which had two people doing all of the project work (including the project management) and a 'Steering Committee' of seven people overseeing it. Another had 21 on a Project Board (equivalent to a PSG) to oversee a team of about eight staff.

❏ **Realism:** Checking that the Business Case is realistic and that plans are achievable rather than just wishful thinking.

❏ **Compliance:** Checks to ensure that the project will comply with any necessary standards including internal organisational ones such as for project risk management as well as the more obvious external ones such as planning regulations.

❏ **Deeds not words:** During the project, checks to make sure that controls are actually being put into effect and then that they're working.

❏ **Your task:** Focus too on what you are actually being asked to do for audit on this specific project so you don't end up doing the normal quick health-check when actually you were required to do detailed audit on this business critical project.

Outline Charter Audit Checklist

There's some initial work in Kick Off to produce an Idea and then a Recommendation. At that point the perspective is a business one. When the Outline Charter – or just 'Outline' – is produced later on in Kick Off, things get rather more serious and project experience is called on as well as business experience. Because the Outline lays the foundation for the project, this is the first point where you are likely to be called in as a Project Auditor to make sure that everything's okay.

The Outline is important because it lays the foundations for the project, as explained in the last paragraph, but also because it's the last major point where it's easy to stop. Although the project could be halted in the Planning Stage, considerably more resource will have been expended by then, so your check here is more than a little important.

Predictably there are quite a few things for you to watch out for and check on, but a key one – so worth singling out here – is that the project really is justified. If it's justified by benefits, look particularly carefully at the projections to ensure that they are realistic and that the project hasn't been 'talked up'. Having made that point, here's the checklist with the full detail:

- ❑ **Clear boundary:** Ensure that the boundary of the project has been spelled out clearly. Check that the 'negative scope' (what the project won't include) information is clear so that people will be in no doubt as to what the project won't cover as well as what it will if there could be any misunderstanding.

- ❑ **Sensible scope:** Check that the scope is sensible and makes for a good project. Look for anything that doesn't seem to align with the rest, then check for any gaps where it appears that an area has been left out but it's either essential or desirable.

- ❑ **Clear deliverable:** Make sure that the Outline defines clearly what the project will deliver, whether that is a product, some service or other outcome.

- ❑ **Time estimate:** Using your knowledge of the organisation and the capability of project staff, is the project timescale realistic? Pay particular attention to any lead times that may have been overlooked, such as getting approval for something as part of the project. Getting legal approval, even internally from a large organisation's legal department, can be a long process and it's often underestimated. However the time needed to get approval to things like technical specifications is often underestimated too.

Don't forget that your checks here are on the Outline Project Charter, not the full Charter. The Outline is much more detailed than the Recommendation that preceded it, but it's still a 'sketch' document. Don't push a project into going into too much detail too early by making audit points saying that the information is insufficient when in fact you have the full Charter in mind, not the Outline.

❑ **Cost estimate:** Is the cost estimate realistic based on your knowledge and on records of any previous projects which were similar in whole or in part?

❑ **Resource:** Check that the resource estimates are realistic and that the people to be involved (or it may just be skills such as 'power engineers' at this point) are actually available.

❑ **Justification:** Is the project justification in the Business Case accurate and sound? Have a look at Chapter 5, Checking the Justification and Benefits, for more on project justification and note that a project may be justified on something other than benefits.

❑ **Benefits:** Where the Business Case does list benefits, are the levels realistic and are the benefits correctly categorised? Again see Chapter 5 for more on the Business Case and benefits.

❑ **Roles:** Check to ensure that proposals have been made for filling all of the project roles and that the people suggested are both suitable and sufficiently available.

❑ **Business impact:** Ensure that the impact on the business and on stakeholders outside the immediate area of the project has been evaluated and considered. It's easy to underestimate the business impact both in extent and in degree.

❑ **Ancillary work:** If significant work will be needed elsewhere in the organisation to accommodate what the project is delivering, has this been thought through? Then have sufficient checks been made that the necessary work can actually be resourced and done, and in good time?

Planning Audit Checklist

Towards the end of Kick Off the Stage Plan for the first project stage, the Planning Stage, is created by the Project Manager – he's creating a plan for the planning. Given that inadequate planning is a known cause of project failure, it's a key area for you to check on in project audit. Use this checklist to help evaluate if the plan for the planning is up to scratch.

In the Planning Stage, three key documents will be prepared. The three are the full Project Charter, the Project Management Plan (PMP) and the Stage Plan for the first Delivery Stage. The Stage Plan for the Planning Stage covers the work needed to produce all three.

❑ **Balance:** Does the plan reflect the control needed on the project? Under-planning is likely to lead to problems of course, while over-planning just wastes resource.

❑ **Completeness:** Check that the Stage Plan covers the production of all of the required elements of the Charter and PMP.

❑ **Realism:** Check that the Stage Plan is realistic and achievable overall. It's unlikely that a multi-million dollar, split site, business critical project can be planned by one person in a planning stage that's just two days long, even if they stay up all night.

❑ **Risk:** A spotlight to check specifically that enough time has been allocated for risk analysis and planning. That's particularly important, obviously enough, if the project is a high-risk one.

❑ **Quality:** Another spotlight as the work involved in specifying and planning quality control is often underestimated.

❑ **Business Case:** A third spotlight on specifics, this time to check that sufficient time is included in the Stage Plan to produce a sound Business Case. In turn that will depend on the project justification and the amount of work already done for the Outline.

❑ **Planning resource:** Make sure that the staff resource needed to create the plans is included in the Stage Plan and that the people involved are actually available. That may include subject specialists such as engineers and also Team Leaders.

❑ **Planning time:** Check that the Planning Stage is long enough to build effective plans. For example, ensure that sufficient time has been allowed for resource levelling and calculating the budget. Check that the Project Manager hasn't reduced the planning time in response to ill-judged pressure from senior managers to 'get on with the real work' in the Delivery Stages.

❑ **PSG involvement:** Check that the resourcing for the plan includes PSG members. That may be in a Planning Workshop or to work on individual elements of the plan. The Project Manager can't create the Charter and PMP in a vacuum.

Project Charter Audit Checklist

Once the three key documents of Project Charter, PMP and the plan for the first Delivery Stage have been produced in the Planning Stage, you may well be asked to check the project over. The next checklist is for the first of the documents, the Project Charter. The Project Charter is developed from the Outline Charter developed during Kick Off. You should look out for the same things as in the Outline Charter Audit Checklist earlier in the chapter, but now there are a few additional things to look for and some areas where you need to dig a bit deeper – just so you feel that you're still needed.

❑ **Basic checks:** Have a look at the checklist for the Outline Charter earlier in the chapter and make sure that in the full Charter those things haven't been compromised.

❑ **Scope:** Check that the scope statement is crystal clear on what is in the project and what isn't. Then check that the scope aligns with the project level Work Flow Diagram.

❑ **Requirements:** Check that any requirements for the project are listed together with the source (such as a legal requirement) and that they've been covered in the scope and documents such as the Quality Plan.

❑ **Business Case:** The full Business Case in the Charter is an essential item for the PSG. Ensure that it's complete, well considered and that the calculations behind the figures (notably cost, time, resource and benefit levels) are correct. Pay careful attention to any non-quantifiable benefits to check that they haven't been exaggerated.

❑ **Organisation:** Check that the organisation chart is correct and shows the people actually taking part in the project. Some appointments may have changed since the suggestions in the Outline.

❑ **Constraints:** Look at the constraints to make sure that they really are constraints. Challenge any that are not, for example an arbitrary delivery date imposed by a Senior Manager who thinks every project should be put under pressure to meet a chosen date. Unnecessary constraints can damage a good project, for example when quality ends up being cut to meet a fixed deadline, when really another week on the project wouldn't have mattered that much.

❑ **Acceptance arrangements:** Make sure that the acceptance arrangements for the handover of project products are clear and as simple as possible. Check also to ensure that the people responsible for acceptance have been named, or at least that their position, such as 'Production Manager', has been stated.

PMP Audit Checklist

The Project Management Plan (PMP) is made up of a lot of component plans and you can find checklists for them in this chapter. This first short checklist relates to the PMP as a whole before you go on to look at the specific plans.

❑ **Complete:** Check that all the component elements needed for the project are included in the PMP. Not every project needs all of them and in particular the project might not need a separate Procurement Plan.

❑ **Clear:** Check that the component plans are clearly written. A lot of people in the project, such as Team Leaders and PSG members, will need to refer to the plans as well as the Project Manager. The plans must therefore be clear and understandable to all, not written in some abbreviated form that only the Project Manager can understand.

❑ **Concise:** To accompany the last point that plans should be clear and properly explained is the counterbalance that they should then be concise. Unnecessary detail and complexity in the plans results in too much resource being used to create them (although that's water under the bridge now), but importantly those plans must be maintained through the project, taking up more unnecessary resource.

❑ **PSG involvement:** Although the PMP is primarily the Project Manager's document, the PSG must check that the controls are sufficient and must input some of the information such as the availability of staff and finance. Ensure that PSG members have been involved in the production of the PMP and that they agree with it from a project governance perspective.

Project Plan Audit Checklist

As a Project Auditor you should be familiar with product, activity, resource and financial planning. From your experience you'll know the sort of things that planners can miss, but here are a few reminders of the main areas to help you cover all the bases.

❑ **Accuracy:** Check the plans for technical accuracy, such as that products have been correctly modelled. Inaccuracies can lead to errors in control.

❑ **Completeness:** Check that plans are complete including, for example, management actions not just the product construction activity.

❑ **Consistency:** Ensure that the plans are consistent with each other. For example, for every team product on the product plans, are there corresponding activities on the activity plans to build that product?

❑ **Quality checks and rework:** Make sure that work to test products, including staff resource, is included and also time and resource for some re-work. Not every product will pass test first time.

❑ **Resource:** Check that the people shown as resource on the plans are actually available when the plan shows that they are needed. Check too that non-working days (such as public holidays and booked annual holiday for particular staff members) are accounted for on the plans.

❑ **Realistic:** Take a critical look at the plans to ensure that they are realistic and achievable. Check that staff members aren't allocated 100 per cent unless the activity durations allow for some non-working time.

Nobody can work 100 per cent of the time so it's unrealistic for Project Managers to have that in their plans. People chat when first arriving in the office, read company emails, take holidays and – shock, horror – even go sick sometimes. For more on availability you might like to look at the classic *The Mythical Man-month* by Frederick P. Brooks, Jr. published by Addison Wesley Longman, but you'll find productivity stuff on the internet too.

❑ **Timing:** Is the timing sensible on the activity plans including, where appropriate, lag times? You can't do induction training for newly recruited project staff the day after the contracts have been sent out – people who already have a job need to work a period of notice with their current employers. It's not uncommon for Project Managers who are focused on project activity to miss these important lags.

❑ **Contingency:** Check that there is sufficient contingency in the plans. It should really be visible and clearly labelled 'contingency' rather than hidden in inflated estimates.

Risk Plan Audit Checklist

The controls in the Risk Plan must be clear but also appropriate for the project. A common problem in projects is that insufficient attention is paid to risk management, and projects get into unnecessary difficulties or even fail as a direct result. However, it's important that Project Managers and PMP members don't make the opposite error with excessive risk management and control that simply isn't justified for the project. Unnecessary control just drives up project overheads both in terms of cost and wasted time.

❑ **Standards:** Ensure that the project risk approach complies with organisational standards, but also that exemption from such standards has been obtained where they are inappropriate for the project.

❑ **Procedures:** Check that the risk procedures are clearly set down, such as how a team member should report a newly identified risk.

❑ **Reporting:** Check that risk reporting requirements are clear, such as including information on the status of key risks in the regular progress reports that the Project Manager gives to the PSG. This aspect may be covered in part in the Communications Plan.

❑ **Escalation:** Ensure that the escalation trigger is clear when a risk changes to a degree that the Project Manager must inform the PSG immediately.

❑ **Review:** Check that the risk review strategy is clear, such as that each risk will be reviewed every four weeks on a rolling program with 25 per cent done each week.

❑ **Recording:** Ensure that the contents of the Risk Log have been specified and are appropriate (avoiding excessive detail for a low-risk project but including sufficient detail where a project is higher risk).

❑ **Interfaces:** Are the interfaces with organisational risk management clear? For example, referring a risk identified in the project to the organisational risk management system if it has wider implications.

Quality Plan Audit Checklist

Quality isn't a game to just 'go through the motions' and make things look good and your audit should check for such superficiality. The Quality Plan should show how the required level of quality will be achieved and how genuine checks will be performed to ensure that. Thorough quality management can be simple though, so in your audit you should be looking for effectiveness not complexity. Indeed simple controls are often the best because everyone in the project can understand them.

❑ **Required quality:** Check that the required quality level has been clearly stated in terms that those working on the project will understand.

❑ **Level:** Is the specified level of quality appropriate? Specifying excessive quality is wasteful while specifying too low a level will lead to problems at best and is downright dangerous at worst.

❑ **Standards:** Check that all relevant standards have been listed in the plan. That includes internal organisational standards as well as external ones such as safety regulations.

❑ **Records:** How will tests and other quality actions be recorded so that it's clear that they've been done and not forgotten?

❑ **Regular checks:** Check that the plan includes how regular checks will be done to ensure that the required quality is actually being delivered. That could simply be the Project Manager and Team Managers examining the Quality Checklist from time to time but a high quality project will need more.

❑ **PSG checks:** Ensure that project controls include the PSG checking on the delivery of quality at Stage Gates. This can be done simply by including it on the standard agenda for the Stage Gate meeting.

❑ **Double checks:** If the project will include very high quality products, check that that the quality procedures are sufficient. For example, a signature that a test has been done may not be enough (people have been known to sign things anyway) so routine second testing of key products may be sensible.

Project Controls Audit Checklist

Checking that the project controls are appropriate is a tricky business and one for which it is hard to provide a checklist; so much will depend on the characteristics of the project. However, here are a few things to look out for.

❑ **Balance:** The balance this time is to check if the degree of control is right for the nature of the project. Look out for excessive control that will merely drive up overheads for no gain, and at the other extreme for insufficient control that will put the project in danger. Part of your evaluation will be based on the experience of the Project Manager and the PMP members.

❑ **Project Manager authority:** Check that the Project Manager has 'room to breathe' to get on and do his job. Watch out for excessive controls demanded by a nervous PSG that is trying to micro-manage.

❑ **Clear authority:** Check that the Project Manager's authority is clear so he knows when he can make a decision and when something must be referred to the PSG.

❑ **Stage checks:** Make sure that effective controls are in place to check on the progress of a stage and get early warning of any problems. That will be the Project Manager's own checks, but also progress reviews by the PSG.

Stage Audit Checklist

You may be asked to do intermittent – possibly random – checks while the Delivery Stages are running. For example, you may be asked to do two random checks during the life of the six-stage project. It's unusual to require multiple checks in every stage in the project. The focus of your stage check will to be to make sure that the controls specified in the PMP are actually being operated and that the information is correct. For example, where the Project Manager is reporting to the PSG that the stage is on target for delivery on time and to budget, do the calculations and evidence support that?

 Clearly the Project Manager will be very busy and focused on the project during Delivery Stages. You need to come alongside with the minimum impact while at the same time getting your job done. If you do it right, the Project Manager will welcome you as 'another pair of eyes' to check that everything is okay.

❑ **PMP controls:** Unless you're very familiar with the PMP for the project, check it before you start your audit to be quite sure that you know what controls are supposed to be operating and when.

❑ **Plans:** Check that the Stage Plan is up-to-date with *actuals* (time actually taken for work and money actually spent) being entered regularly.

❑ **Progress reports:** Check at least the last Stage Progress Report given to the PSG by the Project Manager. Check the facts reported and find the evidence behind them. Look, for example, to see when products have been completed and look at the Project Manager's records and calculations.

❑ **Team data:** The Project Manager's progress reports will be based partly on data provided by the teams (actuals). Examine some team member timesheets to see if the information looks realistic.

I once worked in a large company where a very senior and authoritarian manager reprimanded the junior managers in his section for having their staff working extra hours. He said that if the staff couldn't do the work in the standard week that showed very poor management control at the lower level. His junior managers took the hint, and to protect their own careers instructed their staff to enter work totalling exactly 37.5 hours a week on each timesheet (the standard working hours). Unfortunately this data was also used for project calculations and to help develop bids for future work. The underreporting of work hours had very severe consequences.

❑ **Spending:** Check that spending is properly recorded and that reports of the financial position of both the stage and full project are correct. Check that projections for future spending are realistic and correctly calculated.

❑ **Quality:** Check that the required quality is being delivered. Have the planned tests all be done on products completed to date, or have some been 'forgotten', and were they done by the right people? Has any necessary remedial work been carried out?

❑ **Standards:** Following on from the previous point, where products must comply with a standard (external such as electrical safety or internal organisational standards) is there evidence that the right checks were done to confirm compliance?

❑ **Risk:** Check that risks have been reviewed at the frequency set down in the Risk Plan. Have any new risks been reported and if so have they been handled correctly, not overlooked?

❑ **Business Case:** If the Business Case should be being checked by the Project Manager at intervals during stages, not just at stage end, look to see if the checks have been done. Such checks will probably involve benefit projections and a final cost estimate but it could be more – the PMP controls will say.

❑ **Project Memos:** Where Project Memos have been sent in, does the Project Log show that they have been considered and any necessary action carried out? Where action is required, has it been carried out or have things got forgotten?

❑ **Referral:** Check that the Project Manager is working within the limits of his delegated authority. If something should have been referred to the PSG (such as a scope change) check that it was.

Stage Gate Audit Checklist

There are two areas to focus on if you audit the project as it approaches a Stage Gate. The first is to check that the reported information is correct and that everything is up-to-date for the stage just finishing. The second is to look at the plan for the next stage and any changes to the project controls that will be used in that stage. As always the exact checks you carry out may vary according to the nature of the project and any organisational standards, but here's a list to help you think across the important areas.

❑ **Closing data:** Check the figures on the Stage Completion Report to make sure that they're accurate. That will include cost and team hours, but there may be figures on things like productivity levels as well.

❑ **Product completion:** Check that all products that were supposed to have been delivered in the stage have been delivered.

❑ **Quality:** Check to ensure that all of the planned tests and checks were carried out correctly. Also ensure that if a product needed correction then it was tested again after that work to be sure that it was then okay and met its quality criteria.

❑ **Business Case:** Ensure that any necessary update of the Business Case has been done and that the Business Case correctly represents the project as it is now, not how it was at the start. This document is vital for the PSG to assess if the project is still viable.

❑ **Benefits:** If any quantifiable benefits came on stream during the stage and were due to be measured and reported, check that they have been.

❑ **Risk:** Check that the risk assessment has been updated so that the PSG will have accurate information on the level of risk as it is now and on the status of individual key risks that will significantly affect the rest of the project.

❑ **Stage Plan:** Check the new plan for the next stage and ensure that it is accurate, realistic and achievable. Make sure that the Project Plan has been updated if necessary to keep the plans consistent.

❑ **Resource:** Following on from the last point, specifically check that the resource shown on the new Stage Plan is available. You might do this by looking at confirmation received by the Project Manager or you might check with the Project Supplier, Project User and the staff themselves.

❑ **Project Charter and PMP:** Check that the Charter and PMP have been reviewed and updated where necessary. For example, there may have been a change of some staff at the end of the stage which should now be shown on the organisation chart.

❑ **Controls:** Ask questions to assess if the control in the previous stage was adequate. If not, make sure that adjustments to the controls have been talked through between the Project Manager and PSG members and the PMP updated accordingly.

Project Closure Audit Checklist

Your audit work at closure will be similar to the end of a stage, except that you are now checking data covering the whole project and there is no check of plans for the next stage – because there isn't a next stage. You want to be sure that the figures are accurate, such as the final cost and number of staff hours, but also that the information in the Project Closure Report is complete.

❑ **Closing data:** Check the figures in the Project Completion Report to make sure that they're accurate. Watch out particularly to ensure that all costs are included. There may be bills that have still to be paid by the Finance Department and so some spending may be not yet show up against the project cost code on a computer report from the finance system.

❑ **Product completion:** Check that all products across the whole project have been delivered. That should be quick to do if you have been doing checks at the end of each stage.

❑ **Quality:** Check that any necessary certifications have been obtained, such as for electrical safety.

❑ **Handover:** Ensure that all necessary handovers have been done, and that any documentation related to them is complete.

❑ **Benefits:** If any quantifiable benefits that came on stream before and at the end of the project were due to be measured and the levels reported in the Project Completion Report, make sure that they have been.

Not all benefits will be measurable at the end of the project. Even where a quantifiable benefit is measurable, someone may have decided to leave the measurement for a while until things are more stable, and the figure will be more reliable. Look in the Business Case to find when individual benefits should be measured and reported.

Chapter 20

Finding Useful Techniques

. . . .

In This Chapter

▶ Techniques for planning

▶ Control techniques

▶ Techniques for the Business Case

▶ Risk management techniques

. . . .

*H*ow often have you struggled to do something and eventually found a way through? Then, after you've finished, you find that there was a great technique that you could have used to make the job both simpler and faster.

Project management has been around for a long time, and in that time a lot of people have come up with a lot of ways of doing things. Then a lot more people have found a lot more ways of making those techniques even better. You benefit from all that experience when you use techniques that are well tried and tested. In your projects then, don't struggle to do something when by looking at this chapter you could find one or two techniques that will make your life a lot easier.

The techniques listed in this chapter are to give you a starting point. If one looks like it might be useful, have a look around in places like the internet and project management books to find out more about it. There are many more techniques than listed in this chapter, but the set summarised here are mainstream ones that are useful in a lot of projects.

Following the normal checklist format in this book, each list has the item – in this case a technique – followed by some explanation. For each technique the explanation tells you a bit about what the technique is and in some cases gives you a tip on where you can use it.

Planning Techniques Checklist

There are a lot of planning techniques out there, and they're really powerful. The one that you may be most familiar with is the Gantt Chart, popularised by Henry Gantt almost 100 years ago and now at the hub of most project management software. However, that's just one in an array of powerful techniques in this checklist that you can, and often will, want to use together.

This checklist starts with product techniques then moves on to activity planning techniques, following the 'product based' approach recommended in this book.

❏ **Work Flow Diagram:** Also known as a Product Flow Diagram, you use this network diagram to show what the project will produce (the deliverables) in the order that you will do them. It shows product dependency where an arrow shows that you can't build one product before another is complete, but it also shows lack of dependency where, importantly perhaps, you can build more than one product at the same time. It's an extraordinarily powerful diagram and useful for control and risk management as well as for planning.

❏ **Work Breakdown Structure (WBS):** You can sometimes use this diagram as a listing tool to set down the products which you will then show in the Work Flow Diagram. It's a hierarchical diagram showing the products grouped in categories and, sometimes, sub-categories. Some variants of the diagram have an activity breakdown in this hierarchy instead of a product breakdown.

❏ **Product Definitions:** Forms that are used alongside the two diagrams at the start of this checklist. The Product Definitions say exactly what each product is and specify things like what skills will be needed to build the product and, very importantly, what quality criteria it must satisfy.

❏ **Activity Network:** There are two variants of the activity network. The PERT Chart (Programme Evaluation Review Technique) is one but it's rarely used now. The more common variant is the Precedence Network. As its name suggests, the Activity Network is a network diagram showing the activities in rectangles and then arrows to show the order in which the activities will be performed.

It also shows the timings and which activities have spare time on them (usually known as *float*) and which don't.

❏ **Critical Path Method (CPM):** The CPM technique follows on from the Activity Network. The network will have many paths through it, but one is the longest path of dependent activities, and that is the *Critical Path*. The Critical Path is significant because if you have a delay somewhere along it, you make the longest path longer so the project end date goes out. Every project has a longest path through it, so for your project your only choice is, do you want to know what it is or not? Most of us say, 'Too right I want to know!'

❏ **Gantt Chart:** This activity chart was popularised by Henry Gantt, an American management consultant. However, similar work was also done by the Polish management specialist Karol Ademeiki. The chart lists activities on the vertical y axis with time along the bottom x axis. Bars on the chart then show the activities and their durations and the positioning of the bars reflects any dependencies between activities.

❏ **Time Line:** A simple but useful diagram to show the main parts of the project without the technicality. It is a line stretching horizontally, or off into the distance, with markers or pictures showing key events such as design, build, test and implementation. This diagram can be really useful for communicating with business staff and other stakeholders who need to see the main parts of the project but don't need the detail shown on a complex Gantt Chart. See Figure 20-1 for a typical Time Line.

❏ **Resource Histogram:** A bar chart with vertical bars showing the amount of resource required against the time of the project which runs along the bottom x axis.

❏ **Resource smoothing:** Following on from the Resource Histogram, you'll have a problem if a bar showing required resource is up above the line of available resource. You need to chop the tops off the 'hills' and thrown them into the 'valleys' by resource smoothing. You may achieve part of the smoothing by scheduling an activity to start later when the staff involved have finished other work.

❏ **Critical Chain:** A technique devised by Eliyahu M. Goldratt where he combined the Activity Network with resource; clever move.

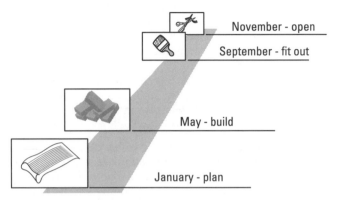

Figure 20-1: A simple Time Line.

 If you'd like to know more about the Critical Chain technique, have a look at Eliyahu Goldratt's book which is called, perhaps not surprisingly, *Critical Chain*. It's published by Avebury.

 For some hints and tips on estimating the durations of activities have a look at Chapter 23 in the Part of Tens.

Control Techniques Checklist

There are some powerful techniques around to help you control your project once it's underway. That control includes monitoring progress but also keeping an eye on things like the spending. Have a look to see if any of the techniques in this checklist may be useful to you on your project. Using the Work Flow Diagram for progress monitoring is especially powerful and, happily, extremely easy to interpret, so Project Steering Groups (PSGs) like them –as do Project Managers and team members.

❏ **Earned Value Method (EVM):** A way of associating progress with spending. You compare the value of work scheduled to be done by a point in time with that actually done. You can also compare budgeted costs with actual costs to see whether things are costing what you expected. For example, suppose you'd budgeted to spend $30,000 by now. You've done ('earned') $30,000 worth of work at the costs set down in the plan, but it's actually cost you $35,000 to do it. By comparing the figures you can determine that at this point in time you're on schedule but over-budget.

❏ **Exception management:** An approach where someone is given delegated authority to manage something within set limits, typically time and cost. If the projection for completion of the work goes outside these limits, the stage or project is 'in exception' and the matter must be reported immediately to the next level of management.

❏ **S Curve:** An ordinary line graph that shows the planned spend on the vertical y axis against time on the horizontal x axis. You plot the actual spend as you go along so you see the actual cost plotted against what you expected and you can also include a forward projection for the spend through to the end. The graph is called an S Curve because of its typical shape with a lower rate of spending at the start and end of the project, with more rapid spending in the middle.

❏ **Work Flow Diagram:** This is the 'jewel in the crown' of progress reporting. Useful initially in project planning (so the technique also appears in the planning list earlier in the chapter) it also has great applications for progress control. By colour coding the products on the diagram you can show which are complete, which are under construction, which haven't been started yet and which are overdue or expected to be overdue. Using the diagram and the product status for control is powerful because it is fact-based reporting, not an estimate of 'percentage complete'.

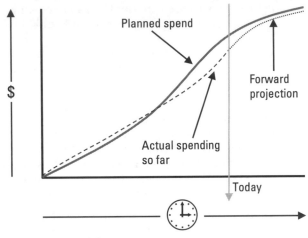

Figure 20-2: The S Curve

Business Case Techniques Checklist

The next checklist covers techniques that you can use for calculations associated with your project's Business Case. Some may seem complicated at first sight, but don't panic because you'll find that they're quite straightforward once you've had a go with them.

❑ **Cost–Benefit Analysis (CBA):** Usually set down on a spreadsheet showing the costs of the project and then ongoing costs set against savings, year on year for a set number of years, often five. The CBA shows when the project will pay back; the point at which the cumulative savings become greater than the cumulative costs.

 Some projects will never pay back but you have to run them anyway, such as for legal compliance. In that case the CBA will show the final cost after the offsetting of benefits, if any.

❑ **Direct Payback:** See Cost–Benefit Analysis above. It's a term associated with CBA but refers just to the point where the costs will be offset by the financial benefits. It doesn't take account of the future value of money, as covered by the next point on the checklist.

❏ **Discounted Cash Flow (DCF):** Also known as Net Present Value from the spreadsheet function @NPV. DCF shows money in future years as less valuable than that in earlier ones. So a project costing $5 million, and paying back nothing before Year 5 when it will make a one-off saving of $5 million won't actually pay for itself.

If you find the DCF concept awkward to understand at first, consider this simple example. Imagine – and please note carefully the 'imagine' – that I were to give you $10,000. I could transfer the money directly into your account today, or I could transfer the $10,000 into your account in five years' time. Which would you prefer? Well, you'll say 'today please'. You know that in five years' time the money won't have the same spending power. Even if you put the money into a savings account you'd end up with more than $10,000 in five years' time because you'd get some interest. The Discounted Cash Flow technique just reflects that reality with the discount factor increasing year by year so that the further you go into the future, the less value the money has.

❏ **Internal Rate of Return (IRR):** Related to DCF, you can use this technique to look at different possible projects to see which offers the best return. You set a date, such as 5 years, then increase the discount factor until there the project exactly pays for itself. The higher the discount factor needed to get to the zero, the better the return of the project. However, see the Remember point below.

❏ **Return on Investment (ROI):** A simple formula to compare the financial return from the project (financial benefits) against what it costs to run the project. So an ROI of 2.0 would mean the return would be double the investment. You should also specify a period of time. An ROI of 2.0 would be more impressive after ten months than after ten years.

The techniques used for making calculations on benefits and on investments are financially based. Remember that there are other reasons to run project, although a benefits justification is the most common. If you're not familiar with the different justifications, have a look at Chapter 5, Checking the Justification and Benefits.

Risk Techniques Checklist

Risk management is a vital area within project management and it's also an area with a very large number of techniques that can help you with risk analysis and risk management. Here's a checklist with some that are particularly suitable for use in project risk management.

❑ **Decision Tree:** A branching diagram that shows possible decisions (such as a risk management actions) and then, for example, the cost of each branch. Each branch may then divide, and divide again with further costed options for lower level decisions.

❑ **Interviewing:** It's easy to overlook this powerful technique in risk management. Go and talk to people with different interests in the project such as users, team members, PSG members and stakeholders and ask them what risks they see in the project.

❑ **Ishikawa (fishbone) diagram:** This diagram, named after its inventor, is also called a fishbone diagram because it looks like a fish with a spine, primary bones and then secondary bones. It's a 'cause and effect' diagram, but you can use it in projects by putting a risk impact as an effect, such as overspending. Then the primary bones are risk categories such as people risk, technical risk, business risk and so on. Using the secondary bones you then show the risks that you identify in each of the category areas. This technique works really well in a risk workshop (see later in this checklist for more on risk workshops).

❑ **PI Matrix:** There are different names around this technique, but at its simplest it's a 5 × 5 grid with probability (P) on one axis and impact (I) on the other. You rate each risk on a scale of one to five and write its reference number on the grid. You can then monitor any movement as you review risks. The grid also indicates the need for action, especially for risks towards the top right of the grid with high measures for both impact and probability.

❑ **Risk Anatomy Diagram:** a simple but powerful diagram that you can use for mapping out the three elements of a risk, the threat or opportunity (sometimes referred to as the trigger and shown with an arrow), the risk itself (shown in a rectangle) and then the impact (shown in a circle). You can use the diagram to think through risks by modelling things such as multiple triggers to a single risk, multiple impacts, chain reactions where the impact of one risk forms the trigger for another, and combined impacts where two risks occur at the same time.

❑ **Risk Checklist:** Simply a list of risks that can affect projects in your organisation and project circumstances. Don't use it first though or you will be so focused on the list that you fail to spot a new risk staring you in the face. Use other techniques first, then the checklist as a safety net to see if there is anything that you've missed. If you spot a new risk that could affect future projects, add it to the risk checklist.

❑ **Risk workshop:** This technique has two powerful advantages. You get together a group of people representing the different interests in the project; in a small to medium project you may include everyone who will be involved. Then they think of risks. The first advantage is that a risk that one person comes up with sparks other thinking, and other people then come up with risks which wouldn't otherwise have been spotted. The second advantage is that everyone is now aware of the risks because they were there when the risk was first identified and talked about.

❑ **Risk Proximity Frame:** A constantly changing diagram as you keep it up to date. The left hand side of the frame is 'today' and the x axis is then time into the future. You model different risks according to their severity, showing them in different sized circles. You can then see how soon the risks can affect the project and how significant they are. You might, for example, see that there are a lot of high-severity risks that are now just six weeks away. As a refinement you can go on to colour code the circles to show which risks are very controllable, which are partly controllable and which ones can't be controlled at all (such as weather conditions). Figure 20-3 shows an example.

❑ **SWOT Analysis:** A four-segment square to help think through the strengths, weaknesses, opportunities and threats to something, such as the project or a business area in your organisation.

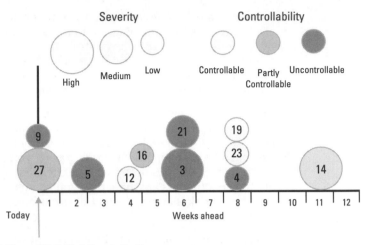

Figure 20-3: Risk Proximity Frame

❏ **Work Flow Diagram:** The Work Flow Diagram is a planning technique but it has two powerful uses in risk management. First, it allows you to see where the project is dependent on products coming in from outside, such as from suppliers and other projects. Second, it gives a structure for a systematic review of what risks are associated with the building of the different project products.

Part VI
The Part of Tens

In this part . . .

✔ Translate tricky project terminology.

✔ Get the lowdown on planning effectively.

✔ Estimate accurately and efficiently.

Chapter 21

Ten Sets of AKAs

*S*tandards in projects can be a bit of a problem. If you've learned one, you're reading a book based on another but your new company uses a third one, then don't be too surprised if your head starts to spin.

This Part of Tens chapter is to help you pin down what's what and to find a way through the maze of terminology. In each section the term used in this book is listed first and after it the AKAs – 'also known as'.

> *What's in a name? That which we call a rose*
>
> *By any other name would smell as sweet.*
>
> Juliet, in Romeo and Juliet by William Shakespeare

Generally speaking the underlying concepts for parts of the project and for documents are the same, and it's just the names that you find are different. One or two exceptions do occur though, where you need to be more careful. You'll find a comment or two in this chapter where that is the case.

Kick Off

Kick Off: Project Start Up.

Outline Charter: Project Brief.

Planning Stage

Planning Stage: Initiation Stage.

Project Charter and Project Management Plan (PMP): Project Definition Document (PDD), Project Definition Report (PDR), Project Initiation Document, Project Initiation Documentation (PID).

The International Standard ISO 12500:2012 and approaches that are aligned with it, such as the Project Management Institute (PMI) and the PRIME project method, separate out the strategic view of the project which is set down in the Project Charter from the tactical view which is in the PMP. Others combine them into a single document such as a Project Initiation Document (PID). In one sense it doesn't make any difference because the overall content is pretty much the same. However, it's arguably much neater to have the strategic separated from the tactical. I'm biased, but I think that the international standard has it right here. The two elements are used in different ways, and I think that the approaches that combine them are not as effective.

Plans

Activity Network: Precedence Network, PERT Chart.

Float: Slack, safety.

Product Definition: Product Description, WBS Dictionary (see the note below for more on the WBS (Work Breakdown Structure) Dictionary.

Resource levelling: Resource smoothing.

Work Breakdown Structure (WBS): Product Breakdown Structure.

Work Flow Diagram: Assembly Diagram, Product Flow Diagram, Milestone Diagram.

At the start of the chapter I noted that some of the AKAs are not exact equivalents, and that is particularly true of some of the terms in this section.

The term 'activity network' is a generic one. The two AKAs are actually different types of network. One has the activities 'on the node'. The activities are drawn as rectangles with arrows between them showing the order in which those activities will be done. That's the Precedence Network. An older approach is the PERT Chart (Project Evaluation Review Technique) which has the activities on the line and the nodes as marker points between them. The nodes are drawn as circles with figures inside showing the timings. Modern approaches use the Precedence Network because it avoids diagramming problems with the PERT. However the terms are included in this chapter because you may hear the activity network referred to as a PERT Chart, even when actually it's a Precedence Network.

The next confusion is with the WBS itself. Some, including some project planning software, use a WBS as a hierarchical decomposition of activities. So you take the whole project as one giant activity, break it down to sub-activities, then sub-sub-activities and so on. When you have reached a reasonable level of detail, you transfer those activities or tasks onto your Gantt.

Other forms of Work Breakdown Structure are a decomposition of products, not activities. It's not a country-by-country divide either. In the USA where many use an activity decomposition, the space agency NASA uses a product decomposition with activities only at the lowest level. Still confused? Try reading the UK edition of *Project Management for Dummies* for an explanation of product planning and the use of the WBS.

The WBS Dictionary is a commentary on elements in the Work Breakdown Structure (WBS). Although the equivalent is Product Definitions, Product Definitions are generally more thorough and useful, especially where they form a part of the overall product based planning approach.

Organisation

Project Steering Group: Project Steering Committee, Project Committee, Project Board.

A lot of organisations use the term 'Project Board' for the group of senior managers charged with oversight of the project. Often the organisation has picked up the term because it is the one used by one of the leading project methods. However, watch out for problems if your organisation uses the term 'Project Board'. The problem lies with the word 'board' because it brings with it the idea of a management board. Unsuitable people (whose careers, let's face it, will never reach the heady heights of the management board) may want to be a board member because it sounds prestigious. That leads to Project Boards filling up with unnecessary people who want, or 'need', to be there.

It's important to keep Steering Groups 'lean and mean' and big ones are trouble. Most big Steering Groups never actually meet because if you have 10 or 15 people involved there are bound to be one or two missing at any one meeting, and often more than that.

Another problem with the prestige view is that if 'important' people think that they must be on the Steering Group because of their grade in the organisation, they expect that to be their only input. In turn that means that these group members start to 'do' the project in the group meetings, taking it completely off track and making for very long meetings. The function of the Steering Group or Project Board revolves around the management of the project, not in doing it. The doing part is in the teamwork. You can have very senior and important people on teams and that's where they should be, getting on with their 'doing' there, not cluttering up the PSG and diverting it from its true purpose.

To help you keep the PSG 'lean and mean', here are three things to help. First, keep the membership focused on roles. If someone says 'Oh I don't want to be one of the roles but I should be on the PSG.' then they don't belong there – keep them out. The PSG is a working group, not some theatre with an audience. Second, listen out for managers saying 'I need to be on the PSG because I must have an input to the project.' No, that's an argument for being on a team, as noted in the previous paragraph. People can have an input by being involved or by being consulted without them being on the PSG. Third, 'I must be on the PSG because I need to know what's going on.' Knowing what's going on may be an entirely valid need, but it's a communications need, not part of the management of the project. Use the Communications Plan to think through and then decide on suitable communication products such as news sheets and briefings.

Project Roles

Project Sponsor: Project Director, Project Executive, Executive, Senior Responsible Owner (SRO).

Project User: Senior User.

Project Supplier: Senior Supplier, Project Provider.

Team Leader: Team Manager.

The chairperson of the Project Steering Group should always be the Sponsor – or the equivalent title. Most organisations use the term Sponsor, but be careful not to confuse this with the user interest, covered by the Project User.

Of the three views referred to in the ISO standards, amongst others, are the business view, the user view and the supplier view. The Sponsor has the business view and must ensure that the project is worthwhile from a business perspective. A user may want something, but it may not be justified in terms of benefits. If the Sponsor is covering the user viewpoint as well, he may get diverted onto the 'nice to have' rather than what is justified.

To help the people involved in the project understand their roles and responsibilities, you can find checklists in Chapter 6.

Support services

Project Audit: Project Assurance.

Project Office: Project Management Office (PMO), Project Support Office (PSO).

'Project Assurance' is a poor term because although it is accurate in one sense, few people can readily understand what it means. Because just about everyone is familiar with the idea of a financial audit, the term 'Project Audit' immediately gives a clear picture of the service involved.

Communication breakdown is a common cause of project failure. It therefore makes sense to use terms that people can readily and accurately interpret. To help avoid comms problems, think critically about naming conventions in the context of your organisation's projects, and especially your current project. Is any term potentially misleading or confusing? If so, you might want to change it.

Even the leading UK project method which promotes the term 'Project Assurance' confuses the work of the role by involving the auditors in project decision-making, as pointed out in Chapter 19 which is written primarily for Project Auditors.

To really hammer this point home, financial auditors don't help write the accounts and then audit those same accounts; that would be pointless, since their independence would be totally compromised. If your organisation uses the term 'Project Assurance' make sure that those involved are crystal clear on their true role and maintain an independent view; and that's no matter what your chosen project method tells you.

Stages

Stages: Phases

Stage Completion Report: Stage Report, End Stage Report.

Stage Gate: End Stage Assessment (ESA).

Control

Logs: Registers.

Project Memo: Project Issue, Issue.

Quality Control: QA (Quality Assurance, but see the warning below).

Version control: Versioning, Configuration Management.

Quality control is testing. Watch out for some environments, notably IT, where people refer to something being 'in QA' (quality assurance) when it is being tested. Although this term is included here as an AKA, it is nevertheless a wrong use of the words. Assurance in the context of a project effectively means 'audit' – checking that the tests and quality procedures have been done, not actually carrying them out.

Some approaches use the term 'Register' instead of 'Log' and refer, for example, to the Risk Register. The content and use of the log is the same though. One approach in particular uses the term 'Log' for informal documents that are for the Project Manager's use only, and 'Register' for the more formal ones that are checked by others. However, using both terms introduces, in my view, unnecessary complexity because everyone involved in the management of the project knows full well what the documents are and how they are used.

The term 'Configuration Management' makes more sense in engineering and IT circles where the 'configuration' of equipment is important. However, the use of the term in the context of project management is a source of much confusion to people who are not engineers or IT specialists. If you ask business managers what Configuration Management is, most will be unable to give a meaningful reply. Ask them what version control is and they won't have a problem.

Configuration Management is more sophisticated than mere version control, but for many projects the difference is not significant. If you're in an environment that needs the greater degree of sophistication, then you're probably already well aware of that because of your knowledge of the project, organisational standards and procedures.

Closure

Project Closure Report: End Project Report.

Evaluation

Evaluation: Post Project Review (PPR), Post Mortem.

The term post-mortem (autopsy if you're American) is here for completeness, but if your organisation uses the term in this project context then try to get it changed. It is entirely negative, whereas an evaluation should look at the positive as well as the negative.

Chapter 22

Ten Tips for Effective Planning

*I*nadequate planning, or no planning at all, is a well-known source of project problems. Hardly surprising is it? Just about everyone, apart from some senior organisational managers that is, realise that if you want something to go well then you have to plan it, whether it's a holiday, a wedding or a business critical project.

You don't just want any plan though; you want a good one. This chapter gives some tips to help you get the plan right. And if the plan's right, then your project is going to be a whole lot easier to manage.

Balancing the Plans

At the start of this chapter I pointed out the problem of inadequate planning as a well-known source of project problems. Actually it's often the cause of complete project failure. However, the answer to under-planning isn't over-planning, it's correct planning.

Over-planning hits you twice. First, it takes you more time and effort than necessary to do the planning in the first place. Second, you now have to maintain those plans throughout the project and so you'll use up even more time and resource unnecessarily. Unless you like doing unnecessary work for the sheer joy of it, over-planning isn't a very clever option.

When you are thinking about the Planning Stage of a project, one of the first things you have to do is decide how much planning you'll need. In turn, that will depend on the characteristics of the project and how much control you're going to have to exercise. The more control you want, the better the plan you'll need for that control, and the higher the cost. If you need less control, you won't need such detailed plans, and the time and cost of planning will be less.

The degree of planning needed this time around should be agreed between the Project Manager and the Project Steering Group (PSG). The PSG is responsible for the overall governance of the project, so the decision must involve PSG members as well as the Project Manager.

Using Planning Levels

Many project approaches have different levels of planning, and those levels are not there by accident; they're logical. You start with planning at the high, project, level. In your Project Plan you set down the entire project from start to finish – if you know what the finish is, which normally you will. Then, as you approach each stage, you develop a more detailed Stage Plan. If any Work Packages (work assignments) are complex, then it may be necessary to go to a third level of planning for at least some of them.

Don't get sucked down into the fine detail when you are looking at the whole project – and it happens so, so easily. Unless you have overwhelming reasons not to, stick to the high level with the Project Plan and leave the detail for the Stage Planning.

Using Stage Plans

Okay, the last section mentioned Stage Plans so why a second one? Well, it's important to understand the disadvantage of planning the whole project in fine detail at the start. Unless your project is very short, things are going to change while the project is underway. The organisation changes, requirements change, priorities change, technology changes and anyway you find out more about what you are dealing with as the project work progresses.

If you plan the whole project in fine detail at the beginning, you're going to be wasting your time because by the time you get into the project those plans will be out of date. With the stage planning approach you do the more detailed Stage Plan towards the end of the previous stage, based on the very latest information, so it's bang up to date. You then update the Project Plan with the latest information from the new Stage Plan.

 Keep your brain switched on because there are always times when you need to break the 'rules'. In some projects it's necessary to plan the whole thing in detail at the start. An example is a film shoot where scenes are shot in location order, not in the chronological order in which they will appear in the movie. In that case you need everything mapped out at the start and you need to know at the start exactly how it's all going to turn out. That sort of project is relatively rare though, and certainly for just about all business projects you'll find the project and stage planning approach to be logical and productive.

Basing Planning on Products

For each level of plan, start with products – what you need to produce. The normal way people approach project planning is to start thinking about the activities. Most of the major computer tools start at that point too and it feels good when you use them because it aligns with how you think. When you start a project, you start thinking 'I must do that, and this, and I mustn't forget to do that' – do, do, do. That starting point may be comfortable and even natural, but it isn't logical. How can you determine activities and estimate time durations if you're not clear what it is you have to produce? For example, how long does it take to build a wall, and what are the activities involved? Precise answer now, please.

Rather than activities springing to mind along with timescales, you've probably got questions. 'How long is the wall?' 'Does it include the foundations?' 'How high is the wall, because I may need scaffolding?' If questions like that did spring into your mind, then you're convinced. Start with what you need to produce, not with the activities.

Consulting Others

Unless you're very experienced in the project subject area you can't produce plans for the project in isolation. You'll need to consult others to determine what's involved in terms of products, activities and resource. There's no shame in that, so don't be shy about involving others. Your skill is in running projects not in being a subject expert in every project area you deal with.

Even if you do know the project area, it still pays to involve others as a cross check. You'll also get 'buy-in' from potential Team Leaders and project specialists if you involve them in the planning at the outset.

Working Hard At Estimates

Accurate estimation is at the heart of a good plan. It takes effort though, and that's in two dimensions. First, if you have limited experience, you have to think very carefully when it comes to the estimates and perhaps talk to other people who have done this stuff before. Second, make the effort to keep historic metrics from projects in a form that can be used in future projects.

You'll find more help on estimating in the next chapter, Ten Tips for Estimating. You'll never get your estimates exactly right, but the closer in you can get, the more the project will track to the plan and the easier it will be to manage.

Being Brutally Realistic

Following on from the last section, a problem with a lot of project planners is that they play games. Not you though; you want to be professional or you wouldn't have bought this book. That professionalism includes being brutally realistic when it comes to estimating activity durations in the project. If your project is going to take 15 months but the bosses say it must be done in 10, then of course the answer isn't to reduce all of the estimates by a third. The work hasn't reduced and all that will happen is that you'll be late.

Be absolutely realistic with estimates. If the project won't fit the required end date, work at the plans until it will. Have a look at the 'Four Dogs' model in Chapter 8 (illustrated at the start of Part II) to get the project 'canvas' into the right tension.

In *Project Management for Dummies* Stanley Portny advises 'Don't back into your plan.' By that he means don't massage the figures to fit the constraints. It's very good advice.

Levelling the Resource

Resource levelling can take a long time. You need to level the resource where the amount needed is greater than the amount you have available. On a resource histogram, you need to chop the tops off the hills and throw them into the valleys. If someone is only available to your project for two days each week, you can't schedule them for five days work in Week 9. You need to level the resource in the activity and spread the work out over at least two and a half weeks.

Resource levelling is hard work too. It's often tough enough to level the resources within the project, but it's even worse where you have to do it across projects where the same people are working on several projects at once.

The tip here is, don't give up. If three projects all have the same installation team booked for a full week of work in Week 27 then two of them are going to be disappointed . . . and late. The over-commitment of resource is evident at the start and should be dealt with at the start during the planning.

Find and solve the problems on the plan, not in the project.

Adding Contingency

Something is going to go wrong with your project – unless you're running it in a rose-tinted, problem-free parallel universe. To accommodate something going wrong you need contingency time and probably contingency money.

Be prepared to defend the contingency in your plans if you come under pressure to strip it out and deliver earlier. One of the examples of planning at the start of this chapter was that needed for a holiday. Why are there so many hotels around airports? Because a lot people go to the airport the day before to be quite sure of catching their flight. Well, if having contingency is sensible for holiday travel, how much more sensible is it for your project?

Updating the Plan

No project ever goes exactly to plan. Your estimates are never going to be spot on to the millisecond and, anyway, things change. At the start of the project, your plan is vital to work out what is to be produced, what work is to be done, who is going to do it and by when. Once the project is up and running though, the plan becomes a vital control document. However it's only useful for control if it's up-to-date. That means putting in 'actuals' (time actually taken and money actually spent) and adjusting the plan for changes. For example, if team performance is different to what you expected, you'll need to run that forward to look at the impact on the project. Then again, if something happens in the project such as a change of circumstances or requirements you'll need to look at the impact and do forward projections to look at the overall effect on the project.

You can't do any of that forward calculation if the plan is two months out of date. Keep it bang up to date then, and for most projects that will mean inputting actuals and then reviewing it at least weekly. That's going to need some discipline and determination at times when you're under pressure but it will pay back over and over.

Chapter 23

Ten Tips for Estimating

*E*stimating is notoriously difficult . . . in most industry areas anyway. If you find that estimating to be a problem you needn't feel lonely. Some areas, such as IT, have a few techniques to help, but even there you'll often find limitations. An exception is the construction industry. If you ask for an estimate for an extension on your home, a builder will come back with the total cost remarkably quickly. So how does he do that when most people struggle for ages with project estimates?

For a list of techniques, including estimating techniques, have a look at Chapter 20.

The answer to the building estimates question is rather simple. Your local builder looks at the different elements needed for the extension, and then he looks up the estimates in a commercially available book. For each item the book gives a unit, such as a square metre, and then the cost for materials, labour and total. Your builder works out the area of the concrete floor for your new extension, for example, and multiplies that by the cost in the book. When he's costed all of the elements, there's a tiny bit extra to add on for profit and cups of tea, then that's the price.

You may wonder why I've included the construction explanation given that most readers won't be involved with construction projects. Well, the construction example makes two extremely important points when it comes to estimating that could be of real help to you no matter what your industry or business area. Read on in the chapter to see where, and you won't have to read on very far.

Where you don't have recorded data, life becomes a touch more difficult. If you're in the business community dealing with business projects the chances are that you won't have anything much to refer to at all, apart from a few old project plans. Even if you do have some old plans, they may not be much help if the Project Managers didn't keep them up to date with 'actuals' as their projects proceeded. However, read the tips in this chapter for help even if you've got good material to refer to.

Holding Historical Data

The most useful information you can have to help with estimating is 'how long did it take us last time?' So store metrics from your projects so you can use them in the future. Don't lose this valuable data and then have to end up guessing all over again when you come to a similar project, or part of a project, in the months or years ahead.

Most organisations are awesomely bad at storing estimating data, either because they don't see the need for it or because they don't want to devote the resources needed to do it. That includes organisations where senior managers then criticise Project Managers when their projects don't align with the estimates in the plan. Everything takes a different time to that which was guessed at for the plans because the estimates were indeed guesses, as there was nothing better to go on.

If your organisation won't store metrics then you can for your own projects to get at least a limited base of data based on your own experience.

Thinking 'Retrieval'

My wife, who I love dearly, has a strange way of storing information. When we lived in London we used to keep a menu for a Chinese food shop in a clip in the kitchen. One day, I couldn't find it and asked her where it was. She got very defensive and said 'It's all right, I'll get it.' I said not to worry and if she just told me where it was I'd get it. 'No, I'll get it' she replied. I got suspicious and said 'Kath, where have you put it?' She was very reluctant to say but finally admitted that it was in our home filing system in the 'Schools' folder. I was mystified and asked why it was in the filing system and, even if she thought that was the best place, why on earth under 'Schools'? Her explanation was that that the last time we had ordered in a Chinese meal we had been looking at information to choose a school for our daughter. She had gathered up the menu with the school papers and put them in the filing system. Her defence for the filing was 'But I knew where it was.'

Kath may have known where the Chinese menu was, but I didn't and wouldn't ever have thought to look for it under 'Schools'. When considering data, you need to focus on the retrieval of information, not just the storage, and how other people will want to access it, not just you. When you're storing estimating metrics, think carefully about future access and then store it accordingly. Most organisations that claim to have past project metrics available actually mean that they've stored the old project plans. When you come to look for estimating metrics for your new project, you then have to guess which of the previous projects did something similar and then scour the project plans to see whether you can find anything useful.

Going back to the construction industry and the estimates for your house extension, which I used as an example at the start of this chapter, the estimating data isn't stored according to the building projects. Instead the data is held according to type, such as flooring, brickwork and woodwork; it's stored according to the way it will be retrieved.

Maintaining Accessibility

Storing good estimating metrics is one thing, but then they have to be accessible. This tip is a simple but important one. The metrics must be readily available to all the staff who need them and especially Project Managers. It's no good at all having the metrics locked up in the Project Management Office and the PMO staff then saying that they will look up what past metrics the project needs when it is being planned.

If a Change Request comes in, the Project Manager must assess the impact including time and cost. So the Project

Manager will need access to the estimating metrics then, won't he? To have to ask for them each time just involves more people, adds time and drives up project overheads as well creating enormous frustration. Besides which the Project Manager doesn't always know exactly what metrics he needs. The task may be different to anything done before, so he'll look at different estimating metrics before deciding which is the closest one to use as a guide.

Modifying Generic Data

It isn't so much a question of 'How long does it take?' but rather 'How long does it take *here*'? For some industry areas you can get hold of universal data that give the norm for particular work. In the IT industry it's known in systems development, for example, what proportion of a systems development project is usually taken up with analysis.

In the USA the inventor of the superb technique of Data Flow Diagrams (used for mapping system functions), Tom DeMarco joined with Timothy Lister to do research on productivity. You can see the results of their efforts in their book called *Peopleware* published by Addison Wesley. They discovered that the best companies work 11 times faster than the slowest companies when doing similar work. The difference is extraordinary, but totally understandable when you read the book.

When you come to do the estimating for your project, then, the key factor is how long it takes to do that sort of task in your organisation. If you get hold of universal metrics based on an average, you may need to adjust them, in either direction, to take account of your own organisational circumstances and performance levels. In other words, are you one of the organisations that goes 11 times faster, or are you the slowest, or somewhere in between?

In passing, and because you are probably wondering, some of the factors uncovered by DeMarco and Lister were related to the working environment. That fact explains the emphasis in several places in this book on ensuring that your project staff have good working conditions, and taking action to change things if they haven't. It can make a huge difference to staff performance and therefore to your project costs and final delivery, as well as to the wellbeing of the staff involved.

Adjusting universal metrics to the actual performance in your own organisation is vital, even if you get a bad feeling doing it because your organisation happens to be the '11 times slower' one. Remember that the estimates are used to underpin the plan, and if the estimates are wrong then the plan will be too. Your project will veer off the plan almost immediately and it will be very hard to control.

Using the PERT formula

PERT is the Project Evaluation Review Technique and is one of the two forms of activity network. The other form which is the Precedence Network has almost totally overtaken the PERT since it avoids diagramming problems. Associated with the PERT technique is an extremely useful formula. If you're not sure how long something will take, then ask people (see the next tip on the Delphi Oracle). Then take the results and apply the PERT formula.

$$\frac{1O + 4M + 1P}{6}$$

This formula is a weighting and biases the most likely result against the two extremes of the most optimistic estimate and the most pessimistic estimates. As you'll have guessed by now, the 'M' in the formula represents the most likely time represented by the majority view of the people you consulted. The 'O' is the most optimistic estimate put forward while the 'P' is the most pessimistic estimate. So the most likely outcome is weighted at four times that of the most optimistic and most pessimistic.

It's a surprisingly good formula, but it's better still because you can adjust it. Think back to the previous tip and the need to adjust estimates according to how long it takes 'here'. If you find that the formula consistently comes up with estimates that are too high and your project teams are performing better, then adjust the formula. On the top line you might then have 2O + 3M + P.

When I started in project management I was involved in computer systems development. I came to do my first project plan and found that the site had no historical metrics at all.

I worked with my Senior Programmer, Paul, to find programs from past systems development that most of the programming team would know about, and then we selected a high complexity one, a medium complexity one and a simple one. I wrote to each programmer and giving the three examples I asked how long it would take them personally to code and test a programme of that complexity. I then looked at the system design and, working with Paul, categorised the programs into high, medium and low complexity. I applied the PERT formula to the estimates given by the members of the programming team, and put that in as the time estimate for each programme according to its complexity. That approach was the best I could do; I had nothing else to go on. When we finished the build, I compared the actual programming times with the original estimates derived from the PERT formula, and they were amazingly close.

Consulting the Delphi Oracle

If you were an ancient Greek and you had a problem, you might have decided to consult the oracle at Delphi. The way the oracle worked is lost in the mists of time, but one suggestion is that it was a group of wise people who would discuss the problem and then come back with a single answer.

If you need an estimate, you can get together with a group of informed people and simply ask them how long they think each of a range of activities will take. They write down their estimates, you collect them in and then calculate the average for each activity.

If you want to be a bit more refined, you can use 'Advanced Delphi'. First, you do the estimating as before. However, you analyse the results while the group is still in the room. For each item you identify the most optimistic estimate and the most pessimistic one. You then ask those two people to explain the thinking behind their estimates.

The person who gave the longest time for an activity and was the most pessimistic might say 'Well, I've worked on this sort of thing twice before, and both times we came across problems that slowed us up.' The person with the most optimistic estimate may say 'We tried a new approach on a previous project and it saved us time and I think it could work just as well on this one.' Everyone listens carefully to the points, and then estimates again. You collect in the revised estimates, take the average and put it in your plan.

As you may have just realised in a blinding flash of inspiration, you can apply the PERT formula from the previous section to the Delphi results in this one.

Estimating When You're Not Sure

With the best will in the world, sometimes you're simply not sure about the estimates. That can be true where there are a lot of variables. If you find yourself in that position, there's a simple way out when you come to write the explanatory notes in your Project Plan or in the Business Case. Simply record a best case, most likely case and worst case.

The correct name for this process is *three point estimating*. Three point estimating can be really helpful because it alerts people, such as senior managers, to the fact that you're not sure about the estimates. It gives those managers the most likely outcome, but then also gives information on the maximum and minimum too. If the delivery is different from that shown on the plan, managers are not taken by surprise because you'd already warned them that it could be different, and told them the possible range of variation.

Stating Your Confidence Level

You should be very clear and open in your project plans, and that includes being open about the estimates. The people reading your plans, such as members of the Project Steering Group, will find it very helpful to have an indication of your confidence level.

To get the idea of this, imagine that I'm the Project Manager and you're the Sponsor. You read my plans which say 'I am 95 per cent confident that the estimates are accurate and that the activities will take the time shown in the plan.' Compare that to your thinking if you read 'We've never attempted this sort of work before and despite taking a lot of advice I am only 25 per cent confident that the estimates are accurate.'

In the first instance you will be confident in turn about assuring other organisational managers that the project will deliver on schedule. In the second instance, you are very aware that the project is going into the unknown and that the actual timing of activities may fluctuate considerably in either direction as the project proceeds. That fluctuation may be unavoidable, but the point is that as Sponsor you are prepared for it and won't be taken by surprise.

Using the Three Strand Rope

Okay, prepare for ending with a touchy-feely bit and something that I include when delivering project training courses, though I haven't yet seen it ever referred to by anyone else. It's about your feelings and how they fit in.

You can think of the process of estimating in terms of three strands twisted together to make strong rope. The first strand is historical data and that's both important and valuable. The second strand is techniques such as PERT.

Now comes the third strand of the rope, which is how you feel about the estimate. You may think that it sounds rather weird to have 'feelings' as a third strand until you pause and consider what you say to yourself sometimes. 'Hmmm. I don't know about four weeks for that bit of work. It just doesn't feel right somehow.' Your 'gut feel' for something isn't anything to do with your gut at all but everything to do with your subconscious mind. The human mind is, of course, awesomely powerful and sometimes your subconscious is putting things together that your conscious mind hasn't considered. Your gut feel of something being wrong is your subconscious flashing a red warning light.

If your 'gut feel' is telling you that the other two strands are wrong, then stop and try to determine why that is. If you have a fair amount of experience in the type of project then take the third strand all the more seriously. Try to resolve the conflict. More often than you might imagine, you'll realise that your gut feel was right and that you missed something out when working on the other two areas.

This chapter has focused on activity estimating. However, you can apply some of the tips, such as using the PERT and Delphi techniques, to estimating risk and benefit levels too.

Index

• *Q* •

About the Author

Nick Graham is the founder and Managing Director of Inspirandum Ltd, a small and specialised company focused on achieving excellence in project management and in the related areas of project governance and programme management. He's also a director of Anglo-Swiss Projects, the company which manages the new PRIME® project management method of which Nick is also co-author.

Nick splits his time between writing and development on the one hand, and training and consultancy on the other. Although he holds project related qualifications, he's also a qualified teacher which helps him design effective training and communicate simply. His courses are highly practical and those attending Nick's training events have described his style as energetic, lively, fun, very practical and very informative.

If you'd like to talk to Nick about running a project governance or project management event in your organisation, do please contact Inspirandum and he'd be delighted to talk to you – the web address is below.

When not away on assignments, Nick lives with his wife Kath in Hampshire in the UK. Kath also works for Inspirandum and has some input into the courses as she's also a qualified teacher. They met as students when training to teach some (cough, cough) years ago and married soon after. Kath was initially an infant teacher and when she joined the company she attended one of Nick's courses to get a feel for project management. She surprised other people on the course when, in the introductions, she explained that until recently she'd taught small children and thought that projects were things you did in school about dinosaurs! Some were even more surprised when later in the course she demonstrated a very rapid and thorough grasp of product based planning which many people struggle with at first.

Nick is a member of the Institute of Directors (MIoD) and of the Association for Project Management (MAPM).

www.inspirandum.com

Dedication

This book is dedicated to Philipp Straehl, the other director of Anglo Swiss Projects and co-author of the PRIME project method. It's astonishing how well we work together. I value Philipp greatly as an intelligent, constructive and innovative colleague. I value him even more as a friend.

Author's Acknowledgments

Writing a book isn't always easy and it can seem a long path to tread sometimes. For that reason I must thank the amazing people at John Wiley in the UK who work on the *For Dummies* titles. They are so encouraging and that means an awful lot when you're writing a book. They manage to combine genuine friendliness with impressive competence. I've spent a lot of my professional life involved with projects and when you have a team like that it's special and it's valuable.

In particular I must mention Simon Bell at John Wiley whose ongoing support, understanding and insight are all things I have come to value highly. Claire Ruston was a huge encouragement, and full of ideas, when she first suggested writing this book.

At home I must thank my wife Kath for her love, patience and understanding when I am deeply focused for long hours at a computer screen 'on a roll' and not wanting to be disturbed.

Publisher's Acknowledgments

Acquisitions Editor: Claire Ruston
Project Editor: Simon Bell
Copy Editor: Martin Key

Project Coordinator: Sheree Montgomery
Cover Image: ©iStock.com/naumoid

Take Dummies with you everywhere you go!

Whether you're excited about e-books, want more from the web, must have your mobile apps, or swept up in social media, Dummies makes everything easier.

FOR DUMMIES
A Wiley Brand

BUSINESS

978-1-118-73077-5   978-1-118-44349-1   978-1-119-97527-4

MUSIC

978-1-119-94276-4   978-0-470-97799-6   978-0-470-49644-2

DIGITAL PHOTOGRAPHY

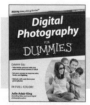 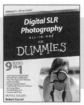 

978-1-118-09203-3   978-0-470-76878-5   978-1-118-00472-2

Algebra I For Dummies
978-0-470-55964-2

**Anatomy & Physiology
For Dummies, 2nd Edition**
978-0-470-92326-9

Asperger's Syndrome For Dummies
978-0-470-66087-4

Basic Maths For Dummies
978-1-119-97452-9

**Body Language For Dummies,
2nd Edition**
978-1-119-95351-7

**Bookkeeping For Dummies,
3rd Edition**
978-1-118-34689-1

British Sign Language For Dummies
978-0-470-69477-0

Cricket for Dummies, 2nd Edition
978-1-118-48032-8

**Currency Trading For Dummies,
2nd Edition**
978-1-118-01851-4

Cycling For Dummies
978-1-118-36435-2

Diabetes For Dummies, 3rd Edition
978-0-470-97711-8

eBay For Dummies, 3rd Edition
978-1-119-94122-4

**Electronics For Dummies
All-in-One For Dummies**
978-1-118-58973-1

English Grammar For Dummies
978-0-470-05752-0

French For Dummies, 2nd Edition
978-1-118-00464-7

Guitar For Dummies, 3rd Edition
978-1-118-11554-1

IBS For Dummies
978-0-470-51737-6

Keeping Chickens For Dummies
978-1-119-99417-6

Knitting For Dummies, 3rd Edition
978-1-118-66151-2

FOR DUMMIES

A Wiley Brand

SELF-HELP

978-0-470-66541-1

978-1-119-99264-6

978-0-470-66086-7

LANGUAGES

978-0-470-68815-1

978-1-119-97959-3

978-0-470-69477-0

HISTORY

978-0-470-68792-5

978-0-470-74783-4

978-0-470-97819-1

Laptops For Dummies 5th Edition
978-1-118-11533-6

Management For Dummies, 2nd Edition
978-0-470-97769-9

Nutrition For Dummies, 2nd Edition
978-0-470-97276-2

Office 2013 For Dummies
978-1-118-49715-9

Organic Gardening For Dummies
978-1-119-97706-3

Origami Kit For Dummies
978-0-470-75857-1

Overcoming Depression For Dummies
978-0-470-69430-5

Physics I For Dummies
978-0-470-90324-7

Project Management For Dummies
978-0-470-71119-4

Psychology Statistics For Dummies
978-1-119-95287-9

Renting Out Your Property For Dummies, 3rd Edition
978-1-119-97640-0

Rugby Union For Dummies, 3rd Edition
978-1-119-99092-5

Stargazing For Dummies
978-1-118-41156-8

Teaching English as a Foreign Language For Dummies
978-0-470-74576-2

Time Management For Dummies
978-0-470-77765-7

Training Your Brain For Dummies
978-0-470-97449-0

Voice and Speaking Skills For Dummies
978-1-119-94512-3

Wedding Planning For Dummies
978-1-118-69951-5

WordPress For Dummies, 5th Edition
978-1-118-38318-6

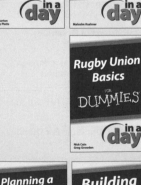